**The Building
Code
Burden**

The Building Code Burden

Charles G. Field
Steven R. Rivkin

Lexington Books
D.C. Heath and Company
Lexington, Massachusetts
Toronto   London

Library of Congress Cataloging in Publication Data

Field, Charles G
  The building code burden.

  Includes bibliographical references.
  1. Building laws—United States. 2. Construction
industry—Law and legislation—United States.
I. Rivkin, Steven R., joint author. II. Title.
KF5701.F5   343'.73'078   73-11675
ISBN 0-669-90423-6

Published simultaneously in Canada.

Printed in the United States of America.

International Standard Book Number: 0-669-90243-6

Library of Congress Catalog Card Number: 73-11675

To Cynthia, Alexandra, and Aaron for
encouragement and patience.

Contents

Appendixes

List of Tables

List of Maps

Preface

The need for greater efficiency in residential construction is becoming increasingly important as Americans face higher housing prices and a scarcity of materials. By tradition, we have looked to the technological ingenuity of American entrepreneurs to provide us with the products we need at costs we can afford. Somehow, this technological innovation has usually been absent from the residential sector of the economy. The authors, looking at the homebuilding industry from a historical perspective, found one consistent explanation for this lack of progress: restrictive building code regulations.

We began our studies of building codes first as independent efforts and finally in collaboration on this book. We were skeptical that good explanations for the dearth of innovative homebuilding could be found in the technical content of codes. Instead, we felt that analyses of the legal, political, and economic dimensions of building code regulation would prove more productive. Steve R. Rivkin's early work focused on building code litigation and legal authorities and appeared in a *Rutgers Law Review* article. He next undertook, for the Department of Housing and Urban Development, two special studies that outlined a number of reform options available to the federal government.

My early work was an analysis of the impact of building codes upon technological innovation. It was my Harvard Ph.D. dissertation, done while I was a fellow at the M.I.T. and Harvard University Joint Center for Urban Studies. It was based upon two national surveys that I conducted—one of some 250 home manufacturers and the other of approximately 1,000 local building officials. During that time I worked closely with Massachusetts State Representatives Martin Linsky (R. Brookline) and Bruce Zeiser (R. Wellesley) on the design of a statewide building code bill that eventually became law. There I had the opportunity to observe and participate in the politics of code reform.

This book represents the natural culmination of our joint efforts to develop a clearer understanding of the building code regulatory system and to advocate effective avenues of reform. I am substantially responsible for the first four chapters, which set forth the background and rationale for building code reform. The survey data and other empirical information was used to demonstrate that a building code burden exists for us all. Steve R. Rivkin is substantially responsible for the probing analysis of the legal and litigative issues of building code reform and of the various approaches to federal preemptive action over state authority found in Chapter Five. My contributions were limited to assistance in developing the role of state governments and to a discussion of the 1974 Housing and Community Development Act.

In the concluding chapter, we present a proposal for building code reform that centers on the need for an effective national product approval system, uniformity of building code actions, and an upgrading of enforcement practices and personnel. The conclusion includes a critical analysis of the weaknesses and strengths of the 1974 legislation and suggests further steps toward reform.

The positions taken in the book reflect our views and are not the official positions or policies of either HUD, for which I work, or the National Science Foundation, which sponsored Steve R. Rivkin's original work.

We are eager to extend our appreciation to those individuals and institutions who have assisted us, either in our earlier efforts or in the preparation of this manuscript. Such acknowledgments are due the International City Management Association for support of the building official survey, the Building Manufacturers for support of the home manufacturers survey, and the Department of Housing and Urban Development for support of several 1973 summer research papers. The National Science Foundation's Research Applied to National Needs (RANN program) supported Steve R. Rivkin's analysis of legal issues with generosity and imagination. We also thank the *Rutgers Law Review* for permission to use Rivkin's article in this book and Massachusetts Department of Community Affairs for permission to use maps prepared by it (for an earlier study) on the basis of our data. When resources were tight, the plight of all Ph.D. candidates struggling through theses, I was generously assisted by the Joint Center for Urban Studies as a Catherine Bauer Wurster Fellow and by the Ford Foundation under a grant to Professors John Dunlop and D. Quinn Mills.

My personal appreciation is extended to Ian Volner for timely advice, to Quinn Mills for early criticism of my work, and to Gene Rowland of the National Bureau of Standards and Arthur Newburg and James McCollum of the Department of Housing and Urban Development for more recent reviews of portions of this work. To John Maxim, a colleague at HUD, a friend, and a probing critic, I wish to extend special appreciation.

Charles G. Field
Alexandria, Va.

**The Building
Code
Burden**

1 Introduction

Not long ago, at ribbon-cutting ceremonies opening a plant for producing modular housing units, the governor of New Hampshire hailed the new enterprise as a welcome addition to the state's economic base. The Governor extolled factory-produced housing and urged manufacturers to bring to the state's citizens the high quality and economy that an industrialized production process can provide. Present were community leaders, bankers, building officials, and interested residents. Special tours of the plant were conducted, with guides carefully explaining the logic of the production line. Modular units in varying stages of completion awaited inspection on the sophisticated assembly line.

To build houses in any of New Hampshire's communities requires a building code permit asserting that the structure is designed to meet the health and safety requirements of the locality. Great care was taken that day to explain to the building officials present what technologies were employed in the structural, electrical, and plumbing systems. All inspectors appeared to be pleased. Buoyed by a successful "open house," the manufacturer began production only to find that in one town the manufactured home was accepted and sold, while in the neighboring town the unit was denied a permit for failing to meet all local code standards. Ironically, the inspector denying the permit was present at the open house and commented favorably on the unit.

After long days of argument and persuasion, the manufacturer gave up the fight for approval; the local veto had prevailed. More often than not, the home manufacturer will take his sales elsewhere rather than fight the costly, timely, and often unsuccessful building code approval battle. Unfortunately, this process all too frequently plagues those who seek to introduce new methods and products of residential construction. Public regulation of economic activity has stifled the growth of an industry. While heavy regulatory control is sometimes in the public interest, misdirected regulation of residential construction works to the public detriment.

The Nature of Our Concern

The objective of this book is to draw the public's attention to the profound impact that building code regulation has upon technological innovation and industrialization in home building. While the dry, technical matters of building

1

codes, standard product testing, and inspection are crucial to enforcing a code system, the public interest in a more efficient and effective housing construction industry demands the fullest attention of public officials to the task of maintaining code currency and of fostering an environment in which innovation can flourish.

The building code is a set of specifications and procedures designed to cover all aspects of construction. The builder designs his homes and brings his plans to the building department for approval. Official sanction is forthcoming if the plans match the provisions of the building code. Here we refer to building codes in their most general sense and also include such specialty codes as plumbing, electrical, elevator, and boiler. If the proposed building meets the standards within the code, construction can proceed. As the building is erected, it is inspected to insure that construction adheres to the code provisions.

Building code approval is a gateway through which all construction must pass. The code often stipulates what products can be used for building, what processes of construction are acceptable, and who can do specific jobs. Codes are thus powerful documents favoring certain ways of doing business and excluding others, which limits competition. Moreover, because codes are legislatively promulgated, they carry the force of law. No wonder many firms in the construction business are vitally concerned with the way codes are written and enforced.

Building codes have been used since colonial days. New Amsterdam local ordinances regulated the construction of chimneys and roofs to minimize the spread of fire at a time when fire posed a major threat to the city's existence—when, in the absence of modern firefighting equipment, a fire in a home or business could easily spread and gut entire city blocks and districts. Within our own century as well, fire has wrought massive distruction on metropolitan areas. In 1906, San Francisco was struck by an earthquake; the resulting localized fires, fueled by highly flammable construction materials, soon spread to ravage large sections of the city. The model building code movement began to appear about this time but it was not until after the Second World war that they came into full use.

Today, almost every community has a code in force. Building code regulation, like residential construction, has long been considered a local activity. Although the constitution grants to states the right to protect citizens through the exercise of the police power, from the very beginning states delegated building regulation to local communities. The exceptions were specialty codes—plumbing, electrical, boiler, elevator, etc.—which were often promulgated as statewide codes. Most recently, state codes covering manufactured housing and mobile homes have been put into effect in a growing number of states. The dominant pattern, though, has been regulatory *laissez faire*, with each community going its own way. Even with state codes, a pattern of local independence

has envolved. Efforts at reciprocity between states have so far proved ineffective.

The consequence of localism has been to foster the belief that local interests are synonymous with the local public interest. This is not to say that over
the decades a public interest was not served. The quality of American residential
construction is one of the highest in the world. While much is still to be desired
in our residential construction technology, the objective of fostering safe and
sanitary housing has in large measure been achieved.

There are multiple goals a building regulatory system should serve. Part
of the public welfare is served by insuring that quality housing is built. The
public welfare also is served when efficiency is served. Our nation is not en-
dowed with unlimited resources of building materials, labor, and capital. Thus,
the watchdog of the construction industry should not only guard against faulty
construction, but also encourage (often by not discouraging) efficient construction technologies. In this book, we shall argue the latter objective is not served
by the existing regulatory pattern; in fact, the present way of conducting
regulatory business discourages efficiency.

Public Interest in Reform

We are a nation struggling to meet our housing commitment. In 1949,
Congress called for "a decent home and a suitable living environment" for
every American family. That goal remains unfulfilled and faces governments
at all levels. There are families, approximately 13 million at last count, who
still live in substandard or overcrowded housing or are paying for housing
beyond their means and have yet to enjoy a "decent home."[1]

Just as lower income families are faced with the day in and day out reality
of inadequate housing, moderate and middle income families are becoming increasingly pressed by rising costs. Labor, material, and land costs continue to
climb, pricing many American families out of the market for new housing and
making prohibitively expensive the renovation of an increasing portion of the
existing housing stock.

The price of the average FHA-insured, newly-constructed single family
house has marched steadily upwards, from $15,789 in 1963 to $23,907 (1963
dollars in 1972.[2] Greater efficiency must become the concern of every American
family, for inefficiences in our residential construction affects us all. The middle
income home buyer is paying a premium price for his house. For the moderate
income family, a new home remains only a dream. And for the lower income
bracket, rising costs of housing translate into fewer government subsidies. Thus,
efficiency in the way we go about the business of homebuilding is a legitimate
concern for one and all.

We feel compelled to write this book, to broaden the focus of the public and of policy-makers from a concern solely for technological solutions or financial minipulations to a concern for the regulatory institutions and practices that guide private entrepreneurial activity. Regulations alone cannot solve the problems of a housing cost squeeze: indeed, they can even raise insuperable barriers to corrective action. The issue now is not whether governments—federal, state and local—should be involved in building regulation; that is a reality. The issue is whether there should be greater and more effective guidance from the federal government in order to rationalize and modernize regulation at the local level.

The national interest in building code reform stems from at least three basic sources: consumer needs, environmental preservation of natural resources, and the fulfilment of national housing goals. Meeting the consumer's needs requires effective economic competition, an environment in which innovative technology has an opportunity to prove its suitability in terms of price, aesthetics, and quality. Otherwise, stagnation results. Fostering competition means finding ways to permit or stimulate additional production options—from "small-stick" fabrication to factory mass production—letting the market decide which technologies are most appealing. Since additional housing options make possible fuller satisfaction of human needs, there is a public obligation to ensure that new ideas can be developed and brought to market.

Environmental protection, the second consideration, also demands the most effective utilization of raw resources—including land, building materials, and labor—and rejects controls that may arbitrarily prejudice such efforts. Forests are not limitless. If lumber supplies are depleted needlessly, other building materials and techniques must be available as substitutes. The pressure on the supply of scarce commodities rises in accordance with heedless use. Labor too, if not used efficiently, is a factor of production whose allocation must be husbanded. Optimal utilization of scarce resources requires conditions permitting factor substitution, and restrictive building regulation stands in the way of society's best use of scarce resources to accomplish a major social purpose.

There is also a special national interest in developing improved efficiencies in energy use. Buildings are major consumers of energy, having made in 1970 about 22 percent of the nation's energy demands, according to the Joint Atomic Energy Committee of the Congress; in absolute terms, that demand can only grow in the years ahead.[3] Residential energy consumption is obviously a large proportion of total consumption. If building codes inhibit the introduction and utilization of new heating and cooling systems (such as solar energy) or of mechanical or insulating designs that reduce overall energy requirements, then code reform is all the more urgently needed. Put it another way: if a market of scale is an inducement to desirable innovation in these areas, impediments to such a market should be speedily removed.

Third, but by no means least, is the urgent need for steps to enhance the housing stock available to the American people. The preeminent right of every American family for a decent home in a suitable living environment remains our ideal.

Is The Need for Reform Real?

Is American building regulation part of the problem or part of the solution to the nation's housing needs? Many critics and housing producers are quick to condemn the rigidity of building regulation because they feel that archaic, diffused, and rigid building codes inhibit acceptance and diffusion of new product technologies. They point out the extreme difficulty of securing affirmative code support for new items like plastic pipe. In contrast, others claim that technological innovation is much more prevalent than is realized. Post-World War II productivity gains in construction were at the national average.[4]

Those in the business, home builders and home manufacturers, consistently see codes as a major problem area. In a 1955 survey of home manufacturers by Campbell McConnell,[5] members of these industries considered building codes their most significant business problem. Fifteen years later, in a national survey of home manufacturers, building codes again appeared as the most important problem affecting innovation.[6] In a 1971 survey of conventional home builders building codes were again voted one of the principal problems.[7]

In 1968, the National Commission on Urban Problems attempted to measure the variation in costs incurred by home manufacturers due to varying code requirements. The Commission reported variations up to $3,500 per housing unit. More recently, estimates based upon a Department of Housing and Urban Development research study of the optimum-valued, engineered, single-family home indicated that building code reforms could produce potential savings of over $1 billion per year. (See Chapter Four). As discussed in Chapter Four, solid evidence is lacking on cost savings through the use of industrialized and innovative housing systems. What little evidence does exist, though, suggests that the impact of technological innovation may be significant, and on that basis alone efforts at reform of the building code regulatory system are justified.

National commission after national commission have concluded that reliance upon conventional building approaches is myopic. Unleashing the potentials of innovation and industrialization in homebuilding is a legitimate act of government.

In 1966, the National Commission on Technology, Automation, and Economic Progress [8] flatly concluded that existing methods are inadequate and emphasis on technological innovation imperative. The Commission on Mortgage Interest Rates stressed the need to reduce the cost of construction as well as the cost of money in order to meet our housing goals.

Urgent as the need is to reduce interest rates, the Commission recognized that this alone will not solve the problems that low and
moderate-income families have in attempting to obtain decent
housing. A one-third cut in interest rates . . . may, of course, be just
enough of a saving to enable some families to move from substandard
into decent housing. But a far greater saving in monthly cost would
be possible if ways are found to produce less expensive housing . . .
The principal key to keeping the monthly cost low should be clear,
however: the basic cost of the house must be low.[9]

The National Commission on Urban Problems,[10] alarmed that private
housing was beyond the financial reach of an rapidly increasing number of
Americans, likewise identified the need to reduce housing costs. Low production
costs would permit far more people to buy or rent decent housing on the open
market without direct federal subsides and thus reduce the total subsidy.

While these commissions agreed on the need to explore the potentials
of housing technology, opinion on the merits of industrialized housing is not
unanimous. Nonetheless, the potential benefits of innovation and industrialization in housing can *never* be known so long as the market rigidities and
exclusions attributable to the present deficiencies of building regulation persist.
Only by removing the building code burden can the prospects of innovation
be fully and fairly explored.

The Setting for Technological Innovation
in Home Building

The extent to which new technology flourishes in homebuilding depends
upon several factors. First is the technical difficulty of the required solution.
By contrast to the exclusive problems of nuclear power for electrical generation,
most technical problems in housing are of trivial complexity. If by innovation
we mean the application of new methods of production, new products, or new
inputs not presently in general use, then numerous technologies are available.
European systems, for example, use many advanced construction methods not
found here. Thus, technological difficulty does not significantly impede advances in construction. By and large, the problems lie elsewhere. A second
factor is the degree to which consumers are willing to accept new technology.
The widespread use of consumer durables within the home attests to a ready
consumer acceptance of industrialized products. However, people mistakenly
and unfortunately equate technological innovation with radical architecture.
Consumer tastes in an architectural/aesthetic sense are generally conservative.
Even so, design is seldom the factor that determines the acceptance or rejection
of innovations. Consumers usually do not much concern themselves about
technological changes in methods of construction, the details of which are often
unknown and unknowable to them. Spacing of wooden studs in load-or non-load

bearing walls, use of off-site assembled plumbing elements, or the use of plastic pipe hold little meaning to the homebuyer. Moreover, whether the housing is built stick by stick on the site or shipped whole to the site from a factory is of little concern. If this were a real problem, sales of mobile homes and manu-factured housing would probably be even lower than they have been over the past five or more years.

The third factor deals with the structure of the market and the extent to which it accepts or rejects new ideas. It is in the marketplace that industrialized housing producers and innovators find their greatest problems. Three market place features, in particular, seriously constrain technological advance.

Instability and uncertainty of housing construction volume are key market problems. Major fluctuations in residential construction imply an environment in which a capital-intensive, high-cost innovation may not survive. When the overall volume of construction activity (residential, industrial, and commercial) is of sufficient volume to justify major investments in products used across all forms of construction, innovation is pursued by building material producers. They can afford the capital and have the staying power to research new prod-ucts and materials that may take ten or more years to find widespread use. But for products used solely in residential construction, in an environment marked by local boom or bust cycles, expensive technologies are less feasible and non-amortizable within the shorter periods of residential construction vitality.

This problem of market fluctuations could be somewhat alleviated if a home producer could market his product over a market area large enough so that an overbuilt district could be balanced by high demand elsewhere. But building code incongruities dictate small discrete submarkets with differing construction requirements; and industrialized processes that require standard-ization flounder in this non-standard market structure.

A second feature of the market is the size and orientation of the firms that constitute the industry. Residential construction is characterized by specialization and smallness. The industry includes thousands of small firms classified as builders, general contractors, specialty contractors, unions, material producers, wholesalers, distributors, local retailers, bankers, and so on. Firms employ specialists with the skills to handle particular jobs: electrical, mechani-cal, plumbing, structural, pipe, and bricklaying. Each firm has tended towards labor-intensity as a means of adjusting to specific projects and to the more general cyclical movement of work activity. Thus, there is a natural, built-in resistance to industrialization or innovation that either displaces skilled workers or requires large amounts of capital. Moreover, there is a resistance to inno-vation and industrialization that redistributes work locally between different types of firms or shifts work away entirely from the local community. But to describe the industry in these terms is not necessarily to condemn it, since the residential construction industry has achieved remarkable adaptability to high-risk, low-profit-margin businesses.

The third significant feature of market structure is the extent to which it is subject to public regulation and stimulation. Residential construction is heavily regulated by thousands of autonomous public agencies with very few or no formal ties between them. Residential construction is regulated down to the last nail. Moreover, while rules in other regulatory systems may merely exclude certain practices, thereby leaving a wide range of permissible behavior, the general pattern in residential construction is to define permissible patterns of construction rigidly, thereby limiting available options.

The government's promotional role has been multifaceted, but not wholly visible to the general public. The most prominent, and least direct, stimulus to technological innovation comes from government-subsidized housing made available over the last 20 years. To a degree, the propagation of Federal Housing Administration (FHA) minimum property standards (MPS) has helped to constitute a market structure for housing innovation, but one no more flexible than prevailing local building codes. The federal government has also sponsored the development of new technologies through direct programs such as Operation Breakthrough and through various defense spin-offs from National Aeronautics and Space Administration (NASA) and Atomic Energy Commission (AEC) Programs.

Whereas innovators and industrialists must learn to adapt to the vagaries of the market structure, certain governmental actions definitely promote greater rationality in the prevailing system. The current building regulatory system can and should be reformed through legislative, judicial, and administrative means. As we set forth in Chapter Five, avenues for judicial challenge exist. Yet while judicial challenge can open the doors to greater flexibility in building code application, substantive and sweeping reform must come through legislative and administrative action. The 1974 Housing and Urban Development Act is a first, major step in this direction. In Chapters Five and Six we argue that in the end, the federal government must take an aggressive stance on code reform. To leave the code pattern as it is, with substantial control in local hands, is to turn one's back on the problem. Continued state action, while desirable, offers piecemeal solutions to a national problem. Now is the time to recognize that federal intervention is required if all consumers are to bear the fruits of what innovators and industrialists can provide in terms of better and less costly housing.

We hope this book will illuminate how deficiencies in building regulation have adversely affected the welfare of our society and how, if complacency persists, important national aspirations will continue to be less than adequately satisfied. This book aims to substantiate, moreover, that reform is not only needed, but attainable. The first step is to focus public concern on present deficiencies and then to heighten confidence in the feasibility of reform. Success will be measured by the extent to which industries, consumers, and governments respond to these perceptions of need and opportunity.

2

Industrialized Housing: Adopting Innovation to Mass Markets

Ultimately, technology exists to serve man. By the same token, one of the purposes of social and legal institutions is to ensure that human ingenuity is directed toward achieving human benefit. Our thesis here is that American regulatory institutions are stifling the prospect that innovation in building technology might serve public and private needs for housing. The focus of this concern is upon producers and marketers of housing provided through industrialized methods—the methods of volume production that characterize modern technology and explain much of its ability to serve human needs. In this chapter, we assess the service potential of home manufacturing and its record of marginal success in the United States, and we develop a perspective on the extent to which institutional reform could stimulate the market for innovation in volume home-building.

The Promise of Innovation and Industrialization

Americans are oriented towards technological change, particularly in material products. We have prided ourselves upon the industriousness and creativity that have fostered rapid industrialization and mass production of goods. Our stores are crammed full of the newest gadgets. The showroom of each auto dealer displays the latest in automotive wizardry, a vehicle that makes yesterday's car obsolete by the fall of each year. We demand novelty and performance in most products of consumption. Thus, it is not surprising that we should look with similar expectations for new product development in residential construction.

To a limited but important extent, these expectations are being realized. New materials, off-site assembly of housing subsystems, and new equipment for construction have come into use. But most changes have had only a marginal impact on the total job of building the home. Sweeping changes that affect the entire building process have been few in number. Most recently, the government, by means of Operation Breakthrough, has been testing the applicability of industrialized techniques to American housing markets. Begun in 1969, Operation Breakthrough is still feeling its way.

The appeal of innovation and industrialization in an era of increasing

9

costs is that of efficiency. We must take it on faith that economies will result
from industrialization of homebuilding, because conclusive evidence of lower
costs does not exist. Presumptive evidence from other industries that have
undergone industrialization implies that innovative homebuilding will produce
substantial savings in cost over conventional techniques. Cost savings could
be of two types: either the initial cost of construction for the same quality
product would be lower due to efficiencies of large scale production, or the
life cycle costs of a home (initial costs and cost of upkeep over the life of the
structure) would be lower. In many cases, higher initial cost due to technically
superior innovation could result in lower life cycle costs. Sampling from a
limited number of studies that attempt to quantify the level of cost savings, we
found that favorable estimates ranged from zero up to 20 percent of initial
costs. (See Table 2-1.) Maximum cost advantage occurred when costs of large-
scale industrial producers were compared to those of small builders. In a limited
number of cases, though, conventional techniques turned out to be more cost
effective. This occurred where large-scale conventional builders were compared
to small-scale industrial producers.

Claims for cost saving innovations appear with each new product and
construction idea. In surveying the literature on building code-induced constraint
on innovation (1973), George Sternlieb estimated that building code reform
would permit innovation that would in turn open the doors to a modest, and
realistic, 3 percent savings in housing costs. Is a 3 percent savings to the consumer worth the struggle for code reform, particularly since the cost savings
are spread out over the life of the mortgage? In this specific case, the answer

Table 2-1
**Distribution of Construction Cost Savings: Traditional vs.
Prefabricated/Industrialized**

% Range	Number of Comparisons	%
Savings favoring conventional construction		
0–5	1	6.7
6–10	1	6.7
Savings favoring Prefabricated/ Industrialized		
0–5	2	13.3
6–10	3	20.0
11–15	2	13.3
16–20	3	20.0
21–25	2	13.3
26–30	1	6.7
Total Comparisons	15	100.0

Source: Computed from Appendix A.

might be "no," for the monthly savings in principal repayment on the mortgage might be negligible; in the aggregate, however, it must be "yes." In 1972, residential construction accounted for $43.1 billion, excluding mobile homes. Three percent of $43.1 is a savings of approximately $1.3 billion. Sternlieb's estimates are based upon presently available technology. More capital intensive technologies could result in up to 8 percent savings. If, as we argue in this book, code reform opens the doors to greater industrialization of homebuilding, potential savings could be significantly higher.[1]

The residential construction environment strongly influences the extent to which and the manner by which innovation and industrialization takes place. Entrepreneurial behavior in residential construction is influenced by two dominant forces: the instability of production volume from one year to the next, and the local nature of demand. Numerous factors influence the volume of production in the short run, but few are as dominant as financing considerations. Because housing is financed on debt, the up-and-down pattern of housing starts is a function of the supply of and cost of borrowing money. The smallest movements in interest rates cause major movements in monthly housing costs. Available money can quickly disappear, and in the competitive arena of the money market, residential buyers, particularly purchasers of single-family homes, are weak bidders. When government and industry capture too large a share of the funds available, mortgage money quickly dries up. In an effort to fine-tune the economy, the government also intervenes directly, adjusting interest rates in order to control the supply of money. The net result of these factors is that a builder, to survive, must be able to sustain very large variations in sales from one year to the next.

Not only must the builder contend with the instability of the market, he must adjust to the extreme local nature of demand. What sells in one community may not sell in the next, for the buyer seeks housing that meets his needs in regard to community, place of work, and public services. Moreover, each community imposes upon the builder its own set of building standards through building codes, zoning ordinances, and subdivision regulations.

Due to localism of consumer demand and of building regulations, the builder must develop an intimate understanding of what is selling in each community. Could he count on a steady flow of local construction, his business problems would be minor. Most builders, however, lack adequate marketing information and pursue a strategy of building what is selling down the street. This strategy quickly leads to overbuilding when market sales are high. Excess construction kills the local market for new housing. Even if a builder has accurate market information, he is usually unable to counter the prevailing trend and is swept along on this roller coaster of local construction by those who fail to read the market signals. Boom or bust is a reality for all builders of local housing; it undermines the sense of stability so vital to a large-scale business.

Plagued by uncertainty of demand and inability to control the building environment, the builder realizes that today's great surge in construction may well become tomorrow's trickle. Therefore, he has used subcontracting to minimize his financial investment. Subcontracting is a rational approach to this business. All concerned share in the risks of the construction process, and each participant makes his own capital investment. It also facilitates the movement of builders from one market to the next. When a builder switches markets, he need not train a new staff and crew, for a network of participants exists within each market. Moreover, the relationships between the various participants—the general contractor, the specialty contractors, labor, and so forth—are generally consistent from one market to the next; only the participants differ. Who has what jurisdiction may vary some from one city to the next, as may work rules and collective bargaining agreements; but on balance, consistency is the rule, with the plumbers doing the plumbing and electricians the electrical work. The builder's problem is how best to tap into this network.

For innovation and industrialization to prosper, several key requirements must be met. First, technological capability must exist and involve both technical knowhow and financial resources. New ideas do not spring into being without years of research and patient marketing to the consuming public. Industrialized housing approaches have been experimental since the turn of this century, and it was not until the 1950s that home manufacturing, discussed later in this chapter, made much headway. Also, technological expertise need not originate in residential construction itself. Often the industry has borrowed technologies developed elsewhere.

Second, any new idea, if technologically feasible, must have willing buyers or respond to a major public need. In a private market system, businessmen must be convinced that sufficient market potential exists to justify investment in research, development, and marketing of new products. On few, but significant occasions, the need to innovate is thrust upon the industry. In a devastated Europe immediately after World War II, housing was in critically short supply. War had taken its toll in terms of both habitable homes and production capacity. Basic industries had been destroyed and equipment formerly used for residential production had been retooled to meet wartime requirements. Europe was faced with the task of building anew its residential construction industry. Many nations sought solutions in industrialized housing. The driving force was less the willing buyer and more the national requirement for technologies capable of delivering large quantities of housing within a relatively short time.

Third, the businessman must perceive not only a willing market, but one large enough to justify his investment decision. The problem is one of market aggregation. The degree of aggregation depends upon the extent of resource investment made into the product or process. Large industrial efforts demand markets in the tens of thousands, whereas the factory production of roof trusses needs only a market in the hundreds. Part of the aggregation issue is spatial in dimension. Willing buyers must live within a reasonable distance of the production facility; otherwise, the costs of transportation will push the price beyond the competitive range. Whereas volume production should lead to declining unit costs, increasing transport distance will result in increased costs unless there are breakthroughs in transportation technologies or transport systems that result in lower per unit mile costs.

Not only does the businessman need volume markets, but markets stable over time to insure continuity of production and sales. He must be able to amortize his capital investment. Where demand for a product is constant over time, the businessman's risks are substantially reduced, but two bad years, back to back, can drive most firms into bankruptcy.

The Flawed Reality

In despair over the slow advances in homebuilding, housing expert Charles Abrams once said:

> Of all the commodities that have been touched by the industrial
> revolution, the house has remained the most impervious to change.[2]

He was making a relative judgment, contrasting the progress in homebuilding with that in other industries.

Major transformations have revolutionized, for example, the automobile industry, taking it from custom manufacture to assembly line mass production. Investment in plant and equipment skyrocketed, production volume increased dramatically, and the unit cost of cars declined. Economies of scale and standardization were realized. In contrast, housing industrialization has lagged behind. Against the American experience, European industrialized efforts stand in strong and encouraging contrast. Industrialized production dominates in many nations, particularly in Eastern Europe. Europeans have made substantial use, since the Second World War, of concrete systems for multifamily housing. Panel systems are in widespread use in Bulgaria, Czechoslovakia, Poland, Rumania, Denmark, France, and Sweden. These panel systems form the heart of Europe's industrialized efforts. Modularized concrete box systems, used in the United Kingdom, East Germany, and Hungary, are less evident. Overall, however, there does not appear to be any abatement in the trend toward industrialized housing.[3] For the cynic who asks whether industrialized housing is possible and sustainable as a business, the answer is obviously yes.

No industrialized system is 100 percent foolproof, nor does industrialization automatically mean high quality. Standards of product performance are still required and their enforcement necessary. One of England's industrialized projects was a 22-floor high-rise apartment built in Ronan Point, England.

Disaster struck in 1969 when an explosion ripped out the wall of one of the building's corner units, triggering a total structural failure. One complete vertical set of apartments collapsed, unit cascading down upon unit. Shockwaves hit the industry, resulting in costly modification to buildings using the same concrete panel system.

Given this European legacy, the logical question is: why has industrialization of major housing systems come so late and in so limited a way to the United States? Systems have existed since the 1950s, but it was not until the late 1960s and under government sponsorship (HUD's Operation Breakthrough) that substantial efforts were first made. Technology was obviously not the problem, given proven European systems. The answer lies in the complex structure of the residential home building industry. As previously noted, in a market characterized by unstable demand, firms have distributed risk through subcontracting of work. The objective was to limit the amount of fixed overhead cost and rely upon other firms to provide diversified services when needed. When demand for new housing decreased, firms were not faced with high overhead costs so typical of heavily capitalized manufacturing concerns.

Thus, centralized decision making has been sacrificed except in the case of large homebuilders, and even the largest are restricted in their flexibility by their relationships to firms that service them. This meant that any radical innovation or industrialization affecting major portions of the house was bound to run into considerable opposition if that innovation or industrialization meant loss of jobs or sales to the firms involved. Major sudden changes were invariably resisted.

This does not mean that the industry stood frozen in existing ways of doing business. Transformation of conventional building practices has been dramatic over the decades, not in the sense of a single sweeping innovation, but in the cummulative effects of many small changes. Whereas a house was once totally built at the site, with raw materials being shipped to the site to be shaped into walls, roofs, foundations, plumbing systems, and electrical systems, many subassemblies are now prefabricated off-site and shipped as units ready for installation at the site. The pre-hung door and roof trusses illustrate current practices. The builder is increasingly becoming a coordinator of subassemblies rather than a carpenter with hammer and nail constructing the house from the ground up. New tools and techniques have been introduced that increase worker productivity. Spray guns and automatic hammers speed up the work process.

Upon closer inspection of successful innovations, most are of the kind that disrupt the fewest workers and firms. Not surprisingly, product changes that substitute one product or material for another are easier to introduce than changes that realign the relationships of firms. This partially explains why many of the innovations accepted by the residential construction industry are changes in materials. Many material producers directly control the production and distribution of their products. Thus, many innovations in product composition or design that are distributed through the producer's normal channels are directly within this control and can be quickly introduced.

Only when the material producer proposes changes that affect other firms in the industry, for example, the plastic industry's proposed use of plastic pipe in lieu of cast iron soil pipe, does resistance appear. In this case, displacement of cast iron by plastic affects the business of cast iron pipe producers, their subcontractors, and the related building trade unions. The potential disruption is great. Recognizing the lower price of plastic pipe, the cast iron soil pipe manufacturers have fought a delaying action in the courts, long enough for them to extend their own product lines into the plastic pipe business.

Taking into account these incremental changes, more could have been done; America has not taken fullest advantage of industrialized techniques. New products still take many years before they are widely used in the market. Large-scale industrialized housing systems have yet to achieve widespread acceptance and use.

A major thrust for change has been in the growth of mobile homes and home manufacturing. The mobile home industry has grown significantly in the past decade, a growth conspicuous for taking place outside the framework of the conventional homebuilding industry. Mobile homes are treated generally as vehicles and are not subject to local building codes (although many states have adopted a nationally recognized mobile home code). Home manufacturing, unlike the mobile home business, has stayed within the residential construction system, subject to all its rules and regulations. As such, it comes closest to being an example of industrialized housing in the United States, and for that reason we now examine it in greater detail so as to better understand the forces that have shaped its growth.

The History of Home Manufacturing in the U.S.

The history of home manufacturing is one of technological promise retarded by capitulation to the economic necessities of the commercial market. Because home manufacturing is an alternative to the conventional system, it has had to overcome resistance from conventional quarters. The problems of change have been less related to man's intellectual ability to conceive of change than to his hesitancy to make those economic and social adjustments that free the system from old production biases and allow for the adoption of new technology.

Although home manufacturing has made inroads into the market, it has never achieved its heralded potentials of significant reductions in costs through industrialization and mass production. When industrialization has been attempted on a significant scale, as in the Lustron experiment of the late 1940s, catastrophic failure has been the result. Yet the quest has not ceased, as indicated by the federal government's current efforts to encourage industrialization of the housing production process.

The history of home manufacturing, which dates back to colonial days [4], can be classified into two distinct time periods separated by World War II. Prewar home manufacturing was sporadic, generally unsuccessful, and failed to make any major contribution to homebuilding. The approach was more experimental than commercial, stressing technology and ignoring marketing. Since the war, home manufacturing has developed to the point where it is now a significant contributor to total housing production.

Pre-World War II Developments

There appeared to be little emphasis upon the development of new construction technologies before 1900. The few early attempts at home manufacturing were aimed at meeting demands not supplied by the traditional homebuilding industry, either because of shortages in materials or the lack of a conventional construction industry. Some homesteaders bound for the barren Western prairies carried prefabricated homes in their wagons, and panelized housing was shipped from the East Coast and the Orient during the 1849 California Gold Rush.[5]

After 1900, technological exploration increased. Grosvenor Atterbury experimented with concrete panels.[6] Thomas Edison built three-story concrete buildings poured in one operation. Buckminster Fuller pursued research on the maximum utilization of a steel house.[7] These technological efforts, though sporadic and uncoordinated, heralded the early stirrings of a home manufacturing industry. During the 1920s and 1930s, research activity increased in both the private [8] and public sectors,[9] but rarely was it translated into production of any magnitude.[10] Where significant production was attained, government invariably played a crucial role.[11] Occasionally, large corporations attempted the business, but their efforts produced negligible results.[12]

The prewar period was an era of exploration into technology, a time when new materials and factory-produced prototypes were investigated and sometimes tested. Fundamental questions were raised, of moving housing construction off the site and into the factory, but little housing was built. In some cases where prefabrication was attempted, it was opposed by the conventional industry,[13] but in general too few attempts at home manufacturing actually got off the drawing boards.

Post-World War II Developments

The Second World War was the midwife of home manufacturing. The Government pressed home manufacturers to deliver housing for defense workers in volume, ordering over 200,000 units—a mass market during these years.[14] For the first time, home manufacturers had the volume necessary for a viable commercial endeavor, the opportunity to establish production lines and resolve basic technical problems of production, transportation, and erection at the site. Emphasis continued to center on technical issues of establishing the production process and delivery system of factory-produced housing.[15]

Nonproduction problems frustrated home manufacturers in the postwar period. Home manufacturing was to enter the postwar housing market on the promise of burgeoning, large-scale demand.[16] Some thought that the conventional homebuilder, after years of relative inactivity during the depression and wartime, would fail to provide for the anticipated increased demand for postwar housing, thus creating a market for industrially produced homes. The sobering reality was the bleak market responses to the manufactured house. Conventional builders responded to demand, the home manufacturer failed. Spoiled by the government's single set of building requirements, the manufacturer was incapable of quickly responding to the totally different environment of the private market. As a consequence, while total housing starts shot up by 700,000 units in 1946, sales of manufactured housing dropped.[17]

Identifying the problems facing the home manufacturer was simple; resolving them was difficult. He was stereotyped early as the builder of cheap housing that was structurally unsafe for habitation.[18] His "staple gun house" would plague him for decades to come. Reaching the potential buy was another problem. Unlike the single buyer involved under government contracts, the private market had many buyers and was highly localized. Few manufacturers, though, appreciated the major differences between selling to the government and selling to the public.[19] The consequence for most producers in the transition from wartime to peacetime markets was the almost total absence of an effective distribution system. The net effect was that many home manufacturers sat back and waited for the flood of orders to come to them, but few came.[20]

The home manufacturer's wartime experiences in financing likewise proved deceptive.[21] Each sale required its own mortgage, and locating enough dependable mortgage funding to maintain profitable operations proved extremely difficult. Uncertainties about manufactured housing clouded the investment picture. Banker conservatism, the unsavory product image, and the localism of lending practices complicated efforts to finance manufactured housing.

One of the manufacturer's greatest problems was the maze of building

code jursidictions and variety of code standards that checkered his marketing
area. Because wartime production techniques were designed to satisfy government contracts for which producers had to meet one set of building standards,
most manufacturers were unprepared to cope with the prevailing kaleidoscopic
pattern of codes. This pattern was antagonistic to the logic of the repetitive
production-line procedure. As a manufacturer approached each new community,
he had to redesign his house to satisfy a new set of code requirements. There
was little room for discretion. Whereas governmental standards were probably
established to meet defense housing needs, local building codes, as we shall
see, were developed to reflect local interests and the traditional way of building.[22]

The extent to which a manufacturer could push new technology was
often limited by antiquated code standards. One of the great challenges
of the day was to unshackle technology from local codes. As Miles L.
Colean warned in the mid-1940s:

> At the present time, construction stands on the threshold of a
> great advance in its techniques, which carries the ultimate promise
> of important cost reductions. Because codes are largely based on
> traditional handicraft methods, and because they usually are slow
> and difficult to change, they often may hold back this progress . . . . [23]

Near Extinction–The Lustron Experience

The most spectacular postwar attempt at industrialization was Lustron.
In many ways, the problems confronting the entire home manufacturing industry were vividly highlighted by this experiment. Lustron was to be to
housing what Ford Motor Company was to automobiles. Production was
highly automated, extending over eight miles of conveyors. The plant was
designed for a capacity of 100 units a day, with break-even production estimated at 30 to 50 units a day or from 7,800 to 13,000 units a year.[24] The
end product was a two-bedroom, ranch-style home of sheet steel construction
enameled in pastel hues and insulated with fiberglass.[25] Included in the package
were built-in finished bathrooms, automatic water heater, furnace, kitchen
cabinets, recessed bookshelves, china cabinets, closets, and even a vanity
table with mirror.[26] The selling price was to be $7,000.[27]

To finance this venture, Lustron turned to the federal government for
most of its capital needs. Aided by strong political support, the company
was able to get $37,500,000 [28] in long-term debt from the Reconstruction
Finance Corporation while putting up only $840,000 in equity.[29] After 18
months of operation, Lustron reported only 2,000 units sold,[30] losses of
$1,000,000 per month,[31] and default on a $22,000,000 loan from RFC.[32]

In July 1950, the company was sold at auction for $6,000,000 [33] following legal action by RFC to recover their investment.[34]

Lustron's problems were typical of the industry's problems, but magnified in consequence. Too much emphasis was given to production and too little to marketing, reflecting the home manufacturer's mistaken faith in the inherent saleability of his product.[35] Local resistance to an unorthodox product complicated Lustron's problems. The house could not pass many local building codes.[36] A weak dealership system also contributed to failure. A dealer was required to handle several homes at one time, requiring him to obtain working capital of $50,000 to $100,000,[37] a prohibitive amount for prefabricated home dealers to raise from conventional sources at that time.

Lustron had its share of technical problems. The production process reduced design flexibility, which was critical at a time of weak public acceptance of prefabricated homes and when scant market research existed on public design preferences. The design of the system also suggested inefficiencies. While the plant was planned for a break-even level of 7,800 to 13,000 units, a bathtub stamping machine, for example, was designed for a break-even level of 120,000 tubs a year.[38]

Though originally scheduled to cost $7,000, the house sold for $11,000, $1,000 higher than a comparably built conventional home.[39] This unexpectedly higher price was due both to higher costs resulting from production problems and higher unit overhead costs due to lower production volumes.

Perhaps Lustron's most serious error was to overestimate the potential size of the mass market. Lustron's break-even volume was in the range of 7,800 to 13,000 units a year, which would amortize the $37.5 million investment. This production level was far beyond that of any large-scale tract builder of the 1940s. Because of an inadequate distribution system, the generally unfavorable public attitude to prefabrication, financing problems, and community resistance to the product through local building codes, the potential market was drastically reduced, making it impossible to achieve profitable production.

The industrial repercussions were significant. The Lustron bankruptcy was to totally discourage, for a long time, any efforts at intensive industrialization. Who would lend the needed capital to finance such a risky business? Numerous severe problems plagued Lustron's effort, and there was no evidence that such an investment would bring down costs. The market judgment was made. Industrialization of the housing process, a quantum leap from the existing methods of construction, was incompatible with the prevailing market conditions for homebuilding. The failure of Lustron did not signal the collapse of home manufacturing; rather it meant that radical industrialization of the home manufacturing process, not home manufacturing *itself*, was incompatible with the prevailing market conditions of the day.

During the 1950s and 1960s a quiet revolution in housing, scarcely noticed by the American public, was underway. Because the marketing strategy of most home manufacturers was to design conventional-looking, single-family houses, the typical industrialized house was easily mistaken for a conventionally-built house. Unless a person actually watched the building progress at the site, it was almost impossible for him to discern the use of manufactured housing. Moreover, most prefabs were of panel construction and shipped in covered vans to the site. Therefore, the unit was not highly visible on the highway.

Reported home manufacturing output (excluding mobile homes) grew from an estimated 38,000 units in 1946 to 316,000 in 1969 (see Table 2-2), an almost eight-fold increase at a time when total national production rose by roughly 50 percent (1,023,000 to 1,499,000). In terms of total market share, home manufacturing began with 3.7 percent in 1946 and rose to 21.0 percent by 1969. Home manufacturing has experienced fairly steady growth over the years. Absolute production gains were scored in all but eight years, and increased market share occurred in all but five.

This growth pattern illustrated the inherent staying power of home manufacturing. Without heavy investment in plant and equipment, the home manufacturer proved himself to be competitive with the conventional builder. The growth in home manufacturing obviously attests to its competitiveness, but the historical patterns suggest that savings did not come from volume production, rather from other benefits of factory production.[40] Because of problems of codes, image, financing, and distribution, to name the most important,[41] few firms had the opportunity to reach large-scale production.

Historical data on size of firm is fragmentary at best, based upon small sample surveys subject to unknown biases. In a 1955 study, only eight out of 39 prefabricators interviewed indicated volumes exceeding 1,500 units; only one firm produced more than 3,000 units.[42] But even these larger firms most likely operated from several plants scattered about the country. Therefore, the economies of scale normally associated with volume production in one plant were not reached, although other economies of scale associated with management or material purchases not necessarily dependent upon a one-plant operation may have been realized. In 1962, only 10 percent of the firms surveyed produced more than 1,000 units per year. By 1962, the proportion increased to 18 percent, but this was accompanied by the growth of small-volume producers, many of which were lumber yards diversifying into the prefabrication of wooden structures—a logical extension of their own business.

The Home Manufacturer Today

Home manufacturing is distinguished by the degree to which on-site labor is displaced by factory production. Manufacturers pre-cut the pieces to size and then ship them to the site for assembly into structural units. The

Table 2-2
Home Manufacturing Production Statistics: 1946–1969

(1) Year	(2) Manufactured Homes (000)	(3) Mobile Homes (000)	(4) Total U.S. Housing Starts (000)	Rate of Growth over Previous Year Manufactured Homes	Rate of Growth over Previous Year U.S.	(5) Market Share (2/4)	(6) Percent Annual Change in Market Share
1946	38[a]	—	1023[b]			3.7	—
1947	37	—	1268	-2.6	19.3	2.9	(.9)
1948	30	—	1362	-18.9	6.9	2.2	(.7)
1949	35	—	1466	16.7	7.1	2.4	.2
1950	55	—	1952	57.0	24.9	2.8	.4
1951	50	—	1491	-9.1	-30.8	3.3	.5
1952	57	—	1504	14.0	9.1	3.8	.5
1953	55	—	1438	-3.5	-4.2	3.8	0.0
1954	77	—	1551	28.6	8.4	5.0	1.2
1955	93	—	1646	17.2	5.8	5.6	.6
1956	95	125	1349	2.1	-22.1	7.0	1.4
1957	94	119	1224	-1.1	-1.0	7.7	.7
1958	110	102	1382	14.5	12.5	8.0	.3
1959	132	121	1531	16.7	9.7	8.6	.6
1960	127	104	1274	-3.9	-20.2	9.5	.9
1961	156	90	1337	18.6	4.7	11.6	2.1
1962	186	118	1469	16.1	9.0	12.7	1.1
1963	198	151	1615	6.1	9.0	12.2	(.5)
1964	213	191	1535	7.1	-5.2	13.7	1.5
1965	233	216	1488	8.6	-3.1	15.7	2.0
1966	230	217	1173	-1.3	-26.8	19.6	3.9
1967	225	240	1299	-2.2	9.0	17.3	(2.3)
1968	240	317	1524	6.2	14.7	15.7	(1.6)
1969	316[c]	413	1499	24.0	-1.7	21.0	5.3

Sources:
[a]National Association of Home Manufacturers estimates. Manufactured homes are housing packages consisting of at least the structural shell. Volume estimates are based on HMA surveys and other surveys by professional journals such as *Professional Builder* and *Automation in Housing*.
[b]*Progress Report on Federal Housing and Urban Development Programs*. Subcommittee on Housing and Urban Affairs, Committee on Banking and Currency. U.S. Senate (Washington, D.C., U.S. Government Printing Office, 1969), p. 2. Total does not include mobile homes.
[c]Estimated from 1970 Survey of Home Manufacturers by Charles G. Field.

AUTHOR: please check manuscript p. 51a. Should there be additional source notes for c, d, and e? If so, please supply.

cutting and assembling of wall units are done by the *panel* manufacturer for assembly and erection on the site. On-site labor remains responsible for much mechanical work and all finishing with either process. Much of this work is done in the factory by the *modular* producer, who goes furthest in off-site assembly of the house by producing volumetric structural units ready for shipment. The assembly of walls, floors, and roofs into 3–dimensional rooms is done in the factory, and the rooms are shipped, like a mobile home, to the site where they are set into place.

In response to steadily increasing costs, part of the industry has moved more and more production into the factory as it has become financially feasible. Sears Roebuck, and Montgomery Ward had great success with pre-cut houses between 1900 and 1940. After the War, panel construction emerged as the dominant form of production. By 1970, 53 percent of firms surveyed were panel producers, pre-cut housing having fallen to only 6 percent; and modular production has begun to move to a prominent position in the industry, representing 25 percent of surveyed firms. (See Table 2-3.)

The same forces that have shaped the conventional industry also constrict the development of the home manufacturing industry. Market instability has imposed a cost-minimizing production strategy upon most home manufacturers. Large-scale investments in a fully mechanized home manufacturing operation require a continuously high level of sales. But the market denies this regularity of volume production. While national housing starts since World War II have fluctuated between one and two million units, regional and local housing starts have behaved more erratically, making accurate market forecasting almost impossible. Unable to forecast accurately future levels of sales and thus smooth out the swings in demand, most home manufacturers have shied away from markets requiring expensive technologies. The home manufacturer has avoided the high-rise market, where investments run between $2 and $3 million. Instead, he has favored the single and low-rise, multifamily markets, where investments need run only $100,000. The high-rise operation would require sales well into

Table 2-3
Home Manufacturers by Basic Form of Production: 1970

Basic Form	Number of Firms Reporting	Percent
Pre-cut	15	6.3
Panel	127	53.4
Modular	61	25.6
Pre-cut and Panel	66	2.5
Panel and Modular	14	5.9
Other	15	6.3
	238	100.0

Source: 1970 Survey of Home Manufacturers by Charles G. Field.

the thousands a year for a number of years, while a single-family, wood-panel operation would require sales only in the range of 100 units annually for a shorter time.[43]

The investment-minimizing strategy also affects the degree to which a manufacturer will commit himself to any given production technology. The techniques he employs remain simple, the equipment unsophisticated, and the materials traditional. The investment-minimizing manufacturer will tend to favor materials requiring minimal equipment. Wood, as opposed to concrete or steel, involves only the most rudimentary tools and is replaced only where greater structural strength is required. According to the survey, wood dominates the industry, being used by 86 percent of the firms surveyed. (See Table 2-4.)

The production process of the single-family house is simple. Raw lumber is drawn from storage areas and cut to size for the particular design. The lumber is shaped into walls and floors as it is moved on jigs from one work station to the next, where specialized crews nail the studs together, or lay in insulation, or cut openings for doors and windows. The most striking feature of the production process is the extensive use of labor. Equipment for greater automation is available, but few producers are willing to bind themselves to these capital costs. The producer can fire the laborer when production drops, but cannot rid himself of owned equipment.

Standardization, a keystone of mass production, has fallen victim to the local market pattern. Not only may consumers in neighborhood markets desire different products, but variations in building codes effectively require variations in structural design between communities. Standardization is impossible when the codes that govern construction rarely agree on standards. The manufacturer is faced with two alternatives. He must either establish a flexible production procedure so that the assembly line procedure is adaptable to any set of standards, or he must build to the strictest set of standards. By qualifying under the most rigorous code requirements, he automatically meets the standards

Table 2-4
Basic Material Used by Home Manufacturers: 1970

Material Used	Number of Firms Reporting	Percent
Wood	209	86.4
Concrete	6	2.5
Plastic	3	1.2
Steel	3	1.2
Wood and Non-wood combination	17	7.0
Non-wood Combinations	2	.8
Other	2	.8
	242	100.0

Source: 1970 Survey of Home Manufacturers by Charles G. Field.

of the other communities. Flexibility results in loss of all standardization, rigor achieves standardization, but at a higher product cost. Neither allows the fullest exploitation of mass production.

Localism of demand has forced upon the home manufacturer a distribution system similar to that used by other manufacturing enterprises. Marketing is expensive because it requires intimate knowledge of local conditions, of consumer tastes, available land, and applicable regulations. As a result, most home manufacturers (59 percent) have developed distribution systems using local builders. (See Table 2-5.) Only 23 percent of reported sales went directly to the final buyer.[44] For the home manufacturer whose sales were distributed over many communities, the costs of analysing the market in each and every community is prohibitively high, forcing him toward some type of arrangement with local builders. Where the home manufacturer acts as his own developer, he sells directly to the buyer.

Large-scale production demands a mass market and continuity of sales, but the attainment of these conditions is blocked by localism and unstable volume. Although the industry has grown in total output, most firms still tend to be small in scale. Half produced fewer than 200 units in 1969, and only 15 percent produced more than 900. (See Table 2-6.) But even for the giants, the principle of minimizing capital investments holds. Most of the largest firms operate as amalgams of smaller plants. By locating his plants in different regions of the country, the large-scale producer reduces the amount of investment dependent upon any one market area.

Production in the thousands is not necessary to justify a home manufacturing operation. Nor does low volume mean that substantial economies are achievable in the low sales ranges. The necessary economic data are not available to make that determination. The industry profile indicates, however, that home manufacturers have minimized their investments in response to market uncertainties and therefore do not require large sales volumes to remain competitive at these low investment levels.

Table 2-5
Major Means of Distribution: 1969

Means	Number of Firms Reporting	Percent
Custom Builders	87	39
Builder-dealers	45	20
Direct to Final Buyer	50	23
Government	6	3
Other	34	15
	222	1.00

Source: 1970 Survey of Home Manufacturers by Charles G. Field.

Table 2-6
Distribution of Output of Home Manufacturers: 1969

Output (Residential Units)	Number of Firms Reporting	Percent
Less 100	58	30
101–200	35	18
201–300	21	11
301–400	21	11
401–600	16	8
601–900	13	7
901–2000	15	8
Over 2000	13	7
Totals	192	100

Source: 1970 Survey of Home Manufacturers by Charles G. Field.

Table 2-7
Type of Residential Production: 1969

Type	Number of Firms Reporting	Percent of Total Firms	Output	Percent	Percent
Single Family	202	84	43,534	35.0	60.0
Multi Family	136	56	28,830	23.0	40.0
low rise			(27,724)	(22.2)	(38.0)
high rise			(1,106)	(0.8)	(2.0)
Mobile Homes	39	16	52,314	42.0	–
			124,668	100.0	100.0

Source: 1970 Survey of Home Manufacturers by Charles G. Field.

The home manufacturer as a minimizer of risks has tended to be a market follower, not a market leader. His attitude is to wait and see which markets open up before investing in plant and equipment. He does not aggressively develop his own new markets. He followed the conventional builder into the single-family market boom of the 1950s and into the low-rise multifamily suburban market of the 1960s. The production mix for 1969 shows that home manufacturers, though lagging, are not far behind the national pattern. Whereas 55 percent of reported U.S. housing starts in 1969 were single-family units,[45] manufacturers reported that 60 percent of their sales were going to that market. (See Table 2-7.) Most of the remaining production went to low-rise multifamily housing (38 percent) and only 2 percent to high-rise construction. While in the 1970s some firms have ventured into the high-rise market, the trend is not strong. This continuing reluctance to enter the high-rise market reflects not only the hesitation of manufacturers to undertake large investments without some guarantee of volume sales, but also the problems some firms encounter from building trade unions.

Out of necessity, most home manufacturers have sought the market with the greatest volume of sales. Few manufacturers have stayed in the low cost market. Investment in plant and equipment, even at a low $100,000, requires a relatively high volume of sales (relative to conventional builder volume) in order to spread the fixed costs over enough units. Because of this investment in plant and equipment, the home manufacturer has a fixed overhead expenditure each year, which he covers by allocating it across units sold. If this volume of sales is low, the same fixed costs must be spread over fewer units, possibly driving the cost of the unit beyond that of the conventional product. Volume in the lower income market is too uncertain, for it depends upon public decisions to appropriate subsidy funds. From the 1950s to the present, the trend has been for the home manufacturer to escape the image of the low-cost builders. The high-income market, in turn, is a weak manufactured home market, because most buyers seek a high degree of personalization in a custom-designed home. Some home manufacturers sell in the vacation home market, but this represents only a small fraction of reported production. The recreation home market by itself is still too small and dispersed to justify investment in a home manufacturing plant. But the middle-income markets, which blossomed after the war, have been ripe for volume producers. That is where Levitt & Sons made a fortune, and where the home manufacturer has staked his claim.

In 1969, the home manufacturer was solidly in the middle-income market. More than half of the houses sold in 1969 (see Table 2–8) were above $15,000. The national average cost of construction for all new housing starts was $14,750 that year.[46] As long as the home manufacturer sold to the middle-income market, he stayed with the traditional and known, and did not strike out in new design directions. Architects were commissioned in the 1950s to design the "conventional-looking" house. That practice continues to this day. Although there are experimental units and new designs on the market, in most instances consumers cannot distinguish between the factory-produced item and the conventionally-built home. As a result, the look-alike design of the manufactured home has masked the true growth of home manufacturing. Since separate statistics were not kept as they are for mobile homes, the lack of distinguishability has blurred public recognition of their existence as a growing contribution to housing production.

Manufactured housing sells throughout the United States. Most sales are concentrated in the Midwest, a reflection of the industrial heritage of this portion of the nation. The Midwest, long considered the cradle of mobile homes, has also nurtured the rise of home manufacturing. It has a tradition of using factory-produced goods. At an early time, farmers made widespread use of Butler Barns, which were prefabricated in factories. Topography also played a key role. The relatively flat terrain facilitated the transportation of

Table 2-8
Distribution of Firms and Sales Volume by Price Class of Output: 1969

Price Class[a]	Number of Firms Reporting[b] Production	Units	Percent	Average output	Firms by Class of Greatest Sale
Under $5000	30	13,196	14.3	440	19
5000–9999	71	17,122	18.5	421	37
10,000–14,999	93	13,859	15.0	149	52
15,000–19,999	119	22,004	23.8	185	43
Over 20,000	101	26,266	28.4	260	59
		92,447	100.0		210

[a]Price does not include cost of land and site development. If the percent of land and site development costs to total sales price is assumed to be 31 percent for single-family homes, the price classes would be under $7,200; 7200–14,500; 14,500–21,800; 21,800–29,000; over 29,000.
[b]Any one firm is generally reported in two or more price classes.
Source: 1970 Survey of Home Manufacturers by Charles G. Field.

housing units. The emerging pattern, though, is for sales to spread throughout the nation, especially in regional growth areas like California, Texas, and Florida. Map 2-1 projects the sale of manufactured homes by states for firms reporting in the 1969 survey of home manufacturers. The higher the projection of the state, the larger the volume of sales made there.

Contrary to the once popularly held notion that manufactured housing was a phenomenon found in small urban and rural markets, it is now found in almost all markets. Producers have pentrated most urban and rural markets, but have failed to develop the large central city ones. The choice of primary markets is not random, but closely associated with the size of the firm. (See Table 2-9.) Larger firms favor the larger urban areas, while smaller firms seek their markets in the smaller urban and rural markets. The potential for volume sales is in the growing urban regions, where increasing metropolitization of the population is creating mass markets within the effective transportation range of the manufacturer's factory. Moreover, the presence of larger, more efficient conventional builders and specialty contractors operating in these major urban markets probably results in competition requiring the manufacturer to make major cost efficiencies, many of which come with volume production. Not surprisingly, the large producers favored medium to large urban markets; smaller producers favored small urban and rural markets.

Home Manufacturing in Perspective

The patterns of penetration by home manufacturers into the housing industry suggest that they have sought some degree of accommodation within

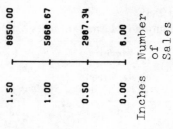

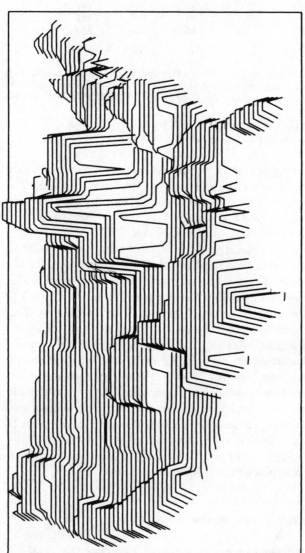

Map 2–1. Where Manufactured Homes Sold: 1969 (Source: 1970 Survey of Home Manufacturers by Charles G. Field)

Table 2-9
Primary Sales Market by Size of Firm: 1969

Volume of Products	Primary Sales Market (%)					
	Large Cities	Suburbs of Large Cities	Medium Urban Areas	Small Urban Areas	Rural and Rural Non-Farm	Total
Less 100	5.5 (3)	9.1 (5)	14.5 (8)	32.7 (18)	38.2 (21)	100% (45)
100-200	7.7 (2)	7.7 (2)	26.9 (7)	23.1 (6)	34.6 (9)	100% (26)
200-300	6.7 (1)	33.3 (5)	6.7 (1)	46.7 (7)	6.7 (1)	100% (15)
300-400	0.0 (0)	22.2 (2)	44.4 (4)	22.2 (2)	11.1 (1)	100% (9)
400-600	14.3 (2)	21.4 (3)	28.6 (4)	21.4 (3)	14.3 (2)	100% (14)
600-900	27.3 (3)	18.2 (2)	27.3 (3)	27.3 (3)	0.0 (0)	100% (11)
900-2000	28.6 (4)	21.4 (3)	7.1 (1)	28.6 (4)	14.3 (2)	100% (14)
2000 +	16.7 (2)	33.3 (4)	33.3 (4)	16.7 (2)	0.0 (0)	100% (12)

Number in Brackets represents the number of firms reporting that category. Percentages based upon row totals of 100%
Source: 1970 Survey of Home Manufacturers by Charles G. Field.

the system. Like all the other participants in the conventional industry, home manufacturers have made their own adjustments to unstable market conditions and localism. The home manufacturer has minimized his investments in plant and equipment, using labor wherever possible. This, in turn, has favored wood technologies to the fullest, for the equipment investment is small relative to that in other technologies. Adjustment to market vagaries has been attempted by seeking the volume markets and by adopting a distribution system that explicitly recognizes the localism of demand. As a result, producers have actively courted the middle-income market, reaching this market (as well as others) by using local builders.

Characteristically, the home manufacturer has adjusted to the home-building industry by seeking a balance between the number of economic functions removed from the site and the degree of effective resistance from local firms. It would be incorrect to assume that all home manufacturers control 100 percent of the construction work on their homes. In larger urban areas where the industrial structure is well defined, the manufacturer does a smaller proportion of the work than he does in smaller urban and rural areas.

He has sought to reduce uncertainties by seeking stable relationships within the conventional homebuilding industry, not by totally displacing it. Establishing ties with local builders has been one approach. Another has been the conclusion of a growing number of labor contracts between manufacturers and the various building trade unions. The firm grants unions jurisdiction within the factory and on the site. The internationals in turn pledge to use their good offices in resolving any problems encountered from local unions. Thereby the firm hopes to sidestep the problems arising when local unions refuse to handle their product. In essence, this is a transformation of the traditional union-subcontractor relationship into a union-home manufacturer one.

Manufacturers have adapted to the prevailing code structure by producing in their plants essentially the same home they would have built on the site. Design flexibility, not only to meet a variety of consumer tastes but also to clear the hurdle of local building code approvals, has been built into the production process at the sacrifice of mass production economies. Although they make adjustments in production, home manufacturers continue to report difficulties with codes.

On the whole, the home manufacturer has followed, not led, the industry. He lets things happen to him. His general inability to shape market forces, a characteristic endemic to the homebuilding industry, prevents his exercising any aggressive leadership. Perhaps the backing of large corporations will produce a new breed of management, but there are no *a priori* reasons for the new breed to be any more effective than the present producers in shaping the industry, because the forces that have molded behavior—market instability, localism, and the existing structure of the building industry—are left unchanged.

It was this failure in industrialized housing combined with rising housing costs and greater production requirements in the late 1960s that prompted a major federal demonstration project to foster the growth of industrialization.

Operation Breakthrough

The Department of Housing and Urban Development's Operation Breakthrough was designed to demonstrate that good industrialized housing technologies were available. In the process, HUD hoped to eliminate or alleviate important constraints like building codes, zoning, and financing that historically have stood in the way of volume production. Operation Breakthrough has just ended and already critics are proclaiming it a failure, or at best a modest success. A full evaluation has yet to be made, but the shutting down of many Operation Breakthrough companies suggests that less than full success was achieved.

Operation Breakthrough was launched in 1969 as a demonstration program under the Office of Research and Technology. The objectives were twofold: first to increase the production capacity of American firms to meet the 1968 housing goals, and second to remove impediments to the aggregation of large markets. HUD asked American industry to demonstrate industrialized housing technologies on nine selected sites around the country. Not only would the government pay for research and development costs, but would also use its regular subsidy program to encourage volume production outside the demonstration sites.

Of 236 consortia responding to the federal call, eventually a cross-section of 22 were selected for the program. Among those selected were major firms like Alcoa, General Electric, Republic Steel Corporation, and TRW. Traditional homebuilders were represented by Boise Cascade Corporation and Levitt Technology Corporation. Home manufacturers were represented by Home Building Corporation and National Homes Corporation. European systems were brought in by the Rouse-Wates Company and Descon/Concordia Systems, Ltd. Building systems ranged from panel construction to module techniques. Materials ranged from aluminum panels and precast concrete panels to plastic wall panels. Thus, the federal effort was to demonstrate a range of technologies from the near conventional to radical departures and pulled together to produce housing for habitation in professionally designed settings.

Development of the prototype sites was a twofold strategy. First, Operation Breakthrough had to demonstrate that high quality, both in construction and site design, was achievable with advanced building technologies—that industrialized housing, properly pursued, was synonymous with quality living. Second, it was expected that Operation Breakthrough would provide the opportunity for HUD to work on removing the constraints to industrialized production. Summarizing his testimony to the Senate Subcommittee on Urban Affairs, HUD's Assistant Secretary Harold B. Finger stated: "Operation Breakthrough is, therefore, not only directed at technological advancement of housing, but also at breaking through the various nonhardware constraints to more efficient production of housing."[47] In the years following this pronouncement, HUD has pursued a policy of working on building code reform, the development of performance standards, streamlining FHA processing as it pertained to industrialized housing, securing labor union agreements, and problems of financing.

There was another face to Operation Breakthrough—one not highly publicized, but equally important. Firms that joined Operation Breakthrough were encouraged to sell their systems in the private market. Armed with federal testing and approval of their prototype site housing systems and with some federal subsidy assistance, the systems producers, it was hoped, would break into the market as volume producers. As of mid–spring 1974, 15 manufacturers of the original 22 were still marketing Operation Breakthrough systems accounting for approximately 34,500 units.[48] While this volume is small relative to total annual construction starts, it does suggest that innovative and industrialized housing systems are viable ventures.

Industrialized housing has yet to catch on to the extent fervently desired by the boosters of Operation Breakthrough. Should the program be called a failure? We must clearly await developments, because industrialized housing, like other innovations in homebuilding, may require years of slow and steady diffusion into the mainstream of American construction activity.

Of the three basic requirements of industrialization and innovation presented earlier in the chapter, the chief one is that of market aggregation, not technological knowhow or market acceptance. This is the lesson of the postwar era. Tested European industrialized systems exist, some of them recently introduced on a limited basis in the United States. Growing purchases of manufactured homes and mobile homes indicate a positive response to innovative housing. Lack of aggregated markets, though, has restricted the fullest use of capital-intensive technologies.

Lack of a stable aggregated market can be overcome if a builder can tap multiple housing markets. When one market is overbuilt, he can balance his business volume by working in markets with excess demand. The large-scale conventional builder has achieved this by scattering projects throughout the country. An industrialized housing producer, by contrast, is typically tied to his production facility, unless it is portable to the project site. He is highly dependent upon demand within the effective transport radius of his plant, and any factor that bars entry to a market and thereby diminishes the effective market area is a highly significant problem.

Local building code regulation has exactly that effect. By reason of prohibitive code provisions, cumbersome approval procedures, fragmentation of the overall market area into hundreds of uniquely defined submarkets, building codes and their regulation have constituted one of the foremost barriers to innovation and industrialization. We now turn our attention to the effects of the building code regulatory system on technology and industrialization.

3 The Regulatory Process

To evaluate the impact of codes upon innovation, it is first necessary to understand the existing structure of the regulatory process. Over 15,000 localities issue building permits, but approximately 8,000 have their own building code, be it a national model code or one locally developed. There are numerous testing organizations and standard-setting institutions, and thousands of producers conducting their own research. In this chapter we describe the nature and functions of this regulatory process. In Chapter Four, the specific consequences for the building innovator and industrialist are described.

The Legal Framework

Unlike many other key sectors of the national economy, the housing construction industry operates in a local rather than a national context. To a large extent, this situation reflects the endurance of nineteenth century *laissez-faire* political and economic thought, perpetuated by the adjustment of markets stabilized under its aegis. Simply put, the construction industry has never escaped from the straitjacket of localism that characterized the early growth of the economy, while other forms of goods and services have increasingly come to flow through national patterns of distribution.

The authority to regulate construction is probably best described in a single comprehensive document that has set the standard for building code lawyers, Charles S. Rhyne's *Survey of the Law of Building Codes*:

> The law of building codes is grounded upon what is called the 'police power' of the state. The police power is *the source of all authority to enact building codes*. It has never been very exactly defined, and indeed the United States Supreme Court has said that it is 'incapable of any very exact definition.' Broadly speaking, it is the power of the state to legislate for the general welfare of its citizens.[1] (Emphasis added.)

Rhyne's 1960 study describes the historic pattern of delegating these exclusively state powers to municipalities:

This power resides in the legislature of the states and enables the legislature to pass laws such as building codes. Some states have done so. But most states have chosen to delegate a portion of their police power to local governmental units such as cities, which are formed by the state legislature and can exercise such powers as are conferred upon them by the state legislature. It is under the police power delegated by the state legislature that local governmental units are able to enact building codes.

To a significant extent, the familiar notion that building regulation is an exclusive preserve of the states represents a conclusion rather than a reasoned statement of what the U.S. Constitution requires or permits. Until the Great Depression forced the assertion of federal powers over wide sectors of the economy, many other aspects of labor and production were similarly considered to be exclusively local concerns. But the need for national action found constitutional support in other provisions of the Federal Constitution, especially the Interstate Commerce Clause, by which the national government may exercise authority over activities "in commerce" between the states. Ensuing judicial interpretations have more or less consistently upheld federal preeminence in areas once considered strictly local. The criterion is a nexus to a specific national interest—from control over production and hours of labor in the 1930s, to civil rights in the 1960s, and control over environmental matters in the 1970s. But federal legislation governing standards of construction has been notably absent, so that the field for state regulation has not been significantly impaired—or "preempted" under the Supremacy Clause of the Constitution. (Subsequently, we shall discuss how federal consitutional doctrine and existing laws may nonetheless be used to attack restrictive building codes. But at this point suffice it to say that federal powers have not expressly invaded the field of building regulation.)

With state authority exclusively occupying the field of building regulation, municipalities and counties have exercised powers over construction delegated either explicitly or implicitly by the states. Notwithstanding the recent enactment of statewide building codes in a number of states—a notable move over the last few years to achieve greater uniformity—municipal bodies have remained the principal locus of authority over building regulation. In many areas, more or less formal procedures exist in the form of Boards of Review supported by a full panoply of procedural safeguards for determining compliance with building codes, but more often authority for inspection and determination of compliance is vested in a single individual, the building inspector.

The content of codes which govern highly technical issues beyond the practical comprehension of state or local legislative bodies, has been the principal source of difficulty in achieving standards amenable to innovation. A degree of uniformity has been achieved through the good offices of model code groups. The principal codes are: *Uniform Building Code* (International

Conference of Building Officials, originally drafted 1927); *Basic Building Code* (Building Officials and Code Administrators, International, Inc.,) *The Southern Standard Building Code* (Southern Building Codes Conference); and *The National Building Code* (National Board of Fire Underwriters, originally drafted 1905). The former three codes were drafted largely by professional groups of building inspectors, and each is periodically updated, normally with annual supplements. All three code-writing groups united in 1971 to publish a Joint Code: *One and Two-Family Dwelling Code* (1971). In addition, the Federal Housing Administration has established minimum standards that serve as guides for federally-financed housing programs and influence the content of the model codes. *U.S. Federal Housing Administration, Minimum Property Standards for Multi-Family Housing* (originally published in 1963).

The establishment of model codes for adoption by local authorities has not, contrary to what one might expect, resolved the problem of achieving market aggregation. First of all, neighboring municipalities may adopt differing model codes as the basis for local regulation. Secondly, periodic revisions of codes promulgated by national code-writing groups may not be adopted by localities for several years, and hence the effort to keep codes current may iself retard the development of uniformity. In addition, municipalities may explicitly decline to adopt specific provisions of model codes, or (as is the case in many large cities) adopt their own variants of key provisions. Finally, even though the letter of codes may be uniform among jurisdictions, the interpretation given to the same language may differ. Thus, the model codes may not be part of the solution to building code diversity, but part of the problem.

Moreover, procedures for enforcement and appeal often reflect little administrative sophistication and considerable informality and arbitrariness. The burden of enforcing such codes rests on local officials in close concert with builders, architects, material suppliers, and tradesmen; and building inspectors may not possess extensive technical qualifications. With respect to appeals on initial determination by building inspectors, affected traditional interest groups often exert self-protective influence. The Douglas Commission commented as follows:

> The construction industry and related interest groups are extremely influential in the operation of appeal procedures. Representatives of the industry frequently are requested to recommend individuals for appointment to appeal boards, and codes and ordinances frequently require that members of appeal boards be architects, engineers, and contractors. Such practices would not appear to provide adequate protection to the public.[2]

While the systems innovator or the architect has a limited voice in such proceedings, the interests of the consumer are largely unrepresented. Generally, appeals may be taken to administrative Boards of Appeal or to a panel of arbitrators. Although judicial review of final denials of relief is not generally specified in enabling statutes, constitutional considerations of due process (and state administrative procedure statutes) appear to compel limited judicial review, to be discussed later.

Finally, note should be taken of the range of sanctions available to enforce building regulations. Generally, owners or architects acting on their behalf, seek permits from municipal building agencies, submitting plans for construction. Permits are not granted if plans do not comply with regulations. After construction begins, building inspectors can make spot checks to ascertain compliance. In many jurisdictions, a final inspection is required before a certificate of occupancy can be issued. Where construction does not satisfy inspection, administrative stop orders can be issued and supported by either summary administrative action, court orders and injunctions, fines, and/or criminal actions.

Thus, in summary, the basic legal framework for building regulation encompasses the following key elements: (1) state enabling legislation, in the absence of federal preemption, exercised either directly by the states or delegated to municipalities and counties; (2) local building codes, often based on a model code but frequently embodying local revisions or omitting up-to-date model revisions; (3) administrative application and enforcement procedures, with significant discretion given to individual building inspectors; and (4) limited avenues of appeal to local appeals boards, to arbitration, or to the courts.

The Regulatory Structure

The building code regulatory system can be schematized as a flow of decisions that begins within a technical framework of standard-setting and testing and ends with more politicized, bureaucratic decisions at the local building code and enforcement levels. Establishing standards, making the necessary product, material, or structural tests, and developing and maintaining model codes all takes place voluntarily. To date, the federal government has declined to play an active and compulsory role in this process.

To say that these activities are technical is to state the obvious. On a more subtle level, there is considerable competition between various interest groups to secure favored code positions. Sometimes the competition is intense, because a technical construction standard can favor one product while cutting another one out of the market.

Promulgating, maintaining, and enforcing building codes are governmental and therefore political acts. The city fathers must vote on the code. It is thus a pass-fail system that carries the force of law. Without code approval, construction or use of a product cannot take place. Without construction, profits and wages are not earned. It is not surprising, therefore, that many in the construction business are vitally concerned with codes. As long as code decisions and approvals support the traditional construction process, firms involved in construction pay scant attention to code activities. But when one party really wants to change established ways of doing business, thus causing redivisions of work, considerable attention and effort are expended to secure code decisions that perpetuate the status quo. In the case of plastic pipe, substantial financial and political resources were brought to bear on the question of code acceptability, because the introduction of plastic pipe meant new pipe producers and potential changes in work hour requirements for organized labor.

Standard-Setting

Standards are the backbone of any building code. They are the technical specifications that determine whether a product, subsystem, or complete housing system meets publicly-defined minimum levels of health and safety. In almost all codes, these standards are expressed in specifications indicating how and/or what the content of an item should be.

A more progressive and technically more flexible approach is to use performance standards. Performance involves a statement of product requirement. For example, in the area of structural fire safety the performance requirement used in Operation Breakthrough's Guide Criteria (the performance-based code developed by the National Bureau of Standards to evaluate Operation Breakthrough housing systems) read:

> The structure should retain its integrity for sufficient time to permit evacuation of the building and for fire fighters to bring the fire under control.

This requirement, though, is too general for application by a building official. Therefore, a level of performance or specification must be set. In this illustration the level set was:

> The fire endurance of the components of the structure should equal or exceed the following: Floor systems over a crawl space or basement, ten minutes: Other floor systems, 20 minutes; interdwelling, bearing walls, 20 minutes.[3]

There are literally thousands of standards in use today covering all aspects of housing. One estimate placed it between 13,000 to 14,000, most having been developed by the various building trade associations. These associations, some 400 to 500 in 1968, represent specialized product groups. For example, the interests of the cast iron soil pipe manufacturers are represented through the Cast Iron Soil Pipe Institute, plastic pipe producers are represented by the Plastic Pipe Institute, and wood interests are handled by the National Forest Products Association.

While these associations conduct, through their membership, the actual research and testing to develop specific standards, certification comes from one of the standardization associations. Two of these, the American National Standards Institute (ANSI) and the American Society for Testing Materials (ASTM), adopt standards through what is termed the "consensus process." Special committees representing industry and public interests meet to consider a proposed standard and eventually reach a consensus on the acceptability of a proposed standard.

The importance of standards is obvious to the innovator. First, standards are established as reference marks for product performance. They set the end targets for product development. Second, standards are then used as the basis for product testing. It is almost tautological that the closer the stated standards to performance requirements, the more directly applicable they are to the innovation and the more applicable the tests.

Inventors and researchers of new housing products need to know what performance is required of their product. Almost by definition, an innovation is a new way of doing something. Thus, standards that specify how and with what types of materials a product is to be built are antithetical to innovation. Unfortunately, almost all codes are specification codes, not performance codes.

A performance code, however, begins with objective statements of functions. Walls should be capable of withstanding certain minimum loads, or plumbing systems should be capable of providing minimum levels of hot water or drainage. The standard is then refined to specification levels. In case of the walls, an absolute minimum level of load bearing capacity will be set. The standards though, do not specify the materials or methods of assembly to be used.

Without performance standards, it is difficult to specify reasonable test procedures, a point discussed below. This void of reasonable construction guidelines severely limits the development, acceptance, and diffusion of radically new housing concepts. As a consequence, most new ideas in housing construction that make it past the standards are only marginally inventive. Though the characteristic pattern of marginal improvements typical of homebuilding is not caused solely by the code structure, the code structure is a definite barrier to meaningful innovation.

The development of specification codes and absence of performance codes is not illogical, given the business environment of residential construction. Violent local swings in construction have led to uncertainty, thus minimizing construction options to subcontracting, specialization and labor intensive strategies. The objective is to make future patterns of business as predictable as possible. Thus, a builder can count on plumbers and electricians to do their jobs, lathers and carpenters to do theirs. A specification code makes predictable the technology, materials, and workers needed to do a job. A performance code, in sharp contrast, leaves all these decisions up to the builder or manufacturer. Thus, a performance code tends to increase rather than decrease uncertainty in an uncertainty-minimizing industry.

To receive favorable treatment when seeking the adoption of new standards, one generally has to be part of the team. The standards associations are often considered by some to be closed shops. To have influence, you must be part of the established industry. Thus, an innovator who generally stands outside the system encounters great difficulty in securing acceptable standards for his product if such standards do not currently exist.

Congress has responded to the national need for performance criteria and standards by establishing a National Institute of Building Sciences, which is mandated to develop, promulgate, and maintain these regulatory elements. We shall have more to say about NIBS in Chapters Five and Six.

Testing

Standards are useless without credible testing procedures. This is the function of testing agencies (like Underwriters Laboratory) developing credible test procedures, conducting product tests, and certifying by label the worthiness of the product. At present there does not exist a rating system for distinguishing between different testing agencies. The assortment of agencies is mixed, ranging from those of high professional standards to those of marginal integrity.

The need for a rating system was recognized in 1971, when the National Bureau of Standards commenced to develop an accreditation project called LEAP (Laboratory Evaluation and Accreditation Project). In 1972, a committee was established in ASTM (E32) to further NBS research into usable criteria standards for engineering evaluation and inspection laboratories. In 1973, an ASTM committee (E36) was established to further NBS research on criteria standards for testing laboratories.

For innovative products and construction processes, testing laboratories play a key role. Many building officials lack the technical knowledge and experience to judge the merits of new products. Therefore, they must and do rely upon the judgments of others. Naturally, they turn to testing laboratories or other similar institutions (i.e., model code associations) when seeking technical evaluations; upon their advice they can approve or disapprove an innovative product. One central problem is that no laboratory's decision is binding. Product approval does not guarantee product acceptance under the code. Building officials are free to ask for new tests, even though the product has been tested, and they often do this.

A major problem in the testing area is the frequent absence of adequate test procedures (and standards) for completely innovative products or processes. Most tests have been designed to specification standards, not to performance standards. There has been a lack of developmental research in this area because money and time have not been available to most testing institutions. In response to this obvious deficiency, the National Bureau of Standards and HUD have sponsored the development of performance standards and testing procedures, but these have yet to receive widespread support in the code-testing community.

One of the more fascinating questions is why the system has been impervious to extensive government efforts to institute performance standards and tests. Clearly, the resources exist in the building products industries to conduct the needed research. If the cost of research is too great for one firm, the industry has demonstrated a capacity and willingness to pool its resources for a given job. This was clearly the case in the Building Research Advisory Board, organized to promote pro-industry public laws and regulations.

Failure in the area of performance underscores two problems. The first is the technical difficulty of developing standards and arriving at a concensus on them. Second is a basic unwillingness by material producers to establish performance standards that open the market to newcomers. The lack of performance standards and analogous tests hinders existing material producers, causing them to expend considerable resources on product development and testing. Many producers have the capital reserves for this, but not small innovators, who are thus prevented from entering the market. Although existing standards may be costly to the material producer, they discourage innovation and preserve his sales market.

Product testing problems fall into two categories—the adequacy of the test itself and the believability of the results. Without adequate performance standards, it is almost impossible to devise a set of tests for innovative products. Old tests have been used to judge new technologies. It is generally acknowledged that much work remains to be done to devise adequate tests related to performance criteria.

As it presently stands, an innovator seeking code approval must submit his product for testing if so requested by the local building official. Unfortunately for the innovator, this is not a one-test system. What is acceptable to one building inspector may not be acceptable to a second, who may not like the testing laboratory or the specification used. While by law the building official must be reasonable and not arbitrary in his use of public power, what is reasonable in a system lacking performance standards is an open question.

Believability translates into product certification or labeling. Because testing procedures are not binding upon a local building official's judgment of a product, credibility of the testing process is a crucial issue. The process becomes more credible if the testing organization is either highly reputable or if it is willing to warrant the product, which none are willing to do. A different approach would be through legislation that provides for automatic code acceptance of a tested product by an approved testing institution. Here the government would assume the basic responsibility by standing behind the institution's certification.

The Pattern of Codes

The efforts of standard-setting and testing institutions become formalized in a building code or in one of the specialty codes (i.e., electrical, elevator, plumbing, etc.). This code is the checklist that a unit or structure must satisfy before it is approved for construction. The code covers all aspects of the residential unit from cellar to attic, from mechanical systems to foundation structure.

Risking oversimplification of a complicated document, we might say that the building code is a composite of three sets of information and requirements: (1) definitions of terms, (2) licensing requirements, and (3) the standards themselves. Each code has sections setting forth definitions of key work areas. These define, for example, what constitutes plumbing or electrical work. While seemingly innocuous, these definitions, when linked to licensing requirements, assume major economic significance to specific groups. The licensing requirements spell out who is authorized to do what work. For example, the International Association of Plumbing and Mechanical Officials code states that only licensed plumbers may do the work defined as plumbing. The significance is clear. Only members of the United Association of Plumbers may do plumbing work under the code, although there are other laborers capable of doing the work. Because codes carry the force of law, the United Associations members are guaranteed the work jurisdiction as long as the code provisions stay in force.

In this the code has served a goal beyond that of health and safety. Job security has been served to the benefit of specific labor interests and to the detriment of others, irrespective of any efficiency gains or losses to the eventual consumer. Long hard battles are fought between competing unions for jurisdiction of work. While the primary means of jurisdictional conflict are resolved through other means, the codes serve either as a battleground between warring building trade unions or as a codification of decisions reached.

The *standards* section, the heart of the code, is the natural and logical conclusion of the standard-defining process. Standards researched by industry and legitimized through concensus, find their way into local codes either through one of the model code associations or through direct lobbying by industry representatives at the local level. This was not the traditional pattern.

Typically, local communities based their codes upon traditional local practice. The test was the test of time. In this way codes were technically conservative documents bearing less the mark of technical feasibility and innovation, more the brand of "what has worked for the past 30 years."

That pattern began to change in the post-World War II period as model codes became more widely used. Model code associations have become one of the gatekeepers of technically current standards. While model code associations have lacked an in-house research capacity, they have often hired professional staff to "monitor" the current technology. Although these associations are also marked by politics and are influenced (some say captured) by building material producers, they are far more professional in judgment than local building officials.

By 1970, all cities, large and small, were regulating homebuilding through building codes. In 1970, 72.8 percent of the cities fashioned their codes upon one of the four model codes (See Table 3-1), whereas in the 1940s, very few of them did. State-based codes (many are based on one of the model codes) were used by 13.5 percent of the cities, and locally-drafted codes by 10.8 percent. Only 2.2 percent of the cities surveyed, accounting for only a small fraction of the population, reported having no building code. Non-code localities were mostly very small urban and rural towns, but even so more than four out of five towns used codes.

The model code associations actively solicit member cities from well-defined regional areas, as if they had agreed upon spheres of influence. While there is some overlapping in market areas, the country is generally blocked out into areas dominated by one of the code associations. The International Conference of Building Officials (ICBO) claim is in the West, Building Officials and Code Administrators (BOCA) in the Northeast, and Southern Building Codes Congress (SBCC) in the South. In the North Central region, BOCA and ICBO actively compete against each other for city members. American Insurance Association (AInA), creator of the National Building Code, is active in three regions, but has no penetration in the West. AInA, unlike the other three code associations, is not an association of building officials. Established in 1905, AInA created the National Building Code as part of their underwriting procedures for ascertaining risk of insurance losses due to fires. Overall, model codes are most evident in the South and West. Ninety-two percent of the West's 224 responding cities say they use ICBO's Uniform Building Code. (See Table 3-1.)

What sharply distinguishes model and locally-drafted codes is the degree to which a community goes outside its political jurisdiction for technical assistance in code drafting. Locally-drafted codes admit to the full play of local interest groups in the development of definitions, licensing requirements, and standards. Jurisdictions using model codes, on the other hand, are basically outward-looking when seeking substantial professional advice. By the same

Table 3-1
Percent of Cities Reporting Code Based Upon:

Classification	Number of Cities Reporting	AIA (1)	ICBO (2)	SSBC (3)	BOCA (4)	State (5)	Locally Drafted Code (6)	No Code in Effect (7)
Total all cities	919	12.2%	31.3%	14.9%	15.1%	13.5%	10.8%	2.2%
Population Group								
Over 500,000	12	0.0	33.3	0.0	25.0	0.0	41.7	0.0
250,000–500,000	12	8.3	50.0	25.0	0.0	8.3	8.3	0.0
100,000–250,000	59	3.4	27.1	25.4	15.3	13.6	15.3	0.0
50,000–100,000	111	8.1	39.6	15.3	16.2	16.2	4.5	0.0
25,000–50,000	225	9.3	34.2	11.6	16.9	13.8	13.8	0.4
10,000–25,000	429	16.6	29.8	15.6	13.1	12.6	10.0	2.3
5,000–10,000	61	13.1	16.4	14.8	23.0	16.4	4.9	11.5
Less 5,000	10	0.0	30.0	0.0	10.0	20.0	20.0	20.0
Geographic Region								
Northeast	185	22.2	1.1	0.0	32.4	21.6	17.3	5.4
North Central	249	10.8	22.9	0.4	27.7	14.9	20.5	2.8
South	241	18.3	2.1	56.4	4.1	14.1	3.7	1.2
West	244	0.0	91.8	0.0	0.0	5.3	2.9	0.0
City Type								
Central	149	6.7	29.5	24.8	14.8	12.8	11.4	0.0
Suburban	414	11.1	33.6	7.2	20.0	12.8	14.0	1.2
Independent	340	16.5	28.5	20.6	9.7	13.8	6.5	4.4
Form of Government								
Mayor-Council	240	17.1	15.0	6.7	20.4	19.6	18.8	2.5
Council-Manager	625	10.2	38.9	17.6	12.8	11.5	7.4	1.6
Other[1]	54	13.0	16.7	20.4	18.5	9.3	14.8	7.4

[1] Includes: Cities with commission government, with town meeting, and with representative town meeting.

Source: Computed from 1970 Survey of Local Building Departments by Charles G. Field and Francis T. Ventre.

token, as a community increases its search for outside professional support, local interest group involvement and influence decreases in the code development process.

Several significant statistics should be noted in Table 3-1. First, a large proportion of the largest cities (defined as 500,000 population or greater) used locally-drafted codes. This was for three principle reasons. The model codes do not typically cover the type of construction—high-rise—used in the larger cities, thus the locality must come up with its own code. These cities tend to have the professional staff and budget resources needed to develop and maintain these codes. Finally, there are numerous local interest groups in the larger cities, for example, unions and specialty subcontractors, who have a vested interest in the specification of the code and prefer not to delegate the code decision-making process to outsiders—the model code associations. Although such groups exist in many communities, their influence is particularly strong and the volume of construction dollars at stake is significantly large in larger cities to justify their involvement in code-writing and enforcement activities.

A second observed pattern is that the older and more industrialized sections of the country are more likely to use locally-drafted codes. The extent to which local groups seek control over codes is probably influenced by the vitality of local construction activity. High and growing construction dollar volume means work to go around and little need to influence code rules that distribute economic activity. Steady or declining activity, on the other hand, probably fosters actions to preserve local jobs and sales. Thus, it is not surprising that the industrially younger and generally faster-growing Western and Southern regions make greater use of the model codes. Neither is it surprising that the slower-growing and more traditionally established industrial Northeast and North Central regions have a greater incidence of locally-drafted codes. Third, in small rural towns coverage is still spotty. Theoretically, they are covered by the state, but in practice you can build what you want there. Now, with the trend toward second homes, extended coverage should be expected.

It was possible to trace recent code pattern changes by taking two national surveys, which traced code changes for 140 cities between 1964 and 1970. Code adoptions during the 1960s emphasized the trends toward model codes and away from locally-based codes. Ninety-one cities adopted one of the model codes, reflecting a search for higher technical quality while retaining full administrative control at the local level. Thirty-seven cities abandoned one model code for another, demonstrating the purely voluntary relationship between the community and the model code association. Thirty-six cities switched to state codes, underscoring the power of states to alter local control of codes. (See Table 3-2.)

Growing dissatisfaction with locally-based codes was reflected in the flight of 74 cities (53 percent of the sample) from local to either model or state codes. (Some of the largest cities have retained local codes because of

Table 3-2
Types of Code Changes 1964–1970

Type Code Used 1964	Type Code Used 1970			
	Model	State	Local	Total
Model	37	15	12	64
State	1	0	1	2
Local	53	21	0	74
Total	91	36	13	140

Sources: Computed from the 1970 Survey of Local Building Departments by Charles G. Field and Francis T. Ventre and the 1964 International City Management Survey of Local Building Departments.

the unique building conditions associated with high-rise, high-density living, but this decision is costly. New York City spent over $1 million to rewrite its code completely.)

Pressures to turn away from local codes have come principally from two sources. The first was growing public criticism of antiquated local code provisions. By the mid- to late 1960s, prestigious organizations like the Advisory Commission on Intergovernmental Relations and the National Commission on Urban Problems had soundly indicted the local approach. The second, and probably more significant cause for change was the increasing pressure by the Department of Housing and Urban Development on localities seeking federally-funded urban development programs to adopt a model code as part of the Workable Program requirements. The policy was not to approve a community's Workable Program unless it contained the *most recent edition* of the regional model code. This persuasion was effective in speeding up local use of model codes, for many federal grants were contingent upon an approved Workable Program.

Having a model code does not imply that the code is current. While model code associations annually update their codes to reflect revised and newly adopted standards, the extent of local revision is much less frequent. This is reflected in Table 3-3, which compares the date of most recent revision stratified by type of code. While model-based codes tend to be updated more recently than state or locally-based ones, there still exists (as of 1970) a substantial lag. Eighteen percent of the communities using model based codes had not revised their codes within the past five years.

Enforcement

The building official, as the chief enforcement official, breathes life into the written code. Whereas the code specifies what type of construction is permissible, the official insures that the standards are met. Often, he must

Table 3-3
Year Building Code Last Revised

Type of Code	No. Cities Reporting	1970	1969	1968	1967	1966	1960 -65	1950 -59	1940 -49	Pre 1940	Total
Model	554	16.6	22.0	15.7	24.0	4.2	13.0	4.0	0.4	0.2	100%
State	89	15.7	13.5	21.3	14.6	7.9	20.2	6.7	0.0	0.0	100%
Local	75	12.0	22.7	9.3	6.7	10.7	20.0	14.7	2.7	1.3	100%
All	718	16.0	21.0	15.7	21.0	5.3	14.6	5.4	0.6	0.3	100%

Source: Charles G. Field and Francis T. Ventre, "Local Regulation of Building: Agencies, Codes, and Politics" in *The Municipal Year Book 1971* (Washington, D.C.: International City Management Association, 1971), p. 150.

interpret the standards when applied to specific building plans. Occasionally, he must determine whether a uniquely-designed building meets the code's performance standards; if so, he will grant approval. Almost every code confers this special approval power. The willingness of the building official to use this power to entertain new products and techniques depends upon the attitudes and personal background he brings to the job.

The building official is responsible for approving building plans, inspecting the construction of buildings, and issuing permits of occupancy. According to one definition, he is

> a law enforcement officer; a highly specialized law enforcement officer 'whose prime mission is the prevention and correction, or abatement of violations . . . [He] designs nothing, repairs nothing. His responsibility is merely to see that those persons who are engaged in these activities do so within the requirements of the law.[4]

This definition, however, fails to take into account the influences that bear upon him. He reacts to different factions of the local building industry interested in securing favorable code decisions. Moreover, his actions are influenced by resources available to him in the form of budget, working conditions, and support from local politicians. Only by placing the local official into his context can we begin to understand his actions and formulate programs to upgrade enforcement.

Disincentives of the Office

Most cities offer a salary and budget that fail to attract good people into code enforcement jobs. According to 1970 data, in only the largest cities do salary ranges for building officials provide monetary incentives for efficiency and fairness in code enforcement. The potential for salary growth is limited. In most cities surveyed, there is a narrow range between beginning and maximum salaries. For all cities, $7,490 is the median for starting salaries and $9,600 for maximum salaries. Only in cities with populations of more than 500,000 did salary schedules offer much chance of job advancement. (See Table 3-4.) The overall median salary for chief building officials in 1970 was only $10,586, surely no incentive for aggressive leadership. Again, larger cities paid better.

Building department budgets are generally too small to support adequate in-house training programs or to undertake ongoing code revision, so crucial in an age of rapidly changing technology. Often the principal source of funding is from building permit fees, which are usually meager. To date, the federal government has committed few of its resources to improving enforcement.

The salary structure of building officials and the economics of construction

Table 3–4
Minimum and Maximum Salaries of Building Officials
by City Size: 1970

City Size	Number of Cities Reporting		Median Salaries		Median Salary of Chief Building Official
	Beginning	Maximum	Beginning	Maximum	
Over 500,000	12	12	$10,002	$15,833	$21,712
250,000–500,000	11	11	7,818	10,683	16,650
100,000–250,000	53	52	7,869	9,956	14,017
50,000–100,000	95	95	7,993	9,995	12,750
25,000–50,000	173	179	7,636	9,653	11,693
10,000–25,000	206	220	7,134	9,085	9,387
All Cities	575	598	7,490	9,600	10,586

Source: Computed from 1970 Survey of Local Building Departments by Charles G. Field and Francis T. Ventre.

combine to foster an environment within which bribes are offered and accepted. Low salary scales with limited growth potential combined with the power to halt construction place a building official in a position to demand payments from people seeking code approval. On the industry's side, the high cost of time for some builders is an inducement to speed up construction at all costs. Greasing the system or the small gift is, according to some, considered part of doing business.

If the satisfactions of work are not to be found in material benefits, perhaps they are to be found in the intrinsic, qualitative aspects of the job. Low income could be offset by the intrinsic reward of challenge of prestige. But prestige is not the lot of building officials. They are generally held in low esteem, often considered to be at the bottom rung of the public service ladder. Their lack of civil service coverage (seeTable 3–10) and the inadequacy of their budgets are indicative of the second-class status they have in the system. They are often accused of accepting bribes; certainly the low salary scales are no protection against bribery. One can only conclude that these job conditions do not attract the most qualified, upwardly mobile and progressive officials. The incentives for becoming a building official must come from elsewhere.

Although the job may offer a step up from blue to white collar status, those who seek it probably are motivated more by the desire to leave construction work than by the opportunities the job offers. Construction is seasonal, exposed to inclement weather, and physically demanding. The building official's job, though lacking salary inducements and bureaucratic status, is year-round, provides a desk, and requires little effort. It should not be surprising that the push of difficult outside work and the pull of easier work attracts older construction workers into the job.

The local building department appears to be a place where careers end rather than begin. One chief building official in seven is over 60, and over

Table 3-5
Ages of Local Officials: 1970

	Number Cities Reporting	Age					Total
		20-29	30-39	40-45	50-59	60	
Chief Building Officer	790	1.6	15.6	30.8	37.8	14.2	100%
Senior Building Officer	471	1.5	12.7	30.6	36.5	18.7	100%
Most Recently Appointed Building Officer	401	8.7	27.4	28.2	28.2	7.5	100%

Source: Computed from 1970 Survey of Local Building Departments by Charles G. Field and Francis T. Ventre.

half of all chiefs are past 50. (See Table 3-5.) Of those officials with seniority in the department, 19 percent are past 60 and 55 percent are past 50.

Limited budget, limited salaries, and limited prestige add up to uninviting job opportunities for bright young professionals eager to do a job. Even those willing to accept the unattractive entry inducements are handcuffed by lack of funds for professional training, comprehensive code revisions, and evaluations of their own enforcement activities.

Progress has been slow in fostering a high level of professionalism in the building official, because the qualifications of officials in office and their reputations for efficiency and fairness are at a very low level. Lacking have been uniformily accepted building official qualifications and educational curricula for their training. The associations of building officials are belatedly recognizing the need for a more formalized and professional approach to the education and training of building officials. The National Academy of Code Administration was incorporated in September 1970:

> to conduct research, develop curricula, establish standards, accreditation and certification, sponsor educational activities and engage in all other scholarly concerns necessary to the development and establishment of a profession.

Part and parcel of upgrading the quality of building officials is the upgrading of their own personal professional esteem.

Parochialism in Orientation

Most officials come out of the local construction industry trained as members of building trades (union or non-union) or as general contractors. (See Table 3-6.) While some experience in local construction is a positive qualification,

Table 3-6
Occupational Backgrounds of Local Building Officials: 1970

	Number Reporting	Union Bldg. Trades	Non-Union Bldg. Trades	General Contractor	Engineer	Architect	Other Govt.	Other
				Percent Reporting				
Chief Building Official	815	28.8	21.4	42.4	26.8	8.6	24.8	14.1
Senior Building Official	522	39.0	29.3	28.8	6.7	2.3	20.9	14.8
Most Recently Appointed Building Official	433	33.1	25.2	29.8	9.9	2.5	20.3	17.5

*Row totals do not equal 100%, because some checked more than one background component.
Source: Computed from 1970 Survey of Local Building Departments by Charles G. Field and Francis T. Ventre.

too much is counterproductive. While inspectors should be receptive to both conventional and innovative construction applications, their experience, bred of the local apprenticeship system, confines their expertise to conventional ways. Because the present regulation system places code approval decisions in the hands of local inspection, proposers of innovative construction approaches face an uphill intellectual battle.

It is not surprising that inspectors by work and social habit are tied to their localities. The officials themselves acknowledge that their most frequent work contacts are with local builders, local building material suppliers, local architects, and local engineers. Their social relationships follow the same pattern. (See Table 3-7.) Thus, the parochial view is reinforced; it is seldom modified by contacts with people outside the community who might hold more cosmopolitan views on construction technology. Except in the largest cities, the building departments are so small that officials cannot hide behind the cloak of bureaucratic anonymity. They are conversant with and known by those in the local construction industry, which makes them susceptible to their influence. While in itself this pattern is most natural, it prejudices building officials against new technologies and innovations introduced by non-local interests.

Sensitivity to Political Influences

Traditional means of achieving job protection—civil service and union representation—are not widespread among building agencies. Seven out of eight building chiefs serve without a specific term of office; they serve at the pleasure of those who appoint them. (See Table 3-8.) More than half of those with specific terms are assured of only one year's tenure. (See Table 3-9.) Only 40 percent of local building departments are covered by civil service regulations (see Table 3-10), most of these departments being found in the larger urban areas. Fewer yet (one in 15) are covered by unions (See Table 3-10). Thus, the normal approaches to job security and grievance resolution are notably absent.

The vulnerability of building officials to the political structure is apparent when we take a closer look at civil service coverage. In a mayoral form of city government, the building official relates directly to the mayor, an elected official. His contact with elected officials in cities with city managers is indirect. In this latter situation, the degree of political influence imposed upon the inspector depends upon the city manager's sense of professionalism and sensitivity to political pressures. In any case, it is clear that the city manager offers some form of political protection to building officials. The lopsided preference of building officials for civil service coverage under mayoral forms of government reflects the uneasiness they feel when they set too close to the political

Table 3-7
Work and Social Contacts by Chief Building Officials

How frequently do you have official business contact with the following individuals?

Contact With	Often (1)	Occasionally (2)	Rarely (3)	Never (4)	No. Cities Reporting
Building Material Producers, and Suppliers Personnel					
Local	28.0	46.4	21.1	4.5	887
Out-of-Town	8.0	49.4	34.8	7.8	862
Prefabricated Home Manufacturer or his Representative	7.2	36.9	41.6	14.3	891
Builder Personnel					
Local	79.1	13.1	2.4	1.6	893
Out-of-Town	37.5	42.3	10.9	2.5	865
Building Trade Union Personnel	4.7	17.0	38.9	32.4	864
Building Officials from Cities:					
Within your county	38.8	36.7	15.7	9.0	855
Outside your county	18.1	48.5	25.6	7.8	874
Building Official from State Building Agency	11.9	38.9	27.3	19.9	865
Representative of a Model Code Group	16.9	32.2	29.8	21.1	882
Architects or Engineers	65.6	28.6	4.8	0.9	858

How frequently do you see the following individuals after work hours?

Building Material Producers, and Suppliers Personnel					
Local	4.4	26.1	37.3	32.2	888
Out-of-Town	0.5	14.6	38.3	46.6	867
Prefabricated Home Manufacturer or his Representative	0.5	8.5	30.0	61.0	879
Builder Personnel					
Local	13.7	38.2	30.3	17.8	884
Out-of-Town	2.8	19.8	43.1	34.3	863
Building Trade Union Personnel	0.7	7.7	25.9	65.7	860
Building Officials from Cities:					
Within your county	11.2	32.3	28.3	28.3	867
Outside your county	6.1	27.4	33.9	32.6	870
Building Official from State Building Agency	1.9	14.5	27.7	55.9	855
Representative of a Model Code Group	3.8	20.1	25.6	50.5	875
Architects or Engineers	9.2	36.1	35.1	19.6	848

Source: Computed from 1970 Survey of Local Building Departments by Charles G. Field and Francis T. Ventre.

Table 3–8

Chief Building Officials Appointed for Term of Office: 1970

Appointed for Term	Number of Cities Reporting	Percent
Yes	117	13.5
No	749	86.5
Total	866	100.0

Source: Computed from 1970 Survey of Local Building Departments by
Charles G. Field and Francis T. Ventre.

Table 3–9

Term of Office for Chief Building Officials: 1970

Number of Years	Number of Cities Reporting	Percent
1	58	51.3
2	25	22.1
3	3	2.7
4–6	25	22.1
7–15	0	0.0
16	2	1.8
Total	113	100.0

Source: Computed from 1970 Survey of Local Building Departments by
Charles G. Field and Francis T. Ventre.

Table 3–10

**Building Officials Covered by Civil Service or Represented by Unions:
By Location and City Sizes: 1970**

	Civil Service %			Union Representation %		
	No. Reporting	Yes	No	No. Reporting	Yes	No
Central City	154	57.1	42.9	153	13.7	86.3
Suburban	410	42.0	58.0	409	6.1	93.9
Independent	320	20.9	79.1	320	3.1	96.9
City Size						
Over 500,000	13	92.3	7.7	13	30.8	69.2
250,000–500,000	12	83.3	16.7	12	33.3	66.7
100,000–250,000	61	60.7	39.3	60	15.0	85.0
50,000–100,000	113	57.5	42.5	113	11.5	88.5
25,000–50,000	223	48.9	51.1	220	6.8	93.2
10,000–25,000	415	22.4	77.6	417	2.9	97.1
All Cities	898	37.1	62.9	896	6.5	93.5

Source: Computed from 1970 Survey of Local Building Departments by Charles G.
Field and Francis T. Ventre.

process. Seventy percent of the chief building officials not covered by civil service under a mayoral form of government desired such coverage. Only 39 percent of officials not covered under a manager form of government expressed a preference for civil service coverage. (See Table 3-11.)

The evidence indicates that building officials are sensitive to both the political structure and the interests of the construction industry in their communities. If interest groups, as we have argued, see themselves intimately bound up with the codes, they will seek all means, including that of political access, to influence code decisions. We would expect building officials to be more responsive to the mayoral than to the managerial system of government when the traditional form of job insulation—civil service—is missing. This is the case. Chief building officials have survived the system. Although they are contracted for very short periods, if at all, they have managed to stay in office for a long time. Chiefs serve in their departments an average of seven years. One out of four has served more than 12 years.[5] Either they never take a controversial position on issues, or they are masters at political survival; neither is likely to be receptive to change.

Conservatism in Judgment

The shortcomings of the formal definition of the building official is its failure to reveal the disincentives of the office and the external pressures that shape the official's behavior. The objective conditions of the office are harsh, which does not encourage the most qualified to enter into public service. The official is the focal point of competitive interests from economic, political, and social quarters, each struggling to get the most favorable public construction projects for itself. Although there are signs that some building officials strive to attain professional standards, they are frustrated in this quest by their work environment, by job insecurity, and by sensitivity to political influence.

Table 3-11
Preference for Civil Service Coverage by Chief Building Officials not Presently Covered by Civil Service by Form of City Government: 1970

Form of City Government	Number of Cities Reporting	Preference for Civil Service		All
		Yes	No	
Mayor-Council	119	70.6	29.4	100%
Council-Manager	349	38.7	61.3	100%
Other	24	58.3	41.7	100%

Source: Computed from 1970 Survey of Local Building Departments by Charles G. Field and Francis T. Ventre.

The typical building department is small—25 percent are one-inspector operations—yet it must be responsible for an astonishing variety of inspection tasks involving elevators, boilers, fire protection, refrigeration, etc. Although the technology of housing does not change from city to city—i.e., housing must have heating plants, electrical systems, plumbing lines, and the rest—single officials in smaller cities must pass judgment on all these subsystems with no staff of specialists to back them up.

The local official is thrust into the position of determining the technical adequacy of a new building practice that is in all probability at variance with the practices he knew and used when he was active in construction. The official is familiar with the old way of doing things, having come up through the local construction economy as either laborer or contractor, and he probably has his own favorite way of building. Few cities have educational programs geared to expose the building official to new techniques, and the programs offered seem to be ineffective.[6] Thus, it is not unusual for an official to resist practices with which he is unfamiliar, since almost all incentives favor the traditional or local way of building, and none favor the innovative. Not surprisingly, his judgments are invariably conservative and in favor of the conventional.

Patterns of Obstruction

Building code regulation has seriously impaired the receptiveness of the housing industry to technological innovation. The patterns that obstruct and retard the introduction of new ways are a consequence, in large measure, of a status quo, risk-minimizing residential construction industry. Significantly abetting these patterns of obstruction was an abdication by state government and an assumption by local governments of the building regulatory function. Without countervailing economic and political pressures there developed patterns of prohibition and code dissimilarity that have frustrated technologists. Similarly, standards and testing procedures have evolved that are not responsive to the requirements of newly-developing housing concepts.

The Unneutral Code:
Prohibitive Standards

By prohibiting specific forms of construction technology, the code can be used to veto new methods. Regardless of what construction advances are accepted by model code associations or other voluntary organizations, in most states the power to adopt or reject them still rests with local officials. The legal action of promulgation is a local prerogative often jealously guarded as a home rule power. Responsibility likewise rests at the local level. Thus, local code drafters are not bound to national models; rather, they are limited by the discretion afforded them by local politics.

One major consequence of this grass roots approach is that local objections to nationally-accepted technologies rule the day. To test this assertion, each city in the 1970 building code survey was asked whether it permitted or prohibited each of 14 construction techniques. All techniques, identified in Table 3-12, were approved construction practices under one or several of the model codes or under one of the nationally-recognized specialty codes. Some techniques were incremental changes from conventional practices, such as the spacing of 2-by-4 inch wooden studs in non-load bearing partitions, others were radical changes, such as the use of plastic pipe in drain, waste, and vent plumbing systems.

Patterns of prohibition were evident. On every code item in question (see Table 3-12), locally-based codes were the most prohibitive form of building regulation. Yet, model and state codes offered little comfort to those advocating new ideas, for on certain types of code changes communities using these approaches to code-writing were also highly prohibitive. Although model code associations had adopted the 14 items as part of their code, the fact that many items were still specifically prohibited demonstrates the strength of local prerogative in setting building standards.

Scoring each city code in terms of all prohibitions against innovative technology illustrates the profound gap between local and model and state-based codes. Each city was assigned a score equal to the number of prohibitions among the 14 items. The higher the score, the more resistant the code to new technologies. Again, local code cities were significantly more unresponsive to new ideas in construction than those using either of the other two forms. Whereas only 3 percent of all local code cities *permitted* all construction practices, 15 percent of both the model and state code cities permitted them. (See Table 3-13.) While most of the model and state code cities were grouped at the non-prohibitive end of the scale, local code communities were more likely to be found in the more prohibitive range

The willingness of a community to revise comprehensively its building codes appears directly related to the progressiveness of the code. The more recent the comprehensive code revision, the less prohibitive the score. Again, the data shows that communities using locally-based codes were least likely to have up-to-date codes. While 83 percent of model code cities and 73 percent of state code cities underwent revision in the past five years, only 61 percent of the local code cities did so. (See Table 3-14.) The decision to undertake such a revision is indicative of a willingness to concede that "what we have today may not be the most current." It indicates a willingness to go counter to certain local vested interests by accepting new standards, an attitude that seems to be absent in most of the local code communities. The decision to revise is also a financial one. Comprehensive revision by a city usually means

Table 3-12
Percent of Communities Prohibiting Specific Construction Innovations: 1970

Code Changes	No. Cities Answering Item	% Cities Answering Who Prohibit Items (A)	By Type of Code			1967 Douglas Survey (E)	Change 1967-1970 (A-E)
			Model (B)	State (C)	Local (D)		
Non-metallic sheathed electrical cable	771	14.7	13.1	9.1	32.5	13.0	+1.7
Prefabricated metal chimneys	832	11.1	9.1	14.0	20.8	19.1	-8.0
Off-site preassembled combination drain, waste, and vent plumbing system for bathroom installation	805	38.5	34.3	47.6	56.5	42.2	-3.7
Off-site preassembled electrical wiring harness for installation at electrical service entrance to dwelling	751	51.7	36.6	59.6	67.1	45.7	+6.0
Wood roof trusses, placed 24" on center	840	5.2	3.8	7.2	12.8	10.0	-4.8
Copper pipe in drain, waste, and vent plumbing systems	818	4.9	4.2	3.8	10.6	8.6	-3.7
ABS (acrylonitrile-butadiene-styrene) or PVC (polyvinyl-chloride) plastic pipe in drain, waste, and vent plumbing systems	826	47.0	42.9	49.5	71.3	62.6	-15.6
Bathrooms or toilet facilities equipped with ducts for natural or mechanical ventilation, in lieu of operable windows (or skylights)	836	2.6	2.5	2.8	3.1	6.0	-3.4

Party walls without continuous air space	750	26.4	25.8	19.6	38.6	26.8	-2.4
Use of single top and bottom plates in non-load-bearing interior partitions	836	20.9	20.2	20.4	26.3	24.5	-3.6
Use of 2" × 3" studs in non-load-bearing interior partitions	833	32.3	29.7	33.3	48.4	35.8	-3.5
Placement of 2" × 4" studs 24" on center in non-load-bearing interior partitions	841	42.6	39.7	38.2	66.7	47.3	-4.7
In wood frame construction, sheathing at least ½" thick, in lieu of corner bracing	834	14.9	13.7	14.7	23.2	20.4	-5.5
Wood frame exterior walls in multi-family structures of three stories or less	819	25.0	19.7	39.0	44.7	24.1	+.9

Sources:
[1] Manvel, Allen, *Local Land and Building Regulations*, Research Report No. 6. Prepared for the National Commission on Urban Problems, (Washington, D.C., U.S. Government Printing Office, 1968), p. 33.
[2] Computed from 1970 Survey of Local Building Departments by Charles G. Field and Francis T. Ventre.

Table 3-13

Prohibition of Scores by Type of Code Used in 1970

Prohibition Score	Type of Code in Use		
	Model	State	Local
0	14.6	15.2	3.1
1	18.9	10.7	4.1
2	18.1	17.0	11.3
3	14.2	17.0	14.4
4	11.7	11.6	15.5
5	9.5	9.8	11.3
6	7.0	4.5	11.3
7	2.8	6.4	11.3
8	2.0	2.7	8.3
9	1.2	3.6	5.2
10	.8	1.8	1.3
11	.3		2.1
12			1.3
Totals	100.0%	100.0%	100.0%
Number of Cities Reporting	639	112	97

Source: Computed from 1970 Survey of Local Building Departments by Charles G. Field and Francis T. Ventre.

Table 3-14

Prohibition Score by Date of Last Comprehensive Revision

Year Last Revised	No. Cities Reporting	Prohibition Score[1]		
		Lower Quartile	Median	Upper Quartile
Pre 1940	2	—	—	—
1940–49	4	—	—	—
1950–59	39	3	5	6
1960–65	105	1	3	6
1966	39	2	4	5
1967	151	1	3	4
1968	113	0	2	3
1969	154	1	3	4
1970	117	1	2	4

[1] See note to Figure 1 for definition.

Source: Computed from 1970 Survey of Local Building Departments by Charles G. Field and Francis T. Ventre.

adoption, at a cost of only several hundred dollars, of the most recent edition of their model code. Comprehensive revisions of a locally-based code, on the other hand, where the city must fund its own staff and research, can be very expensive. As previously mentioned, New York City's new code cost over $1 million.

Although the model code communities tend to do better than the others, the adoption of a model code is no guarantee of code currency five years hence.

Whereas many cities use the model code for its chief benefits, as a means of procuring a professionally-drafted code that is updated annually, just as many cities buy the code and then fail to keep it current. One can speculate that many of these latter cities see the model code as a means of escaping the severe criticism that can beset the locally-drafted code. The model code is a showpiece, but the objective remains the same: stand in the way of innovation. According to the Douglas Commission Study, only 49 percent of the model code cities adopted over 90 percent of the recommended changes, while 45 percent adopted less than 50 percent in the past three years.[7] Cities have used what they wanted from the model code, nothing more or less.

Although all 14 code items face some degree of prohibition, the public has been willing to accept innovative techniques. Diffusion of new technologies has taken place between 1967 and 1970, years for which we have data, as noted by the growing acceptance by jurisdictions of almost all items. Three years of criticism leveled at the obstructiveness of local codes and three years of exposure to the new techniques—at a time when housing costs were skyrocketing—have helped pave the way for adoption.

Since home manufacturers are concerned with multi-community markets, a more meaningful picture of code prohibitions was developed, using the state as the common unit of measure. Each state was assigned a mean prohibition score based upon its surveyed cities, and the scores were plotted for the 48 contiguous states. The states in Map 3-1 were classified into quintiles, while their absolute scores were plotted as projections onto Map 3-2. The vertical height of the state projection indicates the average state prohibition score. The higher the projection, the more prohibitive the codes in the state.

The pattern of state prohibition scores is striking. The highest prohibition scores crowed into the industrial heartland of the country, precisely those locations where locally-based codes were in greater use (the states running from New York and New Jersey, through Pennsylvania, the Midwest, and upper Midwest). As argued earlier, if the degree of industrialization within a state is an index of a measure of the strength of the local construction industry, then the national pattern strongly implies that the stronger the local construction industry, the more likely individual interest groups will seek to protect their own positions by introducing prohibitions against particular standards into the code. If the degree of prohibition is a significant deterrent to innovation and home manufacturing, the national pattern of scores offers little consolation to the proponents of the non-traditional approach to housing.

Fragmentation and Variation:
The Uneven Landscape

As long as the power to decide on code standards and enforcement remains a local prerogative, fragmention and variation will persist. Fragmentation is a direct consequence of the prevailing localism. Decision-making takes place

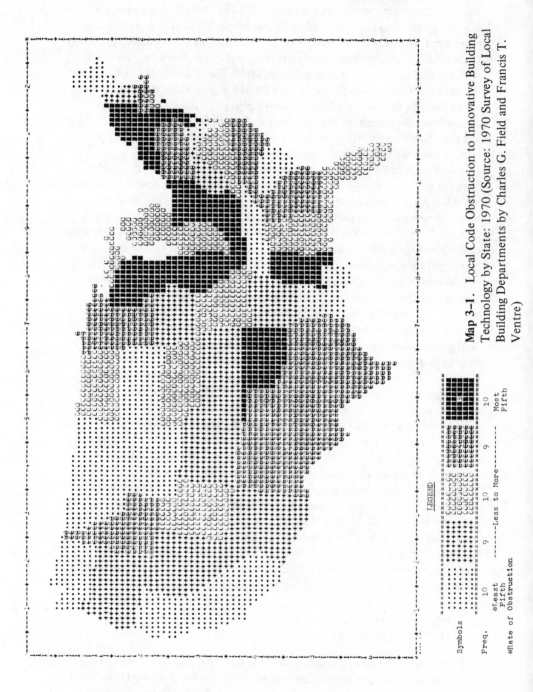

Map 3-1. Local Code Obstruction to Innovative Building Technology by State: 1970 (Source: 1970 Survey of Local Building Departments by Charles G. Field and Francis T. Ventre)

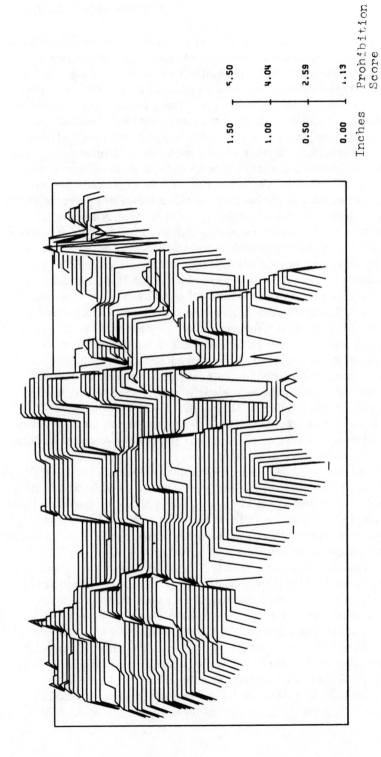

Inches	Prohibition Score
1.50	5.50
1.00	4.04
0.50	2.59
0.00	1.13

Map 3–2. Projections of Local Code Obstruction to Innovative Building Technology by State: 1970 (Source: 1970 Survey of Local Building Departments by Charles G. Field and Francis T. Ventre)

within the community and is subject to its influences. To the innovator seeking market outlets in numerous communities, each new community means a new approval and new negotiations with local officials. Any code change needed to admit the new product or construction process entails an extended effort.

Variation in code provisions from community to community is a logical consequence of fragmentation. Building codes reflect local conditions and local interest group pressures. Because these vary in degree and detail from one city to the next, it is inevitable that there would be variation in substance.

To measure the dissimilarities between codes, cities were grouped into statewide marketing areas. All possible pairs of cities within each state were compared to see whether the two cities agreed on the use of each of the 14 items and whether they agreed on the type of code in use. A dissimilarity score of "0," a perfect match, meant that the pair agreed on all items, whereas a score of "15," a perfect mismatch, meant that there was no agreement on items. The score must be carefully interpreted. A perfect score of "0" did not mean that the two cities had modern codes; rather, that the codes were identical in their pattern of permissions and prohibitions.

Extreme dissimilarity characterized the prevailing state building code landscapes. In Massachusetts, for example, only .4 percent of the pairings were identical and .8 percent off by one, while 18.2 percent differed on five items and 15 percent on six. To be dissimilar on five or six items on a base of 15 meant that the cities differed on from 33 percent to 40 percent of the measurable code items. Massachusetts was not unique; most other states showed as much variation. Admittedly, only 15 out of hundreds of code items were used, items that dealt with innovations. But there is no compelling argument to encourage the belief that the variation scores would drop as more items were added to the comparison.

The national pattern of dissimilarity is shown in Maps 3-3 and 3-4. On Map 3-3 the median dissimilarity score was calculated for each state. States were broken down into nine classes and the scores plotted for the 48 contiguous states. The darker the shading of the state, the more severe the dissimilarity. Map 3-4 is a projection of each state's score by absolute value. The higher the projection, the more dissimilar the state's codes.

Consistently high patterns of wide dissimilarity appear in all regions of the nation except for the Far West and Central Plains states. The sections of the country with the strongest dissimilarities are again shown to be in the industrial heartland of the nation. New England also shared in the strong dissimilarity pattern. The degree of dissimilarity seems closely related to two different factors. The more industrialized the state, the greater the probability that local communities will go their own way in designing their codes. This is consistent with the earlier suggestion that the stronger the local construction industry, the more likely its influence upon the design of local codes. The second factor appears to be the extent of the strength of the model code

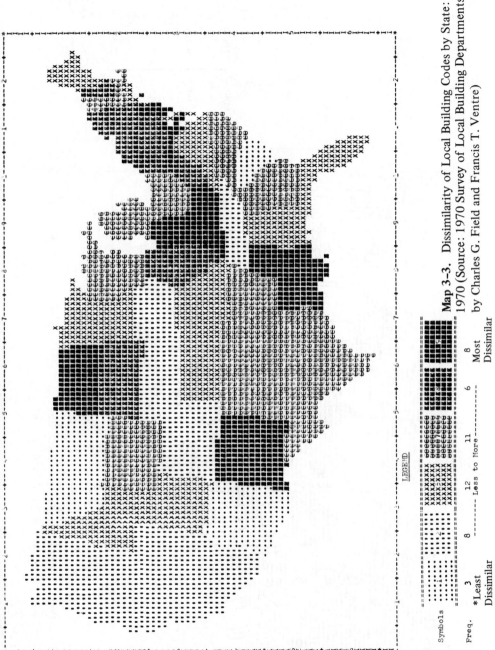

Map 3–3. Dissimilarity of Local Building Codes by State: 1970 (Source: 1970 Survey of Local Building Departments by Charles G. Field and Francis T. Ventre)

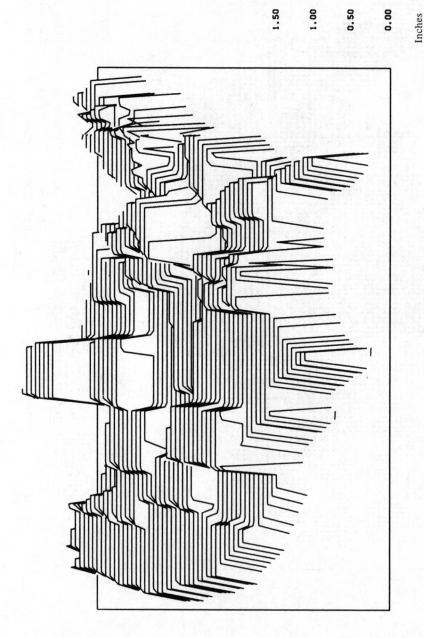

Inches		Dissimilarity Score
1.50	— 10.00	
1.00	— 6.67	
0.50	— 3.33	
0.00	— 0.00	

Map 3-4. Projection of Dissimilarity of Local Building Codes by State: 1970 (Source: 1970 Survey of Local Building Departments by Charles G. Field and Francis T. Ventre)

associations. The West is ICBO country, and from all appearances communities are willing to adopt a code with fewer alterations than in the case of BOCA in the North and East and SSBC in the South.

This may tie in with local attitudes toward professionalism in government. The managerial form of government dominates the West. City managers have a professional orientation and are willing to seek and accept the professional judgments of the model code association. The patterns of political structure are more varied in the South and North, where the mayoral form of city politics is more prevalent. For whatever reasons, the patterns of variation are quite formidable. If uniformity of building code standards is essential to the industrialization of housing, the situation as of 1970 is bleak.

Similarity of standards need not mean uniformity of standards as applied: even if the written standards were *identical* in two communities, the probability of the building officials giving *different* interpretations would be quite high. When asked if interpretation of identical code items varied within their states, building officials responded that it did. When asked how much variations, 37 percent said "very little," 53 percent said "some," and under 10 percent said "much" or "very much." (See Table 3-15.) Model code associations, centralizing the code-writing function, also tend to centralize the interpretive function. When building departments buy a model code, they also buy a common set of standard interpretations. The associations, in an attempt to foster uniformity, publish code interpretations as questions on standards arise. Thus, one interpretation is uniformly recommended to all member cities. In sharp contrast are cities that use locally-based codes. Because each code is a unique product of the community's thinking, it logically follows that the interpretations are locally developed. Often one city will adopt the code of the neighboring town, but unlike the model code case, the adopting city's building officials bring their own interpretations to bear.

The desire for uniform code interpretation is not universal. Many officials

Table 3-15

The Degree to Which Chief Building Officials Perceive Variations in Interpretation of the Identical Code Requirement Between Communities in Their State: 1970

Variation Exists	Number Reporting	Degree of Variation				
		Very Much	Much	Some	Very Little	
Yes	610	3.1	6.6	53.3	37.0	100%
No	6	0.0	0.0	16.7	83.3	100%
Total	616	3.1	6.5	52.9	37.5	

Source: Computed from 1970 Survey of Local Building Departments by Charles G. Field and Francis T. Ventre.

feel that their communities have unique building conditions, and that some flexibility in standard interpretation is thus absolutely necessary. The building official finds it difficult to justify too much variation. As shown in Table 3-16, six out of ten officials who perceived only a "very little" variation thought it desirable. As perceptions of variation increase, support for variation quickly dissipate.

An Overall Perspective

The implicit argument running through this chapter is that the local building code and its enforcement retard the introduction of new techniques into the local construction economy. The total effect of all these forces can be seen in the city patterns of code prohibitions against new technologies. The maxim that technological change is a key ingredient in the competitive struggle also holds in homebuilding. Control over the local building code gives the traditional homebuilding industry a capacity to frustrate competition almost without precedent in other industries. Any technological change can be killed at the city's doors by writing into the code the appropriate prohibitions. Since most residential codes specify materials and techniques, restrictions are easily added.

Just because a monopoly power exists in the exercise of building code regulations, it does not necessarily follow that the code is always used to restrict trade. We have noted that local interests have recourse to prohibitive code provisions when they feel that the innovation in question, if allowed, would jeopardize their well-being. We would now like to test this hypothesis explicitly. Two conditions are necessary. First, the degree of opposition to innovation is likely to be related to the health of the local construction economy. When construction is plentiful and all prosper, few will object to the introduction of new techniques. But in a depressed construction economy, local participants will seek to preserve local business for themselves. Pressing

Table 3-16
Desirability of Variation in Interpretation of Identical Code Requirements by Degree of Perceived Variations: 1970

Degree	Number	Desirable		
Variation Exists	*Reporting*	*Yes*	*No*	*Total*
Very Much	16	–	100%	100%
Much	40	12.5	87.5	100%
Some	292	43.8	56.2	100%
Very Little	214	59.8	40.2	100%

Source: Computed from 1970 Survey of Local Building Departments by Charles G. Field and Francis T. Ventre.

for restrictive codes is one key way of preventing the introduction of new techniques. We can use city location as a surrogate for construction growth. The suburbs have been the high growth locations, while the central cities have had slower if not stagnant growth patterns.

The second condition relates to the potential for local political access. How effectively local participants can lobby for protection depends upon the receptivity of the administrative structure to political influence, with influence being higher in mayoral than in managerial forms of city government. We would expect more prohibitive codes to exist where construction activity is weak and the administrative structure politically sensitive.

Using this simple logic, we would expect that the most restrictive codes, those prohibiting new techniques, would be found in the slower-growing central mayoral cities, and the least restrictive to be found in suburban city manager cities. In fact, however, suburban (not central city) communities with mayoral forms have the most prohibitive codes. (See Table 3-17.) On closer inspection, this is not surprising. Mayoral central cities are typically the older, deteriorating municipalities that are not experiencing major growth. Moreover, their building officials, as shown in Table 3-10, are not likely to be covered by civil service or represented by labor unions, which increases the potential for political intervention in building department functions. As expected, suburban manager cities, typically the fast-growing bedroom communities, stand in sharp contrast. Because the local construction industry is growing, the incentives are not great to seek code prohibitions against new technologies. In fact, such cities might welcome new methods as a means of keeping up with demand. Moreover, the managerial form of administration in these middle-class communities leads to a professionalism that is less susceptible to political influences. Therefore, the codes in these cities should be the most progressive, which indeed they are.

The unexpected good performance of the mayoral central city probably is due to its size and the nature of the bureaucracy. Mayoral central cities are generally cities of over 500,000 population. The bureaucratic maze of

Table 3-17
Prohibition Scores by Political Type and Metropolitan Location

	No. Cities Reporting	Lower Quantile	Median	Upper Quantile
Central City Mayor	48	1	3	4
Central City Manager	94	1	3	6
Suburban Mayor	105	3	6	8
Suburban Manager	291	1	2	5
Independent Mayor	89	1	3	4
Independent Manager	232	1	2	4

Source: Computed from the 1970 Survey of Local Building Departments by Charles G. Field and Francis T. Ventre.

their administrative agencies, of which the building department is but one,
may dilute the effect of local pressure groups working through political channels. In addition, building inspectors in large cities are protected by civil service
regulations (See Table 3–15) and labor representation, and are thus better
insulated from political interference. A final explanation may be that the
largest cities probably have more available resources than smaller cities for
maintenance of codes. For these reasons, codes of mayoral central cities,
in the face of limited construction activity, may not be as restrictive as we
might expect.

4 Surveying the Building Code Burden

We have described various types of innovative building products and systems that could be made available to consumers of residential products. We judge this a potentially dynamic industry on the basis of advances already made, including the industrialized systems in use in various European countries. We have also analyzed the building code regulatory system. Like many regulatory processes, it is complex and influenced by those it purports to regulate. Whether because of centuries of code control at the local level or because of the extent to which regulated firms influence code decisions, the fact is that the regulatory system has ossified over time. It has failed to be fully responsive to change. We shall show that the net effect is one of a potentially dynamic industry frustrated by its regulatory system, which reduces to a trickle the amount of technological change reaching the marketplace.

In this chapter, we demonstrate that both the policy-maker and the public are vitally affected by the building code pattern. The impact is direct, in terms of both cost to the consumer and frustration of public policy. We argue that complacency must give way to concerted action. We establish that the building code regulatory process has a dampening impact upon technological change in residential construction, the consequence of which is to deprive the American consumer of the benefits of improved building processes and higher quality materials.

The burden falls on the public as a whole—not just the individual consumer—because present policy frustrates efficiency in utilizing scarce new materials. For example, solar heating for residential structures is an important alternative to existing heating systems. If codes prevent the introduction of solar heating or comparable energy-saving technologies, then codes are operating contrary to the national interest and must be changed.

We called this book *The Building Code Burden* because our analysis of the system's impact upon residential innovation impels the conclusion that codes impose real costs upon the public. In our view, this burden has two types of consequences. First, the code structure imposes additional costs upon non-conventional products or building processes. Second, the code structure limits the size of market open to innovative products, either through direct prohibitions within the building code or through overly complex code requirements that would be too costly to meet. Exclusion from markets denies

71

to consumers the benefits of the excluded product. These phenomena will be examined in greater detail in the following pages.

Documenting the building code burden has been a difficult task in the past because of the lack of hard systematic data. Anecdotal evidence has abounded, and thus proof of code-induced problems hinged typically upon the experiences of would-be innovators. Perhaps the earliest frontal assaults on codes came with the 1966 study of the Advisory Commission on Inter-governmental Relation's [1] and Allen Manvel's survey of code jurisdictions for the National Commission on Urban Problems. [2] Both dealt solely with building codes. But shortly thereafter, the government began to focus its resources on reducing code problems that related specifically to industrial-ization and innovation under the research umbrella of HUD's Operation Break-through. [3] Operation Breakthrough specifically identified building codes as a principle barrier to the flourishing of innovation and technology in home-building.

To establish the existence of the building code burden, we must establish the existence of four general conditions. These are:

1.   Code regulations are perceived as a problem by housing innovators.
2.   The existing pattern of building codes results in unnecessary higher prices.
3.   The regulatory system is used to restrict the introduction and diffusion of innovations into the market place, and
4.   Socially undesirable consequences result from the present regulatory struc-ture.

Fortunately, our proofs are not reduced to anecdotal information, for the surveys of home manufacturers and building codes described in earlier chapters facilitates an empirical investigation of these allegations. These surveys, because of the intentional structuring of their questions, permit us to compare the reactions of home manufacturers to codes with the cities' descriptions of their codes.

Code Regulatory Practices are Perceived as a Problem by Housing Innovators

If the reality of the code problem mirrors the perceptions of home manu-facturers, one must conclude that codes have been a national disaster. Said one manufacturer: "Because of a lack of knowledge of the industry, local code boards are afraid to endorse anything new. They feel comfortable with the status quo." Another, speaking about the difficulty of obtaining code amendments, referred to the local code people as "hardheaded old men that won't change with the times that are in positions of responsibility." These 1970 observations also prevailed in the 1960s and 1950s, for home manufacturers have consistently reported building codes as one of their principal problem areas. Because perceptions are key factors in molding behavior, we shall take a look at the perceptions of home manufacturers in this section. Later we shall try to quantify these perceptions.

In the 1970 survey, manufacturers were asked specific questions designed to elicit the importance of building codes relative to other problem areas. The intent was to rank codes within the compass of experienced problems, and to differentiate between the problems of current business operations and those of developing innovative products or building processes. Entrepreneurial decision-making differs significantly between these two modes. A business manager attempts to operate efficiently within the given business environment. Thus, he must factor into his decisions such conditions as demand instability, the localism of demand, availability of building materials, and the prevailing pattern of building codes within his market area. An innovator is concerned with the system's capacity to change as well as with the marketing situation of the business manager. Entry problems, obviously, are more salient concerns for the innovator than for the managers of ongoing business operations whose products are already established in the marketplace.

Innovation, by definition, is a new way of doing the job; thus, regulatory acceptance becomes a crucial determinant of how quickly innovations are introduced into the market. The innovator sees the code as his product's first major institutional test. Without code approval, the innovator cannot move to production and the eventual payoff—sales. Innovation flourishes in an environment where performance is the keystone to product acceptance. Thus, in the space effort, we geared technology to the goal of sending man to the moon. Innovation stagnates in an environment where the prevailing regulatory ethic is perpetuation of existing business patterns. This is the case in building code regulation, where high quality performance of the house is neither demanded nor expected. Standards are set and enforced to beat down new challenges to existing routines. To the exponents of change, this regulatory structure appears obstructionistic and discourages technical experimentation.

To capture the dimension of this problem, we asked home manufacturers to identify problems they faced when developing new approaches to homebuilding. They were asked: *"What in your judgment are the* three *most significant problems if you plan to develop* innovative *housing systems or materials?"*

The list of answers included: problems of R & D financing, acceptance by consumers of new residential products, technical knowhow, and obstruction by specific economic interest groups (labor unions and material producers). These were problem areas often cited by both innovators and commentators on residential construction when discussing the technological lag in homebuilding.

The concensus among home manufacturers is striking. Almost seven out of ten manufacturers list codes as one of their top three problems. Adequate funding for research and consumer acceptance were distant, but significant, second and third place problems. (See Table 4-1.) One home manufacturer, explaining his problems with code approvals, said that the main reason was the "lack of qualified personnel administrating as inspectors; local protectionist attitude never for legitimate technical reasons." Others felt that the variations in standards between communities made it impossible to design a new product acceptable to all codes. "Different larger cities have different requirements; therefore a product acceptable in city A is unacceptable in B and vice versa."

While the particular reason given depended upon the production, product orientation and the particular experiences of each manufacturer, the dominant theme was clear. Codes are perceived by home manufacturers as a major deterrent to innovation.

Patterns of perception dramatically shifted when home manufacturers were asked a similar question about problems as they related to business operations. They were asked: *"What were your three most significant business problems in 1969?"* Fourteen different types of responses could have been given, ranging from financial problems to those involving institutional regulations. (These are listed in Table 4-2.) Building codes dropped from first to fifth place, with 28 percent of the 189 manufacturers responding to the question listing codes as one of their top three business problems. Problems of finance, material costs, and labor availability ranked in front of codes.

Because the late 1960s were disastrous housing production years, home manufacturers obviously were more concerned about survival than with the headaches of codes. Volume of non-subsidized production had slid from 1,529 million starts in 1964 to 1,165 million in 1966 and back up to 1,467 by 1969.[4] Labor costs were rapidly rising and mortgage financing was difficult to

Table 4-1

Ranking of Problems Pertaining to the Development of Innovative Housing Systems or Materials

Rank	Problem	Percent of Firms Indicating as One of Their Top Three Problems U.S.
1	Building Codes	69
2	Adequate Financing for Research	52
3	Consumer Acceptance	51
4	Unions	41
5	Technical Know-how	38
6	Business Management	13
7	Other	11
8	Opposition of Material	6
	Number of Firms Responding 197	

Source: 1970 Survey of Home Manufacturers by Charles G. Field.

Table 4–2
Ranking of Home Manufacturer 1969 Business Problems

Rank	Problem	Percent of Firms Indicating as One of Top Three Problems
1	Mortgage Financing	53
2	Material Cost	33
3	Construction Financing	31
4	Lack of Skilled Labor	30
5	Building Codes	28
6	Merchandising and Selling	24
7	Labor Cost	18
8	Construction Cost	17
9	Business Management	16
10	Other	12
11	Land	9
12	Zoning	8
13	Lack of Suitable Land	5
14	FHA–VA Appraisals	5
15	Lack of Materials	5
	Number of Firms Responding to Question 189	

Source: 1970 Survey of Home Manufacturers by Charles G. Field.

secure. Costs of materials, key to home manufacturing, increased steeply during the 1965–69 period. According to the wholesale price index, lumber and millwork products increased by 40 percent and 21 percent respectively during this period.[5] These increases were significant because of the home manufacturer's dependence on wood products. That almost three out of ten still listed codes as one of their top three problems attests to the persistent presence of code problems.

In the code area, the home manufacturer adjusts his production line process and unit designs to maximize the probability of securing building code approval in his market area. Some manufacturers achieve this by designing their products to the most rigorous set of building standards they might typically encounter. Others simplify their production process to the point where each unit is custom-designed to meet the specific standard requirements of the community of sale. If plastic pipe is prohibited in most jurisdictions, manufacturers will use cast iron. Sometimes home manufacturers take a personal approach and invite local building officials to visit and inspect their plant facilities with the hope that familiarity will breed inspector willingness to grant permit approval when requested. While the manufacturer has attempted to make peace with the code structure, peace is made on the terms of the local code. Adaptability has become the hallmark of many home manufacturers. According to one home manufacturer: "We very seldom are able to change codes. We change our product to comply."

The Existing Pattern of Building Codes
Leads to Unnecessary Added Costs

Whereas home manufacturers identify codes as significant problems both for business and innovation, it does not necessarily follow that the consumer is penalized by paying housing costs that are higher than necessary. In fact, building codes may be used as a scapegoat for inefficient home manufacturing operations that cannot compete with conventional builders. While this may be true in specific cases, codes usually do present cost problems. The few studies that attempt to quantify the cost impact of codes indicate that the problem is real and of sufficient scale to warrant corrective action.

If we look solely to studies of the conventional construction industry, the results can be misleading. An early analysis by Sherman Maisel, a 1950 landmark analysis of the San Francisco building industry, measured the impact of scale production upon unit costs. In evaluating the different independent factors, (one of which was the presence of a building code), he concluded that only 3 percent of the variation in construction costs between localities could be attributed to the variations in building codes.[6] Similar estimates were later developed in studies by Richard Muth,[7] and by Leland Burns and Frank Mittleback.[8] Muth's study of single-family, FHA-insured housing estimated that building codes had only a marginal effect upon cost variations, accounting for only 2 percent of them.[9] Burns and Mittleback likewise concluded in their report for the Kaiser Committee on Urban Housing that building codes accounted for less than 3 percent of the average extra cost of the average-priced houses.[10]

These findings are misleading if they are taken as truths about home manufacturing. The authors clearly indicate that their data are statistics on sales of units. No distinction is made between conventional and manufactured housing. Moreover, they do not discuss the production process of firms and how that might change if the code pattern were changed from one of intercommunity differences to a standard set of building requirements throughout the entire marketing area. The production approaches of home manufacturers would certainly change if the producer knew he had only one set of standards to satisfy rather than hundreds. Thus, while the Maisel, Muth, Burns and Mittleback studies conclude that the existing pattern of building codes has negligible consequences for conventional builders, the same conclusion cannot be drawn for home manufacturers.

The few studies made of home manufacturing suggest that codes have imposed significant added costs. A limited survey of home manufacturers in the late 1960s for the National Commission on Urban Problems asked producers to estimate the added cost on a basic $12,000 factory-produced home (built to Federal Housing Administration or prevailing model code standards) due to adjustments necessary to qualify the home under the different code standards within their sales area. The reported penalty was an estimated $1,838 on top of

the $12,000 figure. Added costs stemmed from such things as overly rigid speci-
fications for electrical conduits ($300); specifying plaster instead of gypsum
board ($200); and sheathing requirements above FHA standards ($125). [11]
The added cost varies from one section of the country to the next, from one
producer to the next. Kingsberry Homes, which marketed in the Southeastern
states, reported an average added cost of $2,492, [12] while Home Building
Corporation, which operated in the Missouri-Nebraska-Illinois-Kansas region,
reported excess costs amounting to approximately $3,500. [13] The statistical
reliability of these estimates cannot be checked, but their magnitude is striking.

The 1970 survey of home manufacturers attempted to determine the extent
of the problem. The survey, unfortunately, was not designed to estimate dollars
of added costs due to codes; instead, it asked home manufacturers a judgmental
question about the impact of codes upon their current line of production. Firms
were asked:

Assume you produced your houses to FHA Minimum Property Standards or to the standards of the model code used in your region. Is it
necessary to produce to stricter standards to meet local building code
requirements in your market area?

Fifty-seven percent of the responding firms indicated "yes."

The issue is whether stricter standards translate into significant added costs
to the manufacturer and consumer. Manufacturers, who reported building to
stricter standards, were asked: *"Are the added production costs resulting from
stricter standards significantly large?"* Slightly more than half, 53 percent, of
those responding said yes. While it does not offer detailed figures for the added
costs incurred or tell whether the added cost was occasioned by superior products, the response is indicative of a substantial problem.

As shown in Table 4-3, the responses are not randomly distributed by type
of home manufacturer. The more complex the production process, the less
adaptable that process is to code variations and the more likely the producer is
to report cost problems. Sixty percent of the modular producers who had to
build to stricter standards judged that such regulations resulted in significantly
higher costs. Only 36 percent of the panel producers responded the same way.
Modular construction entails closed wall systems, whereas panel can be open.

This means that a modular producer must disassemble his unit if the construction standards are called into question. A panel producer often leaves his
panels open, to be closed at the site. An inspection to him is much less of a
burden. No wonder the modular producer will build for the strictest set of standards in his marketing area, thereby hoping to minimize the inspector's need to
make a physical inspection. The game plan, therefore, is to minimize any code
objections by inspectors by overdesigning his product.

A more recent study/demonstration by the National Association of Home
Builders Research Foundation indicates that substantial cost economies would

Table 4-3
Incidence of Stricter Standards and Added Costs by Characteristic of the Home Manufacturer (1969)

	Stricter Standards			Added Cost		
	Number of Firms Reporting	Yes	No	Number of Firms Reporting	Yes	No
Basic Form						
Pre-cut	9	100%	66.7	33.3 / 10	100%	60.0	40.0
Panel	80	100%	52.5	47.5 / 70	100%	35.7	64.3
Modular	50	100%	72.0	38.0 / 45	100%	60.0	40.0
Percent of Sales Price						
0–25	49	100%	42.9	57.1 / 27	100%	48.1	51.9
25–50	69	100%	50.7	49.3 / 43	100%	27.9	72.1
50–75	35	100%	68.6	31.4 / 24	100%	54.2	45.8
75–100	72	100%	65.3	34.7 / 52	100%	63.5	36.5
Type of Market						
Single-family	65	100%	47.7	52.3 / 38	100%	52.6	47.4
Single- and multi-family	75	100%	58.7	41.3 / 54	100%	35.2	64.8
Multi-family	41	100%	63.4	36.6 / 27	100%	51.9	48.1
Mobile Home	25	100%	72.0	28.0 / 21	100%	71.4	28.6
Volume						
Less 100	57	100%	49.1	50.9 / 34	100%	38.2	61.8
100–200	25	100%	60.0	40.0 / 18	100%	50.0	50.0
200–400	20	100%	55.0	45.0 / 11	100%	36.4	63.6
400–900	27	100%	48.1	51.9 / 17	100%	41.2	58.8
900+	26	100%	53.8	46.2 / 15	100%	73.4	26.6

Source: Computed from 1970 Survey of Home Manufacturers by Charles G. Field.

be realizable with existing construction technology if building codes permitted the optimum use of known techniques. The study and eventual demonstration model effort was undertaken to determine whether cost savings would flow from the construction of an optimally-designed, single-family, wood frame house. On a $16,000 unit, they estimated savings of approximately $1,650.[14] The bulk of the savings, 65 percent, came from the framing. Assuming an average $1,600 savings per single family unit built, in 1971—with 1.152 [15] million single family starts—aggregate savings would have amounted to $1.84 billion.

These few studies indicate substantial cost penalties imposed by the existing code system. Whether any cost savings from new technologies and more efficient production systems would be passed on to the consumer is a matter of conjecture. That reform of the code system would result in cost savings to the manufacturer is not disputed, for in a competitive industry like home building, cost savings deriving from technological advances will eventually be passed on to the consumer. Given the spiraling costs of housing, cost efficiencies brought about by code reform might not result in reductions in the absolute cost of new housing; rather, the impact might be to slow down the rate of housing cost increases.

The Regulatory System is Used to Restrict
the Introduction and Diffusion of Innovations
into the Market Place

As outsiders to the local construction economy, home manufacturers have pointed an accusing finger at the people who enforce local codes as well as at those who shape code decisions. Behind specific standards or prohibitions unfavorable to their product home manufacturers perceive a competitor in the local construction economy. One manufacturer stated that "building codes are dictated by or written by building trade union people." Another asserted that "home areas are controlled by local contractors that won't allow city council to bend" and that codes were "protection of the local builders or subcontractors by the municipality." The thrust of these comments was always the same—the code shielded local interests against the competitive challenge of the home manufacturer. It was perceived as an agent of exclusion.

To make the case that existing code patterns serve local interests, we need to establish that local code decisions are heavily influenced by local groups and that the consequences of these decisions work to the detriment of outside construction interests. The import of this conclusion, if correct, is that governmental powers are not used primarily in the public interest.

The regulatory powers of the state are being misused to foster special interest groups, rather than to preserve the health and safety of citizens. To determine whether this is true, four questions need to be answered:

1. Do groups outside the building department exert considerable influence
    upon the decisions reached by the agency?
2. Do local interests hold greater influence over agency decisions than
    out-of-towners?
3. Does the existing building code pattern impose unnecessary cost burdens
    upon innovators?
4. Would the elimination of the protective regulatory screen result in negative
    consequences for the local construction industry?

The public power can be used to foster better living conditions for all its
citizens. Presumably, building codes, housing codes, zoning laws, and subdivision
regulations are enacted and enforced with this objective in sight. Public power
can also be used to protect the economic vitality of American enterprise from
undesired foreign competition. The trade tariff and import quota laws have been
promulgated for protectionist reasons. If we can answer the four questions
posed above, building codes appear to foster local protectionism more than the
public's wellbeing.

We shall use the 1970 survey data on home manufacturers and building
code officials to answer the above questions. Both surveys were designed to
facilitate the linking of manufacturer responses on codes to building official
responses about their codes. The link was achieved mainly by identifying those
technology improvements important to home manufacturers in the construction of their units and then determining whether these items were included in
city building codes. Home manufacturers were asked which code items of those
listed in the survey were most important for the production of their own products. Chief building officials, in turn, were asked to provide information about
the various code items, especially about those most difficult to adopt.

According to the manufacturers, four of the five most important code
items deal with mechanical and electrical systems. The off-site preassembled
combination drain, waste, and vent plumbing system for bathroom installation
was noted by 49 percent of the manufacturers. (See Table 4-4.) Just over 40
percent noted the use of the off-site preassembled electrical wiring harness for
installation at the electrical service entrance to the dwelling. Both practices
reflect a growing trend by home manufacgurers to move past the control of
structural systems and to seek entry into the mechanical subsystems, an area
previously closed to them and strongly contested by local interest groups. Their
respective product changes, the use of non-metallic sheathed electrical cable and
ABS or PVC plastic pipe, were fourth and fifth on the list, and noted by 33 percent and 39 percent of all manufacturers responding. The fifth code item was
roof trusses.

Home manufacturers face stiff problems if we look at the response of chief
building officials to the patterns of acceping and the difficulty of adopting these
innovations. The off-site preassembled electrical package was the least accepted

local practice, off-site preassembled plumbing was fourth. Plastic pipe was No. 2, and non-metallic sheathed cable No. 7. Only roof trusses have found wide acceptance in the market place.

Building officials ranked ABS or PVC plastic pipe in drain, waste, and vent plumbing systems as the most difficult to adopt, followed by non-metallic sheathed electrical cable and prefabricated metal chimneys. Of the home manufacturer's top five most important innovations, three were placed by building officials among the top five innovations most difficult to adopt. By objective measure, home manufacturers have a long battle to wage before their products are widely adopted.

We have developed case histories of four of the five top home manufacturer innovations (these are summarized in Table 4–5).[16] The chief building official was given a list of participants and asked what role they played in controversial code changes:

1.   Where did the idea for this change originate?
2.   With whom was it discussed?
3.   Which were the most trustworthy sources of information?
4.   Which groups most supported the change?
5.   Which groups most resisted the change?

The list of participants was designed to be as complete as possible and included builders, unions, material producers, home manufacturers, architects, engineers, and building officials—groups one would expect to have a direct interest in code decisions. Also listed were civic organizations, trade associations, and sources of technical information (government publications, trade journals, etc.). By recording the actual histories of difficult code adoptions, it is possible to illuminate the dynamics of change and show which interest groups had the strongest influence on specific building code decisions. Thus, it was possible to determine who governs the regulatory system. Equally important, it was possible to determine the extent to which home manufacturers influence building code regulation. With this short overview, it is now possible to answer the four questions raised above:

1.   *Do groups outside the building department exert considerable influence upon the decisions reached by the agency?*

The data support the contention that non-agency construction interest groups exert more influence over code adoption decisions than do the staffs of building departments. This is because chief building officials tend to place greater confidence in people outside their agencies when difficult code decisions are made, as can readily be seen by scanning the case histories and noting that the chiefs more frequently looked to interest groups (higher scores on the pro-

Table 4–4
Ranking of Code Items in Terms of Importance to Home Manufacturers, Degree of Local Acceptance and Difficulty of Adoption: 1970

	Importance to Home Manufacturer[1] A	Ranking in Terms of Prohibition by Local Building Codes[2] B	Greatest Difficulty of Adoption[3] C	Expected Greatest Difficulty of Adoption[4] D
Off-site preassembled combination drain, waste, and vent plumbing system for bathroom installation	1	4	4	3
Off-site preassembled combination electrical wiring harness for installation at electrical service entrance to dwelling	2	1	10	8
Wood roof trusses, placed 24" on center	3	12	6	13
ABS or PVC plastic pipe in drain, waste, and vent plumbing systems	4	2	1	1
Non-metallic sheathed electrical cable	5	7	2	2
Wood frame exterior walls in multi-family structures of three stories or less	6	6	9	4
Use of single top and bottom plates in non-load bearing interior partitions	7	8	12	11
In wood frame construction, sheathing at least ½" thick, in lieu of corner bracing	8	9	8	9

	[1]	[2]	[3]	[4]
Copper pipe in drain, waste and vent plumbing systems	9	11	5	5
Bathrooms or toilet facilities equipped with ducts for natural or mechanical ventilation, in lieu of operable windows (or skylights)	10	13	7	12
Placement of 2" by 4" studs 24" on center in non-load-bearing interior partitions	11	3	13	10
Prefabricated metal chimneys	12	12	3	7
Party walls without continuous air space	13	5	11	6

Use of 2" by 3" studs in non-load-bearing interior partitions was deleted because it was excluded in the question asked of the home manufacturer.

[1] Ranking in terms of frequency of mention as being the most essential item to the home manufacturer.

[2] Ranking in terms of frequency of prohibition of the specific item in local codes (# cities prohibiting/all cities with building codes).

[3] Ranking in terms of mention of greatest difficulty of adoption of items already adopted (# time mentioned/#cities already adopted item).

[4] Ranking in terms of expected difficulty in those cities yet to adopt the item. (# time mentioned/#cities yet to adopt item).

Sources: 1970 Survey of Home Manufacturers by Charles G. Field. 1970 Survey of Local Building Departments by Charles G. Field and Francis T. Ventre.

Table 4-5 (a)
The Involvement of Interest Groups in the Fight for Non-metallic Sheathed Electrical Cable
(Percent of Cities Reporting—Based Upon 43 Cities)

Interest Group	Where did the idea for this change originate? (1)	With whom was it discussed? (2)	Role Played		
			Which were the most trustworthy sources of information? (3)	Which groups most supported the change? (4)	Which groups most resisted the change? (5)
Building Material Producers or Supplier Representatives:					
Local	19	30	16	25	5
Out-of-town	16	9	5	11	2
Builder Representatives:					
Local	49	49	16	51	9
Out-of-town	16	14	0	9	5
Prefabricated Home Manufacturer Representatives	11	11	0	16	0
Union Representatives: (identify by trade)					
Local	2	18	0	2	25
Out-of-town	0	7	0	0	7
Building Officials from Cities:					
Within your county	11	35	14	9	14
Outside your county	9	23	7	7	2
Building Department Staff	16	40	11	11	11
Chief Building Official	16	23	7	16	5
Architects and Engineers	4	40	20	20	7

Source: Calculated from 1970 Survey of Local Building Department by Charles G. Field and Francis T. Ventre.

Table 4-5 (b)

The Involvement of Interest Groups in the Fight for Off-Site Preassembled Combination Drain, Waste and Vent Plumbing System for Bathroom Installation (Percent of Cities Reporting—Based Upon 27 Cities)

| Interest Group | Where did the idea for this change originate? (1) | With whom was it discussed (2) | Role Played | | |
			Which were the most trustworthy sources of information? (3)	Which groups most supported the change? (4)	Which groups most resisted the change? (5)
Building Material Producers or Supplier Representatives:					
Local	11	26	15	22	7
Out-of-town	26	15	7	11	4
Builder Representatives:					
Local	11	30	15	33	11
Out-of-town	4	4	0	4	4
Prefabricated Home Manufacturer Representatives	33	22	7	26	11
Union Representatives: (identify by trade)					
Local	0	7	4	4	26
Out-of-town	0	0	4	0	4
Building Officials from Cities:					
Within your county	4	26	18	11	4
Outside your county	7	22	26	0	4
Building Department Staff	7	33	11	15	7
Chief Building Official	15	11	0	15	0
Architects or Engineers	7	18	11	7	0

Source: Calculated from 1970 Survey of Local Building Department by Charles G. Field and Francis T. Ventre.

Table 4–5 (c)

The Involvement of Interest Groups in the Fight for Wood Roof Trusses, Placed 24″ on Center (Percent of Cities Reporting—Based Upon 31 Cities)

Interest Group	Where did the idea for this change originate? (1)	With whom was it discussed? (2)	Role Played		
			Which were the most trustworthy sources of information? (3)	Which groups most supported the change? (4)	Which groups most resisted the change? (5)
Building Material Producers or Supplier Representatives:					
Local	48	42	26	39	3
Out-of-town	26	26	3	6	0
Builder Representatives:					
Local	45	45	10	32	6
Out-of-town	10	0	0	10	0
Prefabricated Home Manufacturer Representatives	42	29	13	26	0
Union Representatives: (identify by trade)					
Local	0	0	0	0	6
Out-of-town	0	0	0	0	0
Building Officials from Cities:					
Within your county	10	32	19	16	6
Outside your county	16	26	23	10	3
Building Department Staff	16	13	6	6	10
Chief Building Official	10	13	6	10	6
Architects or Engineers	32	35	42	19	3

Source: Calculated from 1970 Survey of Local Building Department by Charles G. Field and Francis T. Ventre.

Table 4-5 (d)

The Involvement of Interest Groups in the Fight for ABS or PVC Plastic Pipe in Drain, Waste and Vent Plumbing Systems (Percent of Cities Reporting—Based on 230 Cities)

Interest Group	Where did the idea for this change originate? (1)	With whom was it discussed? (2)	Role Played		Which groups most supported the change? (4)	Which groups most resisted the change? (5)
			Which were the most trustworthy sources of information? (3)			
Building Material Producers or Supplier Representatives:						
Local	35	45	20		41	16
Out-of-town	41	40	13		38	14
Builder Representatives:						
Local	27	49	14		49	9
Out-of-town	7	19	2		17	4
Prefabricated Home Manufacturer Representatives	19	11	1		19	1
Union Representatives: (identify by trade)						
Local	2	17	3		1	26
Out-of-town	0	4	1		0	15
Building Officials from Cities:						
Within your county	9	44	24		16	10
Outside your county	13	42	29		13	5
Building Department Staff	15	50	14		17	10
Chief Building Official	16	15	3		14	3
Architects or Engineers	9	36	16		17	3

Source: Calculated from 1970 Survey of Local Building Department by Charles G. Field and Francis T. Ventre

file) than to agency sources for trustworthy information. For example, in only 11 percent of the cities did the official consider his own staff a trustworthy source of information on non-metallic sheathed electrical cable. (See Table 4-5.) Local material suppliers, local builders, architects and engineers, and building officials from nearby cities all scored higher than the local staff.

Local builders have more need and opportunity to interact with local building officials than do home manufacturers. Thus, chief building officials are more likely to report local builders more frequently than home manufacturers as trustworthy sources of information. The correction process was to subtract from the frequency of discussion the frequency of being reported as trustworthy and then dividing by the former. This new value (column 3 of Table 4-6) can be defined as the drop in credibility. After normalizing the scores, the relationship still held—non-staff exert greater influence in code decisions than staff. The higher the score, the less trustworthy the given source of information.

We found (see Table 4-6) that building officials placed greater reliance upon non-agency groups than upon their own staffs. The drop in credibility for the building department staff exceeded 50 percent. This was due either to a lack of faith on the part of many chief building officials in the judgment of their staffs or, in the case of offices staffed by one inspector, to the need for outisde assistance. The table also shows that interest groups suffered equal if not more severe credibility drops; but to ascribe relative strength to the staff is misleading. Chief building officials were selective when seeking advice on a code change. The interest groups more frequently contacted than building department staff consistently fared better than the staff.

The data substantiates the proposition that the agency depends more upon information from the outside than from within when making code standard decisions. What is written into the codes as standards is often what members of the industry recommend rather than what the staff recommends.

2.   *Do local interests hold greater influence over agency decisions than out-of-towners?*

The argument that the regulatory system is used to restrict the entry of innovators into the market turns on this question. The test is straightforward. The participants were classified into local and non-local groups, and for each group an average decline of credibility was calculated. (See Table 4-7.) A comparison of the declines of credibility for localities and out-of-towners makes the point. Localities (local building suppliers, local builders, local unions, architects and engineers) suffer a smaller drop in credibility than out-of-towners. In all cases, this pattern holds except for wood roof trusses.

Moreover, the home manufacturer scarcely influences the measured code decisions. In the profiles and in the measurement of credibility, home manufacturers consistently performed poorly. One can speculate as to causes. Home manufacturers are not part of the routine construction industry known to the local building official. They do not fit his conception of the traditional sub-contracting system that knits together general contractors to specialty contractors and labor. In addition to not fitting the traditional system, the manufacturer is invariably located a substantial distance from the local community which drastically minimizes the opportunities for contact.

If contact is influence, the home manufacturer is losing ground to members of the local construction industry. Almost no officials knew the home manufacturer. Over half of the chief building officials, 55 percent, reported that they rarely if ever had business contact with the manufacturer or his representative. (See Chapter Three, Table 3-7). Only 7 percent said they had frequent contact. Building officials had significantly higher rates of contact with members of the local construction industry. Thus, communication channels, so vital to the diffusion of new ideas, were closed to the manufacturer but open to those seeking to preserve the *status quo* of conventional construction.

3. *Does the existing building code pattern impose unnecessary costs upon innovators?*

We earlier concluded that the pattern of codes adds unwarranted costs to the price of the house, and that these costs were significant. The implication is that the more manufacturers displaced local construction jobs, the greater the resistance they encountered from codes. There is thus a positive relationship between the value of the manufactured house and the frequency of added costs. The greater the portion of the house produced by an out-of-towner, the more likely the producer would report code problems. As local groups see increasing shares of the economic house being taken away from them, the more prone they are to take protective actions, one of which is to use the building code to ward off such economic invasions. This proposition is generally sustained by the data. (See Table 4-8.) As the proportional control over sales price increased, so did the reported frequency of stricter standards and significant added costs. As the degree of producer control increased from 0-25, 26-50, 51-75, to 76-100, the incidence of significant added costs increased from 20 percent, 18 percent, 33 percent, to 51 percent respectively.

A more serious yet infrequently discussed and subtle impact of codes is their implicit effect on market size. A manufacturer may be able to adjust to a few code prohibitions by altering his production routine, but he reaches a point where they are too many prohibitions to adjust to. The cost of alteration may be too great, the changes may be incompatible with the production routine, or the problems of passing tests for each community may be too difficult. At some point, the manufacturer will say no to a community because of its building code and look for other markets.

To measure this effect, home manufacturers were asked to identify, from

Table 4–6
Average Drop in Credibility on Selected Code Items

Interest Group	With whom was it discussed? (1)	Which were the most trustworthy sources of information? (2)	Drop in credibility (1 – 2)/1 % (3)
ABS or PVC plastic pipe in drain, waste and vent plumbing systems			
Building Material Producers or Supplier Representatives:			
Local	45	20	56
Ouf-of-town	40	13	67
Builder Representatives:			
Local	49	14	71
Out-of-town	19	2	90
Prefabricated Home Manufacturer Representatives	11	1	91
Union Representatives: (identify by trade)			
Local	17	3	82
Out-of-town	4	1	75
Building Officials from Cities:			
Within your county	44	24	55
Outside your county	42	29	31
Building Department Staff	50	14	72
Chief Building Official	15	3	87
Architects or Engineers	36	16	56
Offsite preassembled combination drain, waste, and vent plumbing System for bathroom installation			
Building Material Producers or Supplier Representatives:			
Local	26	15	42
Out-of-town	15	7	54
Builder Representatives:			
Local	30	15	50
Out-of-town	4	0	100
Prefabricated Home Manufacturer Representatives	22	7	68
Union Representatives: (identify by trade)			
Local	7	4	43
Out-of-town	0	1	–
Building Officials from Cities:			
Within your county	26	18	31
Outside your county	22	26	0
Building Department Staff	33	11	67
Chief Building Official	11	0	100
Architects or Engineers	18	11	39

Table 4-6 (continued)

Interest Group	With whom was it discussed? (1)	Which were the most trustworthy sources of information? (2)	Drop in credibility (1–12)/1 % (3)
Non-metallic sheathed electrical cable			
Building Material Producers or Supplier Representatives:			
Local	30	16	42
Out-of-town	9	5	44
Builder Representatives:			
Local	49	16	51
Out-of-town	14	0	100
Prefabricated Home Manufacturer Representatives	11	0	100
Union Representatives: (identify by trade)			
Local	18	0	100
Out-of-town	7	0	100
Building Officials from Cities:			
Within your county	35	14	46
Outside your county	23	7	70
Building Department Staff	40	11	72
Chief Building Official	23	7	70
Architects or Engineers	40	20	50
Wood roof trusses, placed 24" on center			
Building Material Producers or Supplier Representatives:			
Local	42	26	43
Out-of-town	26	3	89
Builder Representatives:			
Local	45	10	0
Out-of-town	0	0	0
Prefabricated Home Manufacturer Representatives	29	13	55
Union Representatives: (identify by trade)			
Local	0	0	0
Out-of-town	0	0	0
Building Officials from Cities:			
Within your county	32	19	41
Outside your county	26	23	12
Building Department Staff	13	6	54
Chief Building Official	13	6	54
Architects or Engineers	35	2	94

Source: Computed from 1970 Survey of Building Departments by Charles G. Field and Francis T. Ventre—calculated from Tables 4–(a)–(d).

Table 4–7

**Average Drop in Credibility on Selected Code Items: Localities
vs. Out-of-Towners vs. Home Manufacturers**

	Locali- ties*	Out-of- towners*	Home manufacturers*
ABS or PVC plastic pipe in drain, waste, and vent plumbing systems	66%	80%	91
Off-site preassembled combination drain, waste, and vent plumbing system for bathroom installation	43%	74%	68
Nonmetallic sheathed electrical cable	61%	86%	100
Wood roof trusses, placed 24" on center	72%	57%	55

*Values are straight averages of column (3) from Table 4–5. Localities include local
building suppliers, local builders, local unions, architects and engineers. Out-of-towners
include out-of-town material producers or suppliers, out-of-town builders, home manufacturers and out-of-town unions.

13 of the 14 construction items,[17] the minimum combination of items
(defined as the prohibitive set) whose prohibition by a city code would *deter*
them from marketing there. The responses were varied, running from one to
several items and reflecting the different requirements of the different housing
systems. With each firm's prohibitive set it was possible to calculate market
exclusion scores. Each manufacturer's prohibitive set was compared with each
city's code status for each item. Where the city prohibited all the items in the
set, the city was defined as being exclusionary. Each firm was given a score
equal to the percent of cities in the total sample (or subsample) defined as exclusionary. If the city permitted at least one of the items, it was classified as
open to the firm. While the calculation is narrowly defined, it is the only
measure available to quantify the impact of codes on market structure.[18]

The exclusionary effects of certain codes bear down heavily upon home
manufacturers. Depending upon the type of manufacturer, anywhere from 20
percent to 49 percent of the market was scored as closed to him. The exclusion
pattern varied by type of city, and type of producer. (See Tables 4–9 and 4–10.)
The most exclusionary cities used locally-based codes. This was expected since
the code is locally written, allowing maximum opportunity by local groups to
insert prohibitions into the code. Cities with the best codes used model and state
codes, but even their market exclusion effects were quite high. Scores in the
40th percentile range were quite common, reflecting the fact that local adoption
of model codes does not preclude item prohibitions.

The type of home manufacturer made a difference. Multi-family producers
had higher scores than single-family producers, 40 percent compared to 32 percent (See Table 4–10.)

Table 4-8
Incidence of Stricter Standards and Added Costs by Degree of Manufacturer Control of Product Value: 1970

Percent of Sales Price Produced in the Factory	Stricter Standards			Added Costs		
	Number of Firms Reporting	Yes	No	Number of Firms Reporting	Yes	No
0–25	49 100%	42.9	57.1	27 100%	48.1	51.9
25–50	69 100%	50.7	49.3	43 100%	27.9	72.1
50–75	35 100%	68.6	31.4	24 100%	54.2	45.8
75–100	72 100%	65.3	34.7	52 100%	63.5	36.5

Source: Computed from 1970 Survey of Home Manufacturers by Charles G. Field.

Table 4-9

Exclusion Scores of Cities by Location and Political Form of Government: 1970

Type of City		Exclusion Scores
Central City	Mayor	37
Central City	Manager	34
Central City	Other	34
Suburban	Mayor	40
Suburban	Manager	35
Suburban	Other	37

Sources: Computed from 1970 Survey of Home Manufacturers and Local Building Departments by Field and Ventre.

Table 4-10

Exclusion Scores by Type of Manufacturer

	Exclusion Scores
Basic Form	
Pre-cut	46
Panel	40
Modular	22
Type of Market	
Single Family	33
Single and Multi Family	38
Multi Family	40

Source: Computed from 1970 Survey of Home Manufacturers and Survey of Local Building Departments by Field and Ventre.

The gap may reflect the recent movement of home manufacturing into low-rise multifamily housing. Whereas single-family producers have had years of market experience in adjusting to the pattern of prohibitions, multifamily producers are still feeling their way.

A surprising result emerges when stratifying by type of product. While we would expect modular producers to encounter greater problems, the exclusionary score facing them was significantly lower than those confronting panel and pre-cut housing producers. The differences were substantial, 22 percent compared to 40 percent and 46 percent respectively. The explanation most likely lies in the product itself. Given the technically more complex modular system and the larger investment costs required for the system, modular producers most likely took greater precautions in designing their units. Because the modular system is often a closed wall system lacking flexibility at the construction site, it must be structurally overdesigned in order to compensate for variations in code standards. As earlier indicated, the strategy of overbuilding is a common means of compensating for variations in codes, seemingly the case here. In sharp contrast, the pre-cut and panel houses offer flexibility, there being room for on-site corrections if the unit is not in full conformance with the local code. One side of the panel may be roughly covered when shipped to the site, allowing access to the interior of the panel if required by the local code inspector. Then there exists a tendency not to overdesign, but to make corrections at the site.

It cannot be deduced from the above statistics that modular producers have less trouble obtaining building permit approval. Quite to the contrary, modular producers report more frequent problems with code approval than other types of producers.[19] As all producers will readily testify, if a building official does not want to grant approval, there is always something in the code he can use to deny the permit. The people problem can be as severe as the formal code problem, if not more severe. Exclusion, therefore, can result either because of the content of the codes or the interpretations and predispositions of local building officials.

Upon analysis, we concluded that the restrictiveness of codes was intimately related to the vitality of the construction industry and to the extent to which political influence could be exerted upon local building officials. Slow-growing, suburban cities with mayoral forms of government had the most restrictive codes. Suburban, city manager cities had the least restrictive codes. If this analysis is correct in relating home manufacturer problems with codes to active opposition by local construction interests, we would expect the slow-growing, mayoral cities to have the most exclusionary codes. That is indeed the case. Suburban, mayoral communities had an average exclusionary score of 40, while managerial central and suburban cities had average scores of 34 and 35 respectively. (See Table 4-9.)

One would anticipate this type of conclusion, since exclusionary scores are, in part, based upon prohibitions within the codes. But the conclusion is not so straightforward, because the exclusion score requires a matching up of what home manufacturers consider important to them and what is prohibited in the code. The results suggest that codes are used by interest groups to serve ends other than the health and safety of the local citizenry. The building code is a politicized document serving special economic ends.

4. *Would the elimination of the protective regulatory screen result in negative consequences for the local construction industry?*

It is extremely difficult to prove that the elimination of building code obstacles would result in negative consequences for the local construction industry. Data that would allow us to calculate cost savings to home manufacturers due to uniformity and non-prohibitionary codes are not available. We can only infer what might happen from recent responses to moves towards the off-site prefabrication and preassembly of housing components. The imposition of local prohibitions need not be a protective response to a potential *real* loss of market share, rather it may be a response to a *perceived* threat of loss.

It is quite clear that in certain situations the introduction of manufactured housing or components results in a loss of local work. The off-site fabrication of electrical and plumbing systems translates into a loss of jobs and/or hours worked for both the unions and the specialty contractors involved. Neither off-site preassembled combination drain, waste, and vent plumbing systems for bathroom installation nor the off-site preassembled combination electrical wiring harness for installation at electrical service entrance represents a substantial product change, but they do represent shifts in the location of the work. If actions are a reflection of local fears, the high incidence of local code prohibitions against off-site preassembled plumbing and electrical systems (see Table 3-12) illustrates the local fear of job loss.

Where codes do not prohibit the preassembled-prefabricated product, some of them nevertheless impose work restrictions that negate any cost savings from the factory process. In Massachusetts, for example, all plumbing is regulated under a statewide code. In a recent regulation, the code's governing body, the State Examiners of Plumbers, ruled that for all plumbing installed in prefabricated buildings constructed in Massachusetts, the work "must be done by Massachusetts licensed plumbers." [20] Moreover,

> all piping installed in the waste vent or water supply system in the plant must be left completely exposed and accessible after the building leaves the plant. [21]

For plumbing installed in prefabricated buildings constructed outside the state, the State Examiners ruled:

> . . . if the building arrives at its point of destination with all plumbing fixtures completely installed, that the *plumbing fixtures* installed *must be disconnected* and removed, and that every inch of piping installed in the waste and vent system shall be exposed, and all open ends capped or sealed in order that the inspector of plumbing may witness and inspect the proper testing of the entire piping system installed to ascertain complete compliance with the provisions of the Massachusetts State Plumbing Code. [22]

Massachusetts is not a unique case. Many local communities use the code provisions, licensing requirements, and definitions to preserve work for special groups. This pattern is repeated in other states with specialized codes (plumbing, elevator, electrical, etc.) and in many local communities. Techniques for preserving work for special groups are sometimes more subtle. Inspectors have substantial discretion in enforcing the codes. Nor is it unusual for plumbing or electrical inspectors, for example, to be members of their respective unions.

Thus, when a question of who controls the work arises, an inspector's judgments are made in favor of the union position.

Sometimes these work requirements do not result from a conscious attempt to block innovations, but from disputes between two competing unions seeking jurisdictional control over the same piece of work. For example, plumbers and laborers have fought over who should install the piping that lies within the property lines but outside the building proper. The United Association of Plumbers has been successful, in a number of cases, in defining the work as plumbing to be performed by licensed plumbers and in this fashion freezing out the laborers. Thus, requirements not designed to inhibit innovation come into the codes and have detrimental affects upon innovation.

The intent of the Massachusetts regulations is obvious—to protect the interests of the licensed state plumbers and the state-based subcontractors from inroads by out-of-state businesses. To require state-licensed plumbers to do the in-state factory work and to require that all installed plumbing units be disconnected and removed for inspection before a permit is issued creates additional work and adds to costs. The effective consequence of these regulations is a tax on prefabricated plumbing and the dissipation of any savings inherent in factory production.

The issue here, perhaps, is not that the dropping of barriers will actually harm local businesses; rather that such harm is *perceived* by localities.

Another useful insight gained from the Massachusetts case is that influence that obstructs innovation is not confined to the local level. State code and code enforcement agencies are just as susceptible to partisan influence as are local agencies. Thus, while the analysis has focused upon local codes, many of the lessons learned are applicable to the state level.

Socially Undesirable Consequences Result From the Present Regulatory Structure.

The extent to which zoning has acted as a barrier to low and moderate-income housing has been revealed in a series of recent court decisions and in press accounts of the activities of open housing organizations. Prompted by fears of low-income families or of increased costs for public municipal services or by a desire to retain existing ethnic characteristics of neighborhoods or by a variety of other motivations, communities have adopted zoning that prohibits the construction of housing that lower income families can afford. The extent to which building codes also screen out this type of housing is little known.

The principal goal sought from industrialization is the production of low and moderate-income housing. The potential contribution that industrialization can make here could be significant if production cost reductions (either absolute or relative to conventional costs) could be realized. This would lead to either a reduced governmental subsidy cost for a given number of units or a greater number of housing units for the same cost. Under the present set of building codes, though, that goal appears unattainable. Home manufacturers, as indicated above, were asked about the code-imposed necessity to build their product to stricter than reasonable standards, and whether the resulting added cost was significant. Added costs due to stricter standards was primarily a low and moderate-cost housing problem. Although most firms reported the necessity to build to stricter standards, the impact was more pronounced for the low-cost than for the high-cost housing producer. As shown in Table 4-11, 60 percent of the firms building in the $5,000-$10,000 class reported encountering both stricter standards and higher costs. The proportion quickly dropped off to 29 percent of the producers in the $20,000-plus class. The drop-off in the less than $5,000 class is attributible to mobile home producers, who accounted for most of that production. In most states, mobile homes are not subject to building code regulations, thus the problem is infrequently encountered. This does not mean that mobile homes are unregulated. They are regulated through standards set by their own association.

Another measure of the impact of codes on low and moderate-income housing comes from the exclusion scores. Just under half of the central cities (48 percent) and suburban communities (47 percent would exclude housing in the $5,000-$10,000 range). Exclusion was particularly severe where local codes were in force—55 percent of those cities. Multifamily housing fared somewhat better, but its exclusion scores were still high at 39 percent in central cities, 40 percent in suburban communities and 43 percent in cities using local codes. (See Table 4-12.)

To this bleak outlook add the indication from the producers of multifamily housing that code approval was a substantial problem and that 52 percent of firms producing multifamily homes indicated that added costs resulted from stricter standards.

This nation has looked toward producers of multifamily housing for subsi-

Table 4-11

The Percent of Firms at Each Price Level who Responded Experiencing Stricter Standards with Resulting Significant Added Costs

Price of Unit[1]	Number of Firms Reporting Stricter Standards Percent of Those Experiencing Added Costs
Less $5,000	42.7%
$5,000–10,000	60.0%
$10,000–15,000	53.1%
$15,000–20,000	46.4%
$20,000+	29.4%

[1] Price excludes cost of land and site development

Source: Computed from 1970 Survey of Home Manufacturers by Charles G. Field.

Table 4-12
Exclusion Scores and the Low- and Moderate-income House

City by Characteristic	Price Class (Percent of all survey cities excluding)				
	Less $5,000	$5,000– $10,000	$10,000– $15,000	$15,000– $20,000	$20,000
Central City	36	48	27	31	35
Suburban	36	47	27	31	35
Independent	39	51	30	34	37
Mayor	36	47	27	31	35
Manager	37	48	27	32	36
Central City					
Mayor	40	52	30	33	36
Manager	35	46	25	30	34
Suburban					
Mayor	42	54	32	37	40
Manager	37	48	28	32	36
Independent					
Mayor	36	47	26	31	35
Manager	36	48	27	32	36

Source: Computed from 1970 Survey of Home Manufacturers by Charles G. Field and 1970 Survey of Building Code Departments by Charles G. Field and Francis T. Ventre.

dized housing, and the location of that housing has typically been the inner cities of our metropolitan areas. If we are to count upon home manufacturers to respond to a public need for lower income housing, we must recognize that these types of producers face severe code problems. Should the existing building code pattern continue, there can be little reason to expect substantial contributions from industrialized production in meeting our lower-income housing production needs.

Conclusion

We have searched the existing literature and sources of data to test whether building codes impose a burden upon the development and marketing of techno-logical innovations in homebuilding. While data were scarce on innovative spe-cialists ranging from building material producers to the inventor working in his garage, fairly good data were available on home manufacturers. American home manufacturers, unlike their European counterparts, do not make major use of plant and equipment to produce a completely new type of housing unit. The American home manufacturer is a producer of residential units, conventional in many respects, who has shifted the location of work from the site and into the factory. Thus, he is an innovator in terms of the production process of housing, but not necessarily in the product itself.

To the home manufacturer, the building code regulatory process is a burden of sizable proportion. Codes affect his business operations by imposing costs higher than those needed to meet nationally recognized standards. His production process is made less efficient because of the need to build in maximum flexibility that will allow him to adjust to changing code requirements, or because he must overbuild the unit in order to meet the differing sets of code requirements.

In addition, the home manufacturer's marketing area is reduced in effective size because of the prohibitions built into the codes. The potential extent of market exclusion can run as high as 50 percent as measured in this chapter.

The building code regulatory process can be misused for economic gain. The real loser is the public. This arbitrary use of public power strains the legal fabric that covers domestic commerce. Moreover, the practice of using the local regulatory power for special interest purposes is destructive to the exercise of governmental power at the local level. It raises the question of whether Americans have the capacity to govern their own local affairs in the public interest. Close contact with building code regulation leads one to the conclusion that this is an area of regulatory policy that is too technical for the average citizen to comprehend. Thus, the local citizen abdicates his responsibilities for policing the use of this power to those groups that understand the meaning of the code. The history has been to abdicate the responsibility to those who have a direct economic, not public, interest in the code, and thus the system has been used to keep new ideas out of the market.

The use of codes is closely analogous to the national use of tariffs and quotas. Drawing the analogy between local building code regulation and national tariffs and quotas helps highlight some of the dynamics of building code regulation. How one equates the local building code situation with the more familiar national tariff and quota systems should be carefully examined. Though the analogies are appealing and meaningful, the two are not exactly comparable. The consequences, we argue, are similar. All three barriers—the tariff, the quota, and the local building code—are legislatively enacted and as such carry the force of law. Their application is mandatory, though the method of application may differ. In this context, both are means of imposing noneconomic public controls upon economic activity. Another similarity is that it is in the best interest of economic groups—be they textile companies, local retail material dealers, or labor unions—to secure legislative conditions favorable to their economic interests. Business incentives in the national tariff may be the preservation of a market share or the avoidance of substantial loss in the face of less expensive imports; the same incentives operate at the local level. Unlike the national tariff, which imposes an explicit tax on imports, the local code does not impose an explicit tax on a particular item; the tax is implicit. Building regulation as a quota is both explicit and implicit, depending upon whether the measure is outright prohibition or more subtle exclusion.

When first written, codes were probably not intended for use against innovations and home manufacturing. More likely, since residential construction was a local activity, the local construction industry simply wanted to keep the door open for its products and labor. But with the coming of new techniques and production processes that threatened local interests, it became obvious that the local code could not only be used to preserve one's position, but also to exclude outside competition. Specification standards served this purpose. By allowing only the specified way of construction, it excluded other approaches.

The problem is less one of product standards themselves than one of interest groups in whose behalf many prohibitive standards are enacted. Local building departments are clearly influenced by outside interest/groups, and in the competition for influence, the "localities" hold much greater credibility than "out-of-towners." Therefore, the structure of each community's code is imbued with local favoritism. Even where model codes are used, variations from the model reflect the local interest. Though local codes may not be consciously designed to exclude the home manufacturer, the consequence of writing prohibitions into the code is exclusion.

Internal tariffs and quotas act at variance with constitutional powers over domestic commerce. Foreign producers enjoy no such constitutional protection. Indeed, tariffs and quotas on foreign goods are specifically intended to block international competition. If the building regulatory process is tantamount to a trade barrier, it is acting contrary to the constitutional provisions of due process and interstate commerce; it discriminates against innovators and home manufacturers who ship their goods interstate. These legal issues surrounding the use of regulatory power are among those to which we now turn our attention.

5

The Legal Framework for Building Reform: Options for Change

For innovation and industrialization to flourish, several key market conditions must exist. As discussed in earlier chapters, there must be markets large enough to justify an innovator's consideration of capital-intensive approaches to building materials and housing system techniques. If his innovation represents a radical departure from established ways of doing business, he must have, in addition, some set of performance standards against which to develop and test his product. Otherwise acceptance of new approaches by building officials becomes rather arbitrary, depending upon their attitude. Finally, the regulatory system must not constitute a continuing harassment to the innovator. Ideally, he should be required to seek code approval once, pay the fees once, and submit to additional approval requirements only when they are explicitly related to site considerations.

In respect to the three critera for equitable regulations, the system of local codes has seriously failed the innovator. The potential market has been Balkanized by hundreds of individual building code systems. Local government has neither the resources nor the political independence to develop and implement performance-based codes. Were such resources available, the certain outcome would be a horrendous jungle of differing performance requirements across communities, a prospect far worse than the existing pattern of variation in standards. Most difficult of all problems to solve is strong local protectionism. Traditional interests make the local system almost completely unreceptive to new ideas. The innovator must battle his way into every new jurisdiction, the task being more difficult as his product becomes more threatening to local economic interests. Thus, code reform does not lie in the direction of resuscitating local building code authority.

The question we face is not how to reform the system from within the framework of local codes. Reform must come from without. At least three broad avenues for future reform appear pertinent. Current trends are toward state solutions, an approach that takes existing constitutional distributions of authority and removes power from local officials by the state's reassertion of primacy over localities in regulating homebuilding for the sake of the health, safety, and wellbeing of its citizens. Another approach is to seek reform through litigation by private parties or government agencies. Judicial intervention can be seen as both a means of securing specific redress for the plaintiff and as a means of buttressing state-level solutions.

A final road to reform is federal action that preempts both state and local codes. Though occasionally discussed in policy circles, federal code action has not attracted wide consideration. Discussion of federal intervention tends to arise only when "all else fails."

To a significant extent, legal parameters govern the economic behavior of the building industry by controlling the pace of innovation and the size of its markets. Over the years, a significant conceptual gap has appeared between the technical and economic interests of most of the builders, craftsmen, and administrators who are direct participants in the regulatory process, on the one hand, and the intricate constitutional and administrative legal niceties that determine how the regulatory process works. With so little practical "interface" between their professional concerns and the conditions defining the market for their skills, it is not surprising that participants in the building regulation process tend to be apathetic about the prospects of significant change.

Lacking clearly defined pressures for reform, regulation of construction has languished in legal obscurity. Indifference to code reform within the legal profession is attested to by the mere handful of scholarly articles that have appeared. But bringing to bear the tools of analysis common to other areas of the exploding field of administrative law would seem to justify considerably greater interest.

Reform from Within: Strengthening
State Authority

In Chapter Three we described the type of code that dominated the country until the early 1970s. Localism was the prevailing code environment both in terms of promulgated codes and enforcement. Conventional builders, innovators—all those who sought code approval—had to deal with the specifics of each local code and the personalities of their enforcers. The most significant change introduced in the past two decades was a growing ascendency of model codes for local use. Still, patterns obstructive to technological advance often remained in force.

By the late 1960s and early 1970s, a promising pattern of state involvement had emerged. Some states were reasserting their consitutional prerogatives over local government by promulgating statewide preemptive building codes. The pattern was not new. States had to some degree administered statewide specialty codes—e.g., plumbing, elevator, electrical, etc.—and model or minimum standard codes. The shift was into the more general building code arena.

This process had gained some momentum in the early 1970s in several very important respects. First was the passage of more state code laws. As of mid-1974, approximately one-third of the states had statewide building code laws, and 25 had manufactured-building laws.[1] While many states have yet to act, progress has been rapid, with most of these laws being enacted over the past five years.

The manufactured-building law provides for the creation of an agency authorized to issue and administer rules and regulations governing design criteria and factory inspection of manufactured housing. Alternatively, the designated agency is an arm of the state executive branch responsible to the governor, or a building code council appointed by the governor but functioning independent of his control, sometimes with the assistance of outside advisory committees. Standards applied are frequently required to be consistent with standards of one or another model code group or with standards applied or recognized by HUD or the National Bureau of Standards. The administrative mechanism by which state standards apply is via the grant of state certification, usually expressed by seals of approval affixed to individual housing units but not extended to local site and foundation work, which must still be approved subject to local regulations.

These laws apply only to manufactured housing, and it is not entirely clear whether the manufacturer has the option of complying with local codes as an alternative. In addition, the disparity of treatment between manufactured housing, which constitutes the lesser part of all construction, and conventionally built housing becomes more glaring as a result of the adoption of special manufactured-housing standards and procedures.

In the late 1960s and early 1970s, state legislators were faced with a growing crisis in housing. Prices were rapidly escalating and were matched by growing public resentment. Pressure was applied to legislators—both from the public and from Washington—to reform the code system radically through state action. The models for action were distinct: either pass a specialized code for industrialized housing or pass a mandatory statewide code covering all forms of residential construction. The former was politically most feasible, for it infringed least upon special interest groups, particularly building trade unions and advocates of home rule.

Building trades had great influence over the state specialty codes whose governing boards (commissions) they controlled. To support a new state code that covered all aspects of construction meant that their control of the board would be dissipated as a broader range of other interest groups were accommodated. According to the model Manufactured Building Act, (developed by a joint committee of organizations and including the Council of State Governments, HUD, and NBS and sponsored by the Council of State Governments), the proposed building code council would have 12 qualified persons: the chief executive officer of the administrative agency, a representative of the general public, one registered architect, one registered professional engineer (structural), one registered professional engineer (mechanical), one registered professional engineer (electrical), one licensed general contractor, one representative of the building trades, one homebuilder, one building code enforcement officer from local government, one mobile home manufacturer, and one building manufacturer.

Home rule advocates resisted anything that would shift back to the state power traditionally held at the local level. But in a public climate demanding some change, opponents grudgingly took the lesser of evils and accepted narrowly defined manufactured-building laws.

Some states have taken that additional step and have adopted statewide building codes that generally eliminate the distinction between manufactured and conventionally-produced housing. The pattern of coverage, though, is uneven. North Carolina has a maximum-minimum code wherein localities may promulgate codes, but with standards that may not deviate from the range established. Explicit permission from the state is required prior to deviations from the code. Virginia is more direct, requiring localities to use the state-promulgated code. Massachusetts also has a mandatory statewide code replacing all local codes including a Boston City code that was recently rewritten at great cost. Indiana, on the other hand, has a mandatory code, but it excludes single and two-family dwellings, and farm buildings. Indiana cities may promulgate their own codes, which must be approved by the state agency.[2]

Just as the pattern of enforcement and coverage varies, so do the basic standards. The pattern is highly dependent upon which model code agency operates within the state. California's code is closely tied to the Uniform Building Code; Massachusetts has tied its code closely to the Basic Building Code. Uniformity between codes therefore largely reduces to uniformity between model codes.

South Carolina [3], West Virginia [4], and Oklahoma [5] have approached statewide coverage differently by adopting legislation that has the effect of approving for construction anywhere within state boundaries any housing system whose use has been authorized by the Department of Housing and Urban Development, preempting contrary provisions of local building codes. All other residential structures are still subject to local codes. Thus, the success or failure of the code depends on the efficacy of HUD actions. Unfortunately, HUD activities in the area of performance standards and certification procedures have not progressed to the point of making these state laws operational. While a promising initial stab at leap-frogging restrictive codes appears to have died stillborn, the precedent established may prove to be of enduring importance. The fact that some states have looked to a cooperative arrangement with the federal government must be viewed as a significant legislative development.

The long battle for statewide building code reform has often been bitter. Massachusetts is a typical example. The Massachusetts statewide housing bill was proposed to rationalize the quiltwork pattern of local building codes in use by local communities. The bill would establish a commission, which in turn would create by administrative power a statewide building code covering all types of construction. The code, after due hearings, would replace all local codes. It also originally proposed that the specialty codes run at the state level would fall under the jurisdiction of the commission. As part of the consolidation of state-level code activities, all code functions were to be lodged within the Department of Community Affairs, the agency directly concerned with the amount and quality of residential housing. This meant the transfer of certain code functions from the Department of Public Safety, which had responsibility for the existing state code (minimum code that allowed local communities to adopt their own codes) and some inspection functions. Finally the bill specified qualifications for building inspectors.

Arrayed in favor of code reform were legislators concerned about the rising costs of housing; architects and engineers who, on the basis of professional judgment, perceived a state code as a more efficient and workable system; local building officials who gained civil service protection under the specific act; certain unions, like the Laborers International, which stood to gain jobs by a more flexible code not controlled by competing unions (plumbers); and state administrators from the Department of Community Affairs, who would pick up the operating responsibilities. In opposition were home rule advocates (legislators), plumbers, general contractors, and state administrators from the Department of Public Safety, who would lose powers under the specific bill. While this list is not exhaustive, it does display the range of interest group involvement.

There were two significant concessions added to the original bill. The first was to include a provision that would place local building officials under state civil service. Support from the state association of building officials was secured with this provision, demonstrating the prime importance of job security to building officials. As local inspectors said at that time, they could not support a code that took power away from the locality for fear of retaliation from local politicians. The second compromise was the removal of key specialty codes from the jurisdiction of the building code commission. This neutralized the opposition of plumbers, electricians, and other union groups that would have lost power if all codes had come under one authority—the original intent of the bill. It took three legislative sessions to get the bill passed.

One of the keys to successful state action is reciprocity. As we have argued, an element essential to a flourishing of technological innovation is a mass market, which means an interstate market. If the prevailing pattern of codes is to be at the state level, there must be an efficient and effective mechanism of reciprocity that permits products or housing systems approved in one state to be adopted without retesting and recertification in other states. Some statutes, like the Washington State Industrialized Housing Law, contain provisions permitting reciprocal certification of systems approved under substantially equivalent standards of other states, where those standards are administered in an approved fashion. This eliminates the need for inspection in other states and facilitates the flow of manufactured housing across state lines.

Reciprocity is not yet a reality among states and is plagued by several significant problems. If each state is to act independently, reciprocity implies a basic similarity in building standards. Without similarity, reciprocity degenerates into chaos, with states that have less strict standards granting reciprocal approval to those with more stringent standards. If states were to regularize standards for purposes of reciprocity, the tendency would be for all states to move up towards the strictest code. Similar problems are involved in the approval procedures used by states. To succeed, interstate cooperation is prerequisite to an effective state building code system responsive to the needs of technologists.

The National Conference of States on Building Codes and Standards (NCSBCS), founded in 1967, is a major step in the direction of interstate cooperation. All 50 states are represented in NCSBCS, by individuals (usually professional building inspectors) are designated by each state, with secretariat services provided by the National Bureau of Standards of the U.S. Department of Commerce. Its activities have carried into areas of standards and evaluation, education and qualifications of building officials, management and regulatory procedures, and reciprocity between states.

In each area, the objectives are to research and develop new and more effective means of conducting building code activities. NCSBCS has no inherent authority over its membership save that exerted by persuasion. Although it is voluntary in structure, NCSBCS can be an important force for reform at the state level. Because it can marshal resources and the good offices of the National Bureau of Standards for technical support, NCSBCS, with its strong statewide bias, serves as an important counterbalance to the locally-oriented, traditional, model code groups.

Yet NCSBCS has yet to prove itself in the area of reciprocity. In part this is due to the limited political pull NCSBCS has within each state, where interest politics in code provisions is quite strong. As with our argument about the localism of local building officials, one can point to the statism of state building officials, whose primary concern is to be responsive to state legislators, the governor's personnel, and state-level interest groups. Support for interstate cooperation, if it comes from anywhere, must sought from the federal government and from material producers and innovators who favor mass markets. NCSBCS is a voluntary organization and as such lacks power to enforce its decisions. Moreover, NCSBCS is a state-funded activity; therefore, state representatives will walk a careful line if developments begin to suggest a federalization of the building code pattern.

Statewide building code laws do not spell the end to problems for innovators and industrialists. The hard experience to date in several states has been that securing building code approval can be as tedious on the state level as on the local level. Home manufacturers who have dealt with New York State code officials constantly complain about the bureaucratic jungle of the code approval process. It can also be quite expensive. Some states, like Maine, used the code approval process as a means of generating revenues, taxing the various manufactured components and thereby pushing up the price of the entire housing unit.

NCSBCS has been developing uniform regulatory procedures that hopefully will reduce the tedium and repetitiveness of code approvals from one state to the next. The extent to which uniformity can be achieved has yet to be tested.

Conceptually, uniform administrative and regulatory procedures should be simple to design and implement. A uniform system can be designed; adoption of the system is more difficult. Each building official is his own expert on administrative procedure. Financing of the state code office differs from state to state, with some states requiring that most of it come from fees, and with other states providing funds from general revenues. Each state building code commission is subject to a different mix of interest groups in private business and the state legislature. Thus, the building commission's response cannot be uniform from state to state.

Finally, and most significantly, there are no substantial incentives for state building officials to act in concert. There are no rewards for adopting similar codes and similar administrative procedures. The only organized voices of collaboration come from the National Conference of States on Building Codes and Standards, and from the federal government. NCSBCS's membership, though, is made up of state delegates representing different state interests. In some cases, they are appointees of the governor representing his office. In other cases they are staff of the state building code commission. Still others represent Departments of Community Development. Membership is voluntary; NCSBCS decisions are not binding on its members, but are merely recommendations. The federal government has, for the present, minimized its pressures for state code reform. Thus, there are few, if any, pressures for the rational development of statewide code systems. Invariably, 50 states with 50 statewide building codes and 50 administrative procedures will evolve without interstate collaboration and reciprocity. While the creation of statewide codes will lead to some amelioration of the overall code burden, we will still need a code system that encourages the fullest use of technology and industrialization.

Litigation

If states are slow in responding to the innovator's need for positive reforms, alternative and complementary approaches can be taken through litigation. If standards of "reasonableness" in administrative action can be judicially imposed on the regulation of construction, greater responsiveness to technological change will result. By establishing a role for judicial interpretations of fundamental standards, interpretations that may legitimize novel building techniques, we may build momentum towards reform.

One cannot expect states to pass perfect codes that will completely reduce legal barriers to innovation. Interest groups do not permit laws and regulations affecting the construction industry to be adopted in a vacuum. Just as at the local level, construction industry interest groups actively lobby for favorable code provisions—often to the detriment of innovators. In the legislative struggle for a statewide Massachusetts building code, the interests of plumbers, laborers, building officials, material producers, architects, engineers and "home rulers" were represented in a strong, but compromise bill. Thus the "best" is rarely passed.

Judicial presence can help to fill these gaps, not only to improve the workings of the administrative mechanism, but also to stimulate legislative action where litigation results in a regulatory vacuum. In this latter sense, successful litigation can be the prelude to administrative and legislative action not previously deemed feasible. Litigation becomes the bridge connecting the present and future code systems.

The expectation of state code reformers is that litigation will provide redress to home manufacturers and prod states to upgrade statewide codes to meet their needs. This expectation is based on (1) the dormant but ever-present threat of federal preemptive action, and (2) recognition that mere promulgation of a statewide code is no guarantee that innovation will be welcomed at the state level. Code reformers believe that litigation can pave the way for legislative and administrative readjustment.

It must be noted that building regulation has not been judicially ignored. Early cases dealt extensively with whether states and municipalities possessed the power to prohibit the erection of structures by property owners. The municipalities' power has long been upheld as an exercise of the "police power" reserved to the states under the tenth amendment to the Constitution.[6] Additional litigation has questioned whether particular states have delegated adequate regulatory authority to municipalities by constitution or statute as an aspect of local "home rule" powers.[7] Other litigated questions have dealt with claims of unfairness arising out of indefinite local regulations,[8] inadequate procedural safeguards,[9] unlimited administrative discretion,[10] procedures for enactment and revision of code provisions,[11] and the validity and procedures of on-site inspections.[12] Overall, although certain standards of reasonable regulatory conduct have been established, the authority of local building processes and the discretion of local building officials have been uniformly upheld against the resistance of property owners.

In a seminal article by Rivkin in the *Rutgers Law Review,*[13] grounds for judicial review are explored in detail. Here we present the major findings of that work as they apply to litigation under the antitrust, due process, and Federal interstate commerce clauses—the principal grounds on which to challenge misuse of building codes.

Principles of *antitrust* are most applicable in the area of standard-setting, where the development or application of standards by economic interests has tended to restrict competition.[14] The test is not whether an economic interest has had a role in the standard-setting process, for business lobbying nearly always abounds. The issue is that of "unreasonable" restraint of competition.[15] An antitrust claim by a product manufacturer whose product was unreasonably suppressed by an industry-dominated code group [16] would suffice to propel a federal court into action.

The prospect of such antitrust litigation reaching a favorable termination at the "summary judgment" stage, that is, prior to a full-scale trial with all its attendant complexities and uncertainties, would seem slim and in any event dependent on the facts of the case. By the same token, raising a Sherman Act claim would expose to review the code formulation process and the reasonableness of regulatory determinations against particular products. Using litigation to determine unreasonableness will not be easy, nor will it lead to an assured result. No such litigation has yet succeeded. In the two most relevant recent attempts, the plaintiffs could not sustain the burden of showing unreasonableness.[17] On balance, the worst cases of protectionist exclusion—resulting in major costs to consumers, colored by arbitrary procedure, and running counter to modern engineering principles—are the best cases for antitrust proceedings.

Due process guarantees a measure of reasonableness for both the substance of building code standards and their mode of application. The federal constitution stands as a safeguard against state-authorized departures from the fifth and fourteenth amendment guarantees of due process. All state constitutions express similar limitations on state conduct, often couched in terms of protecting "property rights."[18] Under these standards, both federal and state courts are available to remedy state action denying citizens due process.

Several cases have potentially strengthened the role of the courts in enforcing due process restraints in the building field. One recent example whose success confirms the validity of such an approach and one that holds implications extending far beyond its own circumstances is the litigation between the Kingsberry Homes division of the Boise Cascade Corporation and Gwinnet County, Georgia.[19] In 1965, Kingsberry began a suit for injunctive relief in the United States District Court for the Northern District of Georgia against the Commissioners of Gwinnett County, who had denied building permits because Kingsberry's manufactured home differed from the permissible standards in two respects. Kingsberry's prefabricated product used plywood of 3/8 inch thickness for roof-decking where the building code provided for 1/2 inch thickness, and plaintiff's product used 1/2 inch intermediate density fibreboard sheathing for corner-bracing where the code contemplated only 1/2 inch plywood wall-sheathing at corners or a traditional system of corner-bracing with two-by-four or one-by-three timber.

Extensive tests of both systems were made for the trial, and testimony was presented both as to the acceptability of plaintiff's approach under other building codes and standards and as to the comparative performance of plaintiff's methods and those approved by the building code in achieving structural strength. With respect to roof-decking, the approach disapproved by the county was acceptable in other jurisdictions under the Southern Standard Building Code and under Veterans Administration, FHA, and other recognized standards.[20] The court found:

It is abundantly shown both by the standards and codes and by direct

evidence of specific deflexion tests conducted by reputable engineering
testing companies that the 3/8" 24/0 plywood used by the plaintiff is
the equivalent of the 1/2" plywood required by the code under the old
system. Thus, except for certain structural groupings not at issue here,
the two requirements are identical and have the same rigidity and
strength. Accordingly, there is no hesitancy in concluding that the
specific requirement of 1/2" plywood decking is unreasonable and
therefore unenforceable, and that the 24/0 requirements of the
Southern Standard Building Code is acceptable in all respects for the
area in question.[21]

A similar finding was reached for plaintiff's corner-bracing methods, though by
a slightly more complex reasoning process. Where the local code provided for
two alternatives, one using plywood and the other using traditional timber
bracing, the court reviewed direct comparison tests between these approaches
and plaintiff's fibreboard method (also sanctioned by the Southern Standard
Building Code) and again concluded that the plaintiff's method, having met
the requirements of the Southern Standard Building Code, was sufficient, and
that therefore the local code requirement was unreasonable and unenforceable.[22] On the basis of these findings, the court granted the injunctive relief
sought by the plaintiff.

In a footnote to the portion of his ruling exploring the comparison between
the plaintiff's fibreboard corner-bracing and the two alternative approved methods, Judge Sidney O. Smith, Jr. suggested an extraordinary, far-reaching field
for judicial review in cases where the facts might differ somewhat from those in
the *Boise Cascade* case. If only the 1/2 inch test had been expressed in the code—
which, Judge Smith found, represented a stricter method than the plaintiff's
method and which itself exceeded the standard acceptable in other jurisdictions—the court would have been unable to find the "equivalency" test
satisfied. However, according to the judge, if the local test exceeded the standard
of "adequacy" established by other competent authorities, it would be unreasonable to prohibit methods employing less, but nonetheless adequate,
structural strength.[23] By complying with, and indeed in this case exceeding,
the standard of another well-formulated code, the plaintiff's method is clearly
satisfactory and prohibition under the local building code unreasonable. The
judge said:

> The indications are that compliance with such a standard [here, the
> Southern Standard Building Code] would establish a *prima facie* case
> of "equivalence," if that were the issue, of "adequacy" if that were
> the issue. Such a showing should not normally yield to anything but
> strong proof of a peculiar extraordinary hazard in the particular area,
> necessitating the higher standard in question.[24]

Thus, the thrust of the court's opinion is that it could have required the county to justify its adoption of a standard stricter than warranted, and that if it failed to do so, a less strict method of construction would be permitted.

The consequences of this line of reasoning are far-reaching. If an authoritative standard-setting agency were established to specify what is adequate, plaintiffs could seek relief from adverse rulings under either local or state-promulgated codes that set standards stricter than those established by the agency.

In the *Boise Cascade* case, there were several circumstances that greatly simplified the court's determination. First, the plaintiff had built a number of houses in the jurisdiction and elsewhere before the code was enforced against it, using the rejected methods of construction with no apparent ill effects. In addition, the county's deviation from the prevailing regional standard was obvious and apparently arbitrary enough to focus the court's attention on the justification for the deviation. Finally, the court felt that the Southern Standard Building Code was a reasonable effort at wide regional acceptance, which, as a practical matter put the burden of persuasion on the county. While the court was careful to buttress its decision by citing the practices of neighboring jurisdictions, it enunciated no logical limits to the types of proof that can be entertained. Thus, the implications of the court's analysis go far beyond the case at hand, inviting any builder to submit reputable testing results not necessarily embodied in any formal code in order to substantiate a claim that building standards are excessively rigid.[25]

Reform of building codes may be considered from another point of view, that of preserving the national economy from undue encroachments by state laws. A federal power under article I of the United States Constitution, to "regulate commerce with foreign nations and among the several states,"[26] vests federal courts with jurisdiction to review the reasonableness of state-authorized building codes insofar as they affect interstate commerce. The national interest that brings the *interstate commerce* clause into play is best expressed in various federal housing laws, beginning with the Housing Act of 1949:

the realization as soon as feasible of the goal of a decent home and a suitable living environment for every American family, thus contributing to the development and redevelopment of communities and to the advancement of the growth, wealth and security of the Nation.[27]

Against these goals must be weighed the states' interests in the health and safety of their citizens and, to a lesser and less well-articulated extent, in its local economy and the employment of its working men. The balancing process, again, is by no means simple. The fact that the nation has hitherto considered construction a localized concern makes somewhat conjectural the claim that local regulation significantly impedes the free flow of goods and services in what has been expansively termed "the continental common market."[28] But the growing interdependence between the economy and society and the rise in public concern over housing needs have generated a legitimate federal interest in removing local barriers to improving the housing supply.[29]

The Supreme Court has ruled that states may not unduly discriminate against interstate commerce in protecting local interests.[30] Laws passed to protect the public health of local citizens, which on first examination appear to be a reasonable exercise of power, have been struck down by the Court if the principal aim was to protect local economic interests and if alternative nondiscriminatory actions would have equally served the public interest. In *Dean Milk Co. v City of Madison*, the Court ruled that the Madison ordinance prohibiting the importing of milk from Illinois (milk could be brought into Madison only from within a 25-mile radius) was unconstitutional. It held: "By thus erecting an economic barrier protecting a major local industry against competition from without the state, Madison plainly discriminates against interstate commerce. This it cannot do, even in the exercise of its unquestioned power to protect the health and safety of its people, if reasonable nondiscriminatory alternatives, adequate to conserve local interests, are available."[31]

Similar issues can be raised in the context of local building regulation. Such issues would obviously turn on the facts of particular cases, some of which might usefully be conjectured. A property owner desiring to build a manufactured home or to install a prefabricated component imported from another state need not be deterred by a local building code provision requiring on-site inspection of homes in the process of construction. He could show some reasonable alternative method to achieve inspection, such as sending a local inspector or obtaining some disinterested third party certification.

A more complicated issue arises where the desired importation of a product, acceptable in other states, is prohibited in the particular jurisdiction. The litigation would turn on whether the local measure discriminates against interstate commerce or merely represents a local safety measure with only incidental effect on interstate commerce. Such safety measures have long been upheld as presumptively within state authority.[32] The outright clash of interests posed by onerous local inspection requirements is absent when all products of a certain type, regardless of origin, are expressly barred. Nevertheless, state measures barring all products of one type are vulnerable where there is a strong national interest in widely disseminating technological innovation and in achieving economies of scale and where there are " reasonable alternative" solutions that protect the public's health and safety without blocking the free flow of goods in a national market.

The balancing tests used by federal courts clearly invite submission of arguments to invalidate local codes on interstate commerce grounds, but tangible evidence of disservice to clearly-drawn national purposes must be presented. The costs to potential suppliers of complying with local idiosyncrasies will be easiest to substantiate where a particular code provision represents a hold-out against change in a regionally integrated market. Any such commerce clause argument will be reinforced by a due process claim, and *vice versa*.

It is one thing, however, to identify relevant legal principles and another to translate them into meaningful progress toward widespread reform, but perhaps a useful beginning has been made. Since the principles identified here have application to all forms of construction, not merely to housing, the economic incentives to engage in litigation are greater. However, the basis of litigation for gaining approval of a specific innovation or building design can never be lightly chosen. The facts of the case must clearly support the theories relied on, not only in the interest of a speedy and successful conclusion to the particular situation, but also to avoid false starts that might undermine such efforts. The hospitality of particular courts and judges to innovative challenges to local customs, their perceptions of relative economic and social interests, and their responsiveness to the subtleties of sophisticated technological issues must also be considered.

Federal Roles to Displace State Authority

Even if the logic for federal action were cogent and the legal issues re-solvable, one would still have to contend with the politics of federalization. A variety of significant public and private interests are at stake. State and local officials are skeptical of the federal government's acquisition of local regulatory powers, for they feel that building code regulation has been the undisputed domain of the state government. Thus, little support could be expected from organizations representing state and local interests. Big business, in particular material producers and labor unions, has a major stake in the way building codes are written. Those who benefit from the current codes would fight bit-terly against any federalization of the system. Of course, there are other material producers and unions who have only a small slice of the construction business and would see in a federal code an opportunity to make further inroads into the market through innovative use of materials and skills.

We have argued the case for reform in preceding sections of this book; we now inquire whether there are proper federal roles to be played and whether these are sustainable under law. Until this year, very little progress had been made towards a substantial federal role. Formative first steps have been taken by the Congress in recognition of the need for code reform. The Housing and Community Development Act of 1974, signed into law August 23, 1974, creates a National Institute for Building Sciences and a National Mobile Home Act. Both are long-waited actions that actively introduce the federal government into building code regulation.

The National Institute of Building Sciences (NIBS) has long been advocated by Senator Jacob Javits (R. New York) and Congressman William Moorhead (D., Pennsylvania) as a link in the code regulatory process that is essential to the introduction of new building technologies. Originally introduced for Congressional consideration in the late 1960s, bills on NIBS failed to gather sufficient support from private construction groups and the administration. Many private construction groups were fearful of massive federal intervention; therefore, they actively lobbied against proposals that appeared to shift substantial authority away from state, local, and private standard-setting authorities. Administration support over the years was complicated by rivalries between agencies that wanted to have direct control over the functions of NIBS or sought stronger ties to it.

In establishing NIBS, the Congress declared that:

> The Congress finds (A) that the lack of an authoritative national source to make findings and to advise both the public and private sectors of the economy with respect to the use of building science and technology in achieving nationally acceptable standards and other technical provision for use in Federal, State, and local housing and building regulations is an obstacle to efforts by and imposes severe burdens upon all those who procure, design, construct, use, operate, maintain, and retire physical facilities, and frequently results in the failure to take full advantage of new and useful developments in technology which could improve our living environment; (B) that the establishment of model building codes or of a single national building code will not completely resolve the problem because of the difficulty at all levels of government in updating their housing and building regulations to reflect new developments in technology, as well as the irregularities and inconsistencies which arise in applying such requirements to particular localities or special local conditions; (C) that the lack of uniform housing and building regulatory provisions increases the costs of construction and thereby reduces the amount of housing and other community facilities which can be provided; and (D) that the existence of a single authoritative nationally recognized institution to provide for the evaluation of new technology could facilitate introduction of such innovations and their acceptance at the Federal, State, and local levels. (Section 809 (a) (1) of the Housing and Community Development Act of 1974.)

The National Institute of Building Sciences is directed to develop appropriate performance criteria, standards, and testing procedures (to include prequalification of products) suitable for adoption by code regulatory agencies. Congressional intent was not to establish an agency with preemptive authority over existing regulatory agencies, rather one that provided technical assistance.

It was clearly Congressional intent that maximum coordination and cooperation should exist between NIBS and code regulatory agencies—be they federal, state, or local.

In contrast to the gentle approach of persuasion, the Congress also passed the National Mobile Act, which gave the Department of Housing and Urban Development the direct authority to establish federal building standards for mobile homes. The Congress found that the purposes to be served

> are to reduce the number of personal injuries and deaths and the amount of insurance costs and property damage resulting from mobile home accidents and to improve the quality and durability of mobile homes. (Section 602 of The Housing and Community Development Act of 1974.)

Unlike NIBS, HUD actions in mobile home regulation are preemptive. Once standards are established for mobile homes, they must be adopted or accepted by states and their political subdivisions. The law reads that:

> . . . no State or political subdivision of a State shall have any authority either to establish, or to continue in effect with respect to any mobile home covered, any standard regarding construction or safety applicable to the same aspect of performance of such mobile home which is not identical to the Federal mobile construction and safety standard (in effect). (Section 604 (d).)

These recent actions by the Congress may usher in long-awaited code reform initiatives. They represent an approach that, if effectively implemented, could result in lasting reform. This is an issue we shall return to in Chapter Five.

There are three modes of federal intervention:

1. Federal promulgation of a national building code;

2. Federal preemption of standards for products and processes tested and certified by an authoritative agency; and

3. Federal quality control through the coordination and certification of state regulatory programs.

These three approaches are not mutually exclusive and could be used in combination. They do represent different degrees to which the federal administrative apparatus may exercise functions now performed at the state and local levels. For any of the three, there would be the need for a single responsible entity—either under one of the existing executive departments (The Departments of Commerce and Housing and Urban Development are logical candidates) or an agency specially created to perform the legislated functions (the National Institute of Building Sciences).

A Federal Code

A federal building code would contain a body of standards, definitions, testing procedures, approval procedures, and permitted uses that would define acceptable construction. To be responsive to the needs of innovation, the code would have to incorporate performance standards and associated test procedures. The federal code could preempt state and local codes, although it is feasible for state and local codes to coexist within the framework of a federal code system, particularly where local variation is warranted by circumstances.

The scope of federal power would depend on economic analyses of the construction industry in the United States by value, by proportion of value added at the site and within the state in question, and by types of construction.

The most comprehensive reason for federal jurisdiction would be a finding that all construction not undertaken by the owner for his own occupancy is a national concern because it affects interstate commerce either directly (as the largest component of a typical family budget) or indirectly (local building "casts a shadow" on interstate commerce). Alternatively, all construction to which federal funds have been committed—either directly or through a federal mortgage guaranty, etc—could be made subject to federal standards only. Additionally, federal regulation could exempt from any definition of applicability certain classes of construction, either statutorily defined or defined by regulation.

A direct precedent for this approach, as mentioned earlier, is the National Mobile Home Act of 1974. In this Act, the Congress has established the preeminence of the federal government in establishing and enforcing building standard regulations for mobile homes. The Act gives the Secretary of the Department of Housing and Urban Development the authority to promulgate, by administrative order, standards for mobile homes that are binding upon state and local jurisdictions. In addition, HUD is given the authority to undertake the necessary research, testing, and development of mobile homes for experimental purposes, as well as the training of personnel necessary to carry out the intent of the legislation.

States may have enforcement roles, if they so elect. To assume enforcement responsibilities, the interested state must file for approval of a state plan consistent with the provisions of the Act. Once the plan is approved, the state can move to implementation, but HUD reserves the authority to rescind its approval should the state plan become inadequate or outdated.

Primary responsibility for compliance with the federal standards rests with the manufacturer, who must certify that his product conforms to the standards. Certification takes the form of a lable or tag permanently affixed to the unit. Prior to manufacture of a mobile home, the manufacturer must certify to the Secretary of HUD that his proposed unit meets all applicable federal construction and safety standards. In turn, HUD is authorized to inspect the plans and manufacturing facilities to verify the manufacturer's representations. If defects are found in the mobile home, the manufacturer must correct them before going into production. If defects are found after production, the manufacturer must make the necessary corrections at his own expense. Fines of up to $1,000 and possible imprisonment of up to one year put teeth into the law.

We should have learned from the experience with model codes that without some strong guidance from above, there are undesirable variations and prohibitions in code standards. While a National Institute of Building Sciences is a desirable first step, other actions must be initiated.

Other precedents for federal regulatory action exist in other fields. Some examples come up in the area of fair labor practices, meat inspection, and mine safety.[33] To establish federal jurisdiction, the Congress established that these cases had aspects of interstate commerce that constitutionally justified federal intervention. Federal code action would also build upon a base of rising concern about and state and local action on building safety. The federal government pre-empts state and local codes when federally-owned construction is involved. Standards and inspection procedures exist, for example, for Government Services Administration construction. The government also establishes minimum standards for private construction where direct government lending assistance or mortgage insurance is involved. The Minimum Property Standards serve this purpose for Department of Housing and Urban Development projects. These, though, do not override state and local codes, although the MPS or its equivalent is mandatory for the builder seeking assistance. Finally, HUD and the National Bureau of Standards have severally and jointly supported research on standards and have encouraged efficient code administration. Thus, the next step to a comprehensive federal code is to determine on what grounds direct intervention could be justified and whether there is Congressional and Administration support for this undertaking.

The vast scale on which federalized building regulation would have to apply would make complete displacement of state and local powers impractical, even though a completely federal process might well be constitutionally defensible. By the same token, any overlay of federal standards upon state enforcement mechanisms must be undertaken with a view to making a partnership approach effective, rather than to replacing state bureaucracies with a federal one.

While a mandatory federal code might completely eliminate the role of state and local codes, its enforcement could and probably should be the business of state and local authorities. The federal government does not have the enforcement reach required of a federally-enforced code. Enforcement takes place at the local level, except where the product is built in a factory and the inspection conducted there. Still, there is a need for local inspectors to approve the way the unit has been set on the lot and connected to the public services provided. A

code enforcement system is already in place. What is needed is not federalization, rather an enhancement of job training, professional inspector qualifications, and a guarantee of job security.

The government can decisively intervene or seek to persuade state governments (the carrot and stick approach) to adopt a federal code. Intervention is
the most drastic step and should be pursued only when the effectiveness of any
other corrective action is highly unlikely. Persuasion, while coercive through use
of sanctions (e.g., reduction of federal grants in the absence of affirmative state
action), leaves some discretion with state government and recognizes that the
states, constitutionally, have a role to play in the regulation of residential
construction.

Federal Product Certification

The second major federal intervention is a product certification system.
There is a proper role for the federal government in establishing standards and
testing procedures leading to certification of innovative products and housing
systems. This certification would in turn be honored by all state and local code
agencies, except where an agency can demonstrate within a reasonable time that
code approval would be detrimental to the health and safety of citizens. The
merit of this approach would be to unify the product approval process; innovators and others must presently seek one approval after another. The immediate
and significant value would be the creation of a mass market free of unwarranted constraints. The local approval procedure would be reversed, with the
burden of non-acceptance placed on the agency. Moreover, the unified system
would build upon the existing system of state and local codes and fill the void of
adequate performance testing.

A federally-supported product approval system is not new. Europeans have
had similar procedures in force for years. France's Agreement System evaluates
innovations and issues certificates that are accepted by building officials, banks,
and insurance companies. Without certification, innovations have little chance
of achieving marketplace acceptance. Over the years, the Agreement Systems of
the various European nations have been coordinated through an International
Union of Agreement that facilitates reciprocity between countries. Thus, strong
national leadership in product approval combined with locally-controlled enforcement is a workable combination.

Federal regulatory precedent exists for national preemption of standard-
setting for products involved in commerce. In the Noise Control Act of 1972,
Congress sought to:

> establish a means for effective coordination of federal research and
> activities in noise control, to authorize the establishment of federal

noise emission standards for products distributed in commerce, and to
provide information to the public respecting the noise emission and
noise reduction characteristics of such products.[34]

The principal thrust of the legislation is that the Administrator of the Environmental Protection Agency must establish regulations, where feasible, governing
noise emission of products on a specified list and may publish additional standards for any other product where he finds that such standards are "feasible and
are requisite to protect the public health and welfare." For such products (de-
nominated "new products" to apply only to products manufactured after the
effective date of the Act), states and localities are prohibited from adopting or
enforcing standards that vary from federal standards, while their rights to impose other controls on environmental noise are unaffected.[35]

The Act's preemption of standard-setting for particular products is a helpful
parallel with respect to such identifiable building "products" as manufactured
buildings, components, or materials intended for a specific construction purpose. Thus, either by statute or by regulation pursuant to statute, a federal
regulatory standard and an approval procedure could be established to certify
that a particular product is fully adequate to protect life and safety when used
in a prescribed fashion, and that any local prohibition on such use would constitute a burden on commerce. This approach would be more intrusive on state
regulation than the Noise Control Act provisions, because state and local authorities would be preempted from prohibiting the use of such products for
specific purposes while permitted to establish other standards "not inconsistent
with" federal standards.

Effectively, this approach would "certify" particular products for particular uses. The list of products covered could be spelled out categorically by
legislation or, preferably, left to the discretion of a competent federal regulator
or regulatory body subject to procedural safeguards under the Administrative
Procedure Act (notice to interested parties, opportunity for hearing, judicial
review, etc.) and aided by research and testing facilities. Whenever a federal
standard for a particular product (tailored to a particular use) is issued, state or
local regulations in conflict with such a standard in its area of applicability
would be preempted.

Any approach of certification with sanction faces Congressional opposition.
As the Housing and Community Act of 1974 moved towards enactment, Congressman Frank Annunzio (D., Illinois) introduced an amendment that would
have forbidden HUD from forcing a community to change a code or standard
that was higher than that deemed necessary by the National Bureau of Standards for public health and safety. The real effect of this provision would be to
deter HUD from liberalizing code provisions through carrot and stick techniques
like withholding housing and community development funds, as HUD had done
in the case of plastic pipe. While the National Bureau of Standards could set the

floor on standards, localities could proceed to establish more stringent and restrictive code provisions without fear of federal intrusion.

The provision was struck from the Act in conference committee, but Congress did go on record that it opposed coercion through the withholding of funds or by denying approval to state or local plans seeking federal funding. The committee stated:

> The conferees wish to state that with the repeal of the workable program provisions of the urban renewal law, the HUD Secretary retains no authority to impose any particular model building or safety code, or any element of such a code, on any community, or to condition or withhold grant funds under any program by reason of the failure of any community to adopt such a code. The conferees believe that the development of more effective building standards should be encouraged primarily through the activities of a National Institute of Building Standards, which would be established for that purpose under other provisions of the conference report.

Within the context of the 1974 Act, Congress has provided for two modes of federal intervention in state and local code activities. One mode is through persuasion by the National Institute of Building Sciences. The second mode would be explicit Congressional intervention establishing the preeminence of federal authority, as also provided in the National Mobile Home Act of 1974. While the Annunzio amendment failed to carry, Congress has made clear to the Department of Housing and Urban Development what types of actions it favors toward reforming state and local codes.

Federal Certification of State Programs

The third major federal role could be to reconcile conflicting state approaches by certifying state regulatory systems against a common set of criteria. Conceptually, this differs from the federal building code approach in terms of emphasis and timing. It places federal authority in a reactive role and puts primary emphasis on the efforts of states to bring their own regulatory programs more into line with national needs. Federal regulatory authority would articulate national needs and goals and help develop state regulatory mechanisms that comply with national policy. Using the federal carrot and stick would be appropriate, but the initiative for reform would rest with the states.

Federal involvement must be more than advisory, for passivity has proved of limited value. For example, the model code movement did not reach full stride until after the federal government had made a modern building code a prerequisite of a local community's Workable Program. (An approved Workable Program would be needed before federal funding of urban renewal and other urban grant programs.) The principle is well established—to have an effective quality control program requires some form of strong federal sanctions. Without such sanctions, state officials will seek solutions responsive to the needs of state-level pressure groups, but not necessarily responsive to the needs of the general population.

One approach would be to prohibit federal assistance to states for housing activities unless a designated federal agency approves their building code regulatory programs. Initially, it should be established that a state will lose federal funds by a particular date unless it has established a statewide building regulatory system (with provisions, of course, for sub-delegation and exemption for particular classes of political subdivision or building construction) permitting public participation in the promulgation of standards, implementation, enforcement and judicial review. In addition, criteria for the approval of proposed buildings should emphasize adoption of uniform standards throughout a particular state and reciprocity with other jurisdictions, initially through adoption of a model code. However, the pace of reform should be pressed both by statutory provisions and by federal regulation. Specifically, a federal administrator could be empowered to make rules—concerning specific building products, materials, and techniques—that must be "substantially reflected" in the criteria used in state building regulatory processes.

A key to the effectiveness of this approach would be a requirement that federal certification of state building regulatory programs be of limited duration, e.g., four years. Thus, in the first phase after enactment of the legislation, states may be required by a particular time (say two years after enactment) to have in being a prescribed process and program with regulatory criteria consistent with a model code. Prior to that time, the responsible agency will have completed promulgation of certain specified criteria—probably stated in the negative (i.e., "No state code may prohibit the use of plastic pipe for the following purposes . . .") and made applicable for the ensuing certification period, with the threat of non-renewal a key to compliance. Such federal criteria would, of course, have to be adopted under safeguards of procedural fairness and judicial review; and participation from the states as well as from industry, labor, and consumers would have to be fostered through an advisory mechanism.

The requirement that states be responsive to federally-imposed criteria would have an organizational corollary for state agencies: that state provisions could be revised by state administrative action rather than awaiting the full legislative cycle (often two years). Otherwise, states could find themselves crippled in their programs, faced with federal sanctions, and without an opportunity to comply with federal standards. In any event, the right of states to contest sanctions through litigation would again have to be confirmed.

We have described three broad approaches to the problem of how a stronger federal role in building regulation might be achieved: (1) federal definition of standards for particular building products, (2) promulgation of a federal building code to be enforced by the states, and (3) federal certification of state processes, mechanisms, and criteria for building regulation within an overall framework of statutory and administrative guidelines. Each approach would require certain conditions:

1. Development of building products standards can be accomplished by a federal instrumentality with minimum participation by the states; promulgation of federal codes and federal certification of state activities require ongoing coordination with the states, justify extensive federal commitments in terms of grants and training support to effectuate compliance, and may require severe sanctions through withholding of funds.

2. While the outright development of federal standards and codes would require the least federal involvement in the activities of model code groups and of traditional interests in the building industry, coordination with these groups and interests may be the key to significant improvement. Thus, preserving and stimulating state initiative in code formation as reflected in the federal certification of state programs may be an attractive and useful reason for legislation following that course of action.

3. The development of a comprehensive federal building code (even if administered by the states) would require a federal reevaluation of traditional building approaches that may well be a distraction from the central aim of stimulating innovative measures. Nonetheless, an opportunity to reassess safety standards (dramatically suggested by the recent series of fires in high-rise buildings and several structural collapses of high-rise buildings under construction purportedly confirming to local codes) may be required. Moreover, it should be recognized that failures of coordination between federal and state agencies may subsequently require the development of a federal enforcement mechanism on a vast scale.

4. In all three approaches, major federal research initiatives are required, not only in developing new building techniques, but perhaps more importantly in designing sound tests for judging innovative technology. Thus, the key to success may well be the extent to which a federal "handle" on performance standards can be achieved, a task that appears justified regardless of the method chosen. Moreover, the political credibility of any novel departure in regulation may well depend on a prior demonstration that improved regulatory methods are actually in reach.

A Legal Basis for Federal Action

Although a need for decisive federal action can be established and several viable alternatives proposed, Congress can do nothing without finding some basis for its action in constitutional law. The traditional view was that responsibility for regulating building construction is constitutionally restricted to the

states. Contemporary constitutional doctrine, though, finds legal justifications
for Congressional action: federal statutes backed by solid court holdings. These
developments have occurred in various fields, all of which come under the sweep
of federal power as expressed in the interstate commerce clause and the powers
of a state permitting local regulation "for the general welfare of its citizens."
Changed, too, is the perception of need for a federal role, the absence of which
made federal initiatives just as unthinkable in 1960 as its presence makes strong
federal action appropriate a decade and a half later.

It is by now a legal maxim that the reach of legitimate federal power under
the interstate commerce clause is far greater than was once perceived—limited
only by the practical requirement that there be some rational connection with
trade and commerce among the states before Congress can invoke the clause.
Perhaps the most vivid demonstration of this change of attitude is expressed in
the recent reenactment of federal narcotics control statutes. Originally, federal
powers were considered inadequate to cover the possession of narcotic sub-
stances, which gave rise to an elaborate (and ultimately constitutionally vulnerable) substitute structure to choke off narcotics traffic;[36] now a simple
provision of the Drug Abuse Prevention and Control Act of 1970 makes it
unlawful to "possess" a "controlled substance" except in accordance with the
provisions of the Act.[37] In essence, a frank recognition that drug abuse
constitutes a national problem prompted Congress to devise a more rational,
comprehensive structure of control. As a result, mere possession by an individual—about as "local" an act as can be imagined—is now an unambiguous
federal crime.

Without a similar perception of need in the field of construction standards,
it is not surprising that a similar comprehensive legislative mandate has not been
sought or secured.[38] Nevertheless, it has been clear, at least since New Deal
days, that federal powers can be exercised over business activities for which a
strong contrary argument could be made on behalf of state powers.[39]

The expansion of the scope of federal regulatory powers has continued to
be affirmed by the courts. With respect to the setting of building products
standards, the Civil Rights Act cases make clear that federal power may be extended to protect products within statutory or regulatory range. In *Heart of
Atlanta Motel v. U.S.*, [40] the Supreme Court upheld the public accommodation provisions of the Civil Rights Act of 1964. The Court found that the
motel in question was easily accessible to interstate highways and that approximately 75 percent of its guests came from out of state, which meant that the
character of the motel's discrimination was precisely foreseen by Congress in
passing the Act. In *Katzenbach v. McClung*, [41] the Act's application was
extended to restaurants serving or offering to serve interstate travelers, or to
restaurants where a substantial portion of the food "has moved in commerce."
The Court said:

where we find that the legislators, in the light of the facts and testimony before them, have a rational basis for finding a chosen regulatory scheme necessary to the protection of commerce, our investigation is at an end.[42]

Four years later, in 1968, the Court refined in *Maryland v. Wirtz* [43] what it meant by "rational basis." Significantly, the Court held that Congress had only to define the *class* of activity (enterprises engaged in commerce, very widely defined) leaving for courts to determine only whether the particular class was within federal jurisdiction. In *Wirtz*, the underlying statute was extraordinarily broad,[44] and the result, the Court found, was to eliminate the claim that an enterprise within the class was exempt because its activities in commerce were trivial. The result of *Wirtz*, in building regulatory terms, is that virtually any connection of a construction project with any federal power (interstate commerce, federal mortgage programs, urban renewal, etc.) is well within the scope of federal regulatory power.[45]

With respect to the setting of building *products* standards, the Civil Rights Act cases make clear that federal power may be extended to protect products within statutory or regulatory range. The breadth of the building *products* class may even be extended to embrace standards for the use of *materials* that have moved in commerce or in whose use a substantial federal interest can be shown. (For example, if the nation is indeed "running out of wood," standards for wood substitutes would be appropriate as a conservation measure.)

On jurisdictional grounds, the federal government may deal with codes and standards at the local level, but does its authority extend to preempting local standards that are more restrictive than those federally prescribed? Deletion of the Annunzio amendment implies this authority. Promulgation of a federal code for mobile homes makes it explicit. This question is crucial, since establishing federal minimums does not prevent state and local authorities from setting standards above such minimums. The consequence, as discussed in Chapters Two and Four, is an inconsistent patchwork system of local codes frustrating the creation of mass markets potentially available through a unified federal system of codes.

Again, the Supreme Court has opened up the door for decisive federal action. In a 1973 Supreme Court decision, *City of Burbank v. Lockheed Air Terminal*,[46] the Supreme Court struck down a local Burbank ordinance imposing a curfew on the operation of jet aircraft after 10 p.m. on the ground that the ordinance conflicted with the Federal Aviation Administration's authority to regulate aircraft noise. Although the powers of the FAA (supplemented by those of the Environmental Protection Agency) did not flatly preempt state and local noise control, the Court read the Burbank ordinance as an interference with federally-protected airline scheduling. The case is relevant and parallel, indicating that federal regulation of a problem common to the nation and the states may be less restrictive than local regulations.

Instead of focusing on the development of a market for specific building products, which the building products standards approach would serve, federal building codes and federal certification of state programs would rest on an explicitly stated national goal of fostering building innovation across the board. This justification would be no different in qualitative terms, merely more comprehensive. But the essential requirement would be that Congress be convinced that the costs of construction nationwide can be lowered and efficiencies raised by removing impediments to a national market—either through total displacement of state and local codes or purposeful coordination among them. In each instance, the goal to be achieved would have much in common with the ill-served aim of the Housing Act.

6

Towards a Policy of National Building Code Reform

If we are to move towards a constructive policy of securing adequate housing for all Americans, building code reform must be rigorously pursued.

While this need has been identified by several Presidential Commissions and private studies over the past decades, public awareness has been slow in developing. It is now generally held that building regulation is not impartial in its effect upon the housing industry. Misuse of regulatory powers has resulted in higher than necessary housing costs, obstruction of new building technologies, inefficient use of scarce national resources, and discrimination against lower-income families. For these reasons, government must act to reconstitute building code regulations as a positive tool of public policy.

Why should consumers bear the burden of unnecessary housing costs? This question has reached an increasing crescendo as inflation continues to dilute incomes and housing costs maintain their steady upward march. Manipulation of codes for private ends was not a consumer issue when housing was available at a reasonable price. When costs increase faster than incomes, we become increasingly concerned about what our dollars buy. We have learned by the checkbook that the prohibitions against innovations like plastic pipe and romex cable only line the pockets of selected producers and unions. Home rule control over building regulations has also pinched the consumer's purse by deterring home manufacturers from developing their factory production processes to the most efficient levels of operation. Home rule has resulted in heterogeneous sets of codes. To meet the varying requirements of local building codes, manufacturers abandon assembly line processes in favor of custom production approaches. Thus, any savings resulting from routinization and scale production are lost.

To secure the benefits of technology for consumers, we must establish market preconditions conducive to technological innovation. Innovators and industrialists seeking to employ capital-intensive mass production techniques need mass markets governed by uniform building requirements. Without mass markets, neither the innovator nor industrialist can amortize his research and development investment over enough sales to make his product competitive.

Recent state code actions have begun to open large markets at the state level, but in most cases these codes apply only to mobile homes and manufactured housing. Only a few states have placed all residential construction under one code. Despite these forward-looking actions, lack of agreement between

129

states on a common set of standards and tests seriously undermines the development of national markets.

Even with uniform markets, technologists need authoritative targets of performance against which to design, develop, and test their products. Lacking these targets, decisions about a new product's code compliance are left to the arbitrary judgment of building officials. The technologist would benefit from a one-stop approval process acceptable to the building regulatory community. Instead he must travel from one product approval process to the next, testing and retesting his product and incurring considerable expense and frustration.

These are not the good old 1950s, when we pursued consumption of goods without thought to the limitations on available resources. Only recently have environmentalists, oil producers, and others driven home the message to the American consumer that we cannot continue indiscriminate consumption without giving consideration to both the price and the availability of goods for tomorrow. In homebuilding, this means we should seek those construction technologies that make the most efficient use of building materials and manpower. When lumber is dear, other more abundant materials should be substituted. As we become more energy conscious, we must be able to build into our homes the technologies that conserve—not waste—energy. Our limited resources have forced us to realize that regulations must encourage new technologies that take that limitation into account.

Perhaps the most pernicious effect of codes is their impact upon the residential opportunities for lower-income families. We have demonstrated that the burden of codes is disproportionately carried by home manufacturers of lower-cost housing for lower-income families. Higher housing costs take lower-income families out of the market. A similar conclusion was reached by the United States Commission on Civil Rights when it identified building codes, along with zoning regulations and highway construction, as public means of excluding or removing low-income and minority families from suburban areas.[1]

Taken individually, these code-induced ills may require only partial solutions at state and local levels. But taken collectively, they demand a national solution. A national solution does not eliminate constructive roles for state governments, because the highly localized nature of most residential construction activity requires a strong local orientation. As we shall argue, responsive state actions are vital to a national solution, but so, too, is the active and continuing presence of the federal government.

After years of nibbling at the edges of direct involvement in building codes, the federal government has finally entered the lists with a significant mandate. The Housing and Community Development Act of 1974 established the National Mobile Home Construction and Safety Standards Act (hereafter called the Mobile Home Act) and the National Institute of Building Sciences (NIBS), about which we shall have more to say. The interesting question is why federal action has taken so long. For one thing, building codes are highly technical.

You have to be a trained architect, engineer or builder to understand the standards governing construction. Thus, the average citizen delegates his responsibilities to "technicians". As a result, there has been no public watchdog to halt regulatory activities that no longer serve the public good.

The explanation for a belated federal response also lies deeply imbedded in the economic structure of the construction industry. Firms in the industry face major business uncertainty from one year to the next. Construction can be vigorous one year and then sink to depression levels two years later. Firms, therefore, pursue multiple strategies to secure their sales volumes, one of which is to use the building code as a means of securing favored positions for their products. Unions, faced with the same industrial instability, use codes to freeze into regulations a determination of who does what jobs. Not surprisingly, there has been strong resistance from those in the conventional industry to new patterns of regulation that throw open the market to competitive, innovative products.

To have ignored regulatory reform despite mounting evidence of harmful consequences would have been to condone the use of state authority to favor some at the expense of others. We would be hypocrites to talk about equal opportunity, to pass fair housing legislation, to enshrine into law the American goal of a decent home and a suitable living environment for all, and then knowingly permit state authority to deny realization of these goals. The Congress has acted. The question before us is whether its response is sufficient to the need.

Strategy for Building Code Reform

Any strategy for reforming building code regulations must be responsive to the needs of innovators and industrialized housing producers, for these sectors of the housing industry have the potential for creating major benefits for consumers. The strategy, therefore, should open the possibilities of mass markets, make effective use of product standards and tests based upon performance criteria, and promote fairness in the enforcement of building regulations.

A prudent approach to the reform of regulation would be to build upon those state and federal actions that give promise of stimulating needed changes. Within this context, state, and federal governments have substantial roles to play, states because of their recent activities in statewide building codes and enforcement, and the federal government because of newly-acquired authorization to develop a performance testing system for regulating mobile home construction.

To the states fall the primary tasks of creating strong statewide building code systems incorporating workable reciprocity procedures, and of developing and implementing sound enforcement policies. In tandem with state activities, the federal government is to establish a product certification process for the testing and approval of innovative products and processes, thereby eliminating the cumbersome and ambiguous approval procedures used at state and local levels. Federal funds would be necessary to support state code actions. Finally, the federal government must be prepared to step into the regulatory process directly should states fail to reach their objectives.

The strategy is simple and straightforward. Establishment of uniform building standards and enforcement procedures is left to the states with the active encouragement of the federal government. Development, promulgation, and implementation of authoritative approval procedures for innovative building technologies, binding upon state and local governments, are primary responsibilities of the federal government.

State Actions

States must expand their activities in the areas of statewide building codes and code enforcement. The strategy requires the states to accelerate the pace of legislative action that reasserts the primacy of state authority over local community code efforts. Localism has been the prevailing pattern investigated in this book, and we have concluded that it has been counterproductive to innovation and industrialization. In effect, the codes have acted like a local tariff. Without statewide codes or a federal building code, mass markets are not achievable. The recent record of state action has been encouraging with states moving aggressively to promulgate mobile home and manufactured housing laws. Although the federal government has now preempted the mobile home field, earlier state actions here demonstrate an ability to act when needed.

Fewer states have taken the more comprehensive approach of a statewide building code covering all forms of residential construction activity. This is because states have found that codes covering specialized forms of construction are more acceptable to state construction interest groups than more general residential code reforms. Thus, states have tended to take the path of least resistance.

Federal pressure for state code action, particularly for manufactured housing and mobile homes, has also contributed to recent state successes. This pressure grew out of Operation Breakthrough and the increasing public concern about the rising prices of new housing. Without federal pressure, it is doubtful whether states would have gone as far as they did. Thus, an important element in the strategy is continuing federal pressure and incentives for state code reform.

Although mobile home and manufactured housing laws are important steps forward, statewide building codes should be the ultimate targets. Public concern about efficiency in residential construction should not be limited to specialized sectors of the residential market. The consumers' interests cover all forms of residential activity. Moreover, it appears somewhat arbitrary to single out mobile homes and manufactured housing as special cases from the rest of residential construction. Mobile homes, manufactured housing and conventional construction are all forms of shelter, sometimes indistinguishable from one another. If we sincerely believe in performance-based concepts, these three classes of construction are just different forms of achieving the same end—a decent home. Reform should span all residential construction activities.

While statewide codes can help create uniform markets, they can be self-defeating if the codes and approval procedures differ significantly from one state to the next. Reciprocity between states, third-party testing organizations acceptable to the states, and simplified and common approval procedures are important matters still to be resolved. These require commitment of state resources and a willingness by states to cooperate in finding mutually satis-factory solutions.

Recognizing the goal of uniformity, Congress has encouraged states to work directly with one another to develop solutions. In the 1974 Act, Congress stated:

> The consent of the Congress is hereby given to any two or more States to enter into agreements or compacts, not in conflict with any law of the United States, cooperative effort and mutual assistance in the comprehensive planning for the growth and development of inter-state, metropolitan, or other urban areas, and to establish such agen-cies, joint or otherwise, as they may deem desirable for making effective such agreements and compacts.[2]

It would be appropriate for states to enter into an interstate agreement to secure uniformity in state code actions. The National Conference of States on Building Codes and Standards has been a first, voluntary step in this direction. Federal encouragement and funding is now available to elevate the importance of this form of interstate cooperation.

States must also upgrade the quality of code enforcement. Building official qualifications have long been ignored. Training programs are almost nonexistent. Information programs have been left to voluntary organizations. Salaries tend to be depressed relative to those of other civil servants. And little has been done to free the building official from local political influence. A few states, like Massachusetts and Ohio, have recognized that a well-functioning regulatory system requires high quality enforcement; the others have done little to improve code enforcement.

One cannot expect innovation to flourish if building officials lack a basic understanding of technical advancements in the industry. Efficient code admin-istration cannot sell a product, but it can stimulate the flow of new ideas into the market.

States should encourage the formation of state building official organizations. This would foster discussion of enforcement problems within a state-wide context. It would also institutionalize a process that could lead to statewide training, qualification requirements, and information dissemination efforts.

Funding of state code development and enforcement activities can be assisted by federal grants. HUD has the authority to provide planning funds for developing state plans and improving state management. Section 701 of the Housing Act of 1954, as amended by the Housing Act of 1974, specifically identifies housing as a central element of comprehensive planning. In addition, the National Institute of Building Sciences is also authorized to conduct programs with states to encourage changes in state laws and to develop in-service training programs for building officials.

Federal Actions

In Chapter Five, we identified three modes of federal intervention: enforcement of a federal code, product approval, and coordination and certification of state building code programs. We have argued that federal intervention must be deliberate, building upon encouraging state actions. Massive federal intervention would probably be inappropriate and politically unacceptable at this time. Thus, a mixed federal role emerges, given the objectives of fostering the fullest use of innovative building products and systems and efficient use of national resources.

The first step would be to create an effective national product approval system. Products would be evaluated for performance by an authoritative testing agency. This evaluation should be acceptable to all state and local code jurisdictions. There would also be a program of coordination and certification of state building code programs. These actions assume strong statewide code systems, but recognize that states have limited capacity to develop performance-based codes and testing procedures, and that state efforts at interstate cooperation need federal encouragement. If states fail to carry forward their side of the reform effort, the second step would be to impose a federal code on state and local governments.

The Housing and Community Development Act of 1974: Does It Meet the Need?

As we discussed earlier, Congress has taken seemingly important steps toward code reform. It has established an authoritative product approval agency, the National Institute of Building Sciences, and mobile home act for all jurisdictions. Both NIBS and the Mobile Home Act address the need for improved code enforcement and provide federal funds and technical assistance for that purpose. (See Appendixed B and C respectively for enabling legislation of NIBS and the National Mobile Home Act.) These actions are a mixed blessing. The Mobile Home Act is a strong piece of legislation that vest HUD with substantial powers to, in effect, promulgate and enforce a national building standards system for mobile homes. HUD, in turn, works hand in hand with state and local governments. This is important, relieving state and local governments from any obligation to deal with non-governmental institutions, whose lack of standing before state and local governments is a mixed blessing. Some of the best codes to date have originated with the model code associations, but there is no necessity for local governments to deal with these associations. Increased local use of model codes attests to the efforts of the code associations and the application of federal pressure through HUD.

The law provides that all state and local governments must abide by the mobile home standards established, that variations from the federal standards are not permissible. This is the muscle of the law. Once the manufacturer certifies that his unit meets the national standard, he can crank up the production lines without fear of rejection for failing to meet the state's set of standards. Nor need he demonstrate to the state through additional testing that the unit meets the national standards. Mobile home manufacturers must be forced to comply with the standards set by HUD. Two forms of sanctions are available under the law. First, there are civil and criminal penalties for non-compliance with federally-established standards and procedures. HUD, as well as individual consumers, can bring action directly against the manufacturer in the United States district courts. Perhaps more persuasive is the authority of state and local governments to deny code approval if the manufacturer's unit does not have an appropriate federal certification. The effort will not be strapped for funds. Resources to develop the code are authorized as needed under the statute. Moreover, the general resources of HUD in terms of dollars, manpower, and expertise are available for the task.

To insure HUD compliance with the law, Congress has mandated that federal mobile home construction and safety standards will be developed and implemented by August 1975. This clearly shows Congressional urgency to get on with the job and some possible skepticism about HUD's willingness to implement a system of standards within a reasonable period of time. The second major federal action was the creation of NIBS. As we discussed in Chapter Five, the thrust of legislation was in the proper direction: to establish an authoritative product testing agency. American innovators needed an institution to which they could relate and whose judgment they could trust as being objective and even-handedly applied. The consumer also needed such an institution whose motivation is to encourage the best technology on behalf of the consumer. NIBS is a vital first step in this direction, but it does not go far enough; it does not have product approval powers that are binding upon state and local governments. Only with such binding authority is it possible to open national markets.

NIBS stands outside the system of power and must act by persuasion. The 1974 Act does not provide a governmental home for NIBS; rather, it provides for a non-profit, non-governmental entity to be chartered by Congress or under the District of Columbia Nonprofit Corporation Act. Moreover, Congress does not require federal, state, and local governments to cooperate with NIBS. Instead, Congress indicates that governments are "encouraged to accept, use and comply with any of the technical findings of the Institute . . . ." NIBS lacks muscle. While it is mandated to develop, promulgate and maintain nationally recognized performance criteria and standards, the Institute is not given the funding capability to accomplish the task with its own staff. Instead, the Institute is ordered to delegate, "to the maximum extent possible," the work needed to perform its mission to outside private and governmental agencies. The legislation capitalizes NIBS at $10 million for the first two years and requires that it depend on fees and assistance received from other federal agencies. Assuming the best, that NIBS is partially persuasive, there may be enough applicants for prequalifications to generate adequate revenues from fees. But if NIBS is not persuasive, one can hardly expect a flood of innovators and producers seeking approval.

In an area where interest group politics has been intense, where the development of HUD's Guide Criteria was an expensive and technically demanding effort, and where there has been no industry support of the Guide Criteria, arming the Institute with powers of persuasion and limited resources is like sending David without his sling to best Goliath.

The hesitation of Congress to move aggressively into the product approval field is attested to by the right of NIBS to prequalify building technologies. This implies that building technologies must still find qualification elsewhere. In this area, limited authority may not be such a liability so long as courts are willing to accept the Institute's findings. Recalling Judge Sidney O. Smith Jr.'s opinion in the *Boise Cascade Case* (See Chapter Five), remedy may be possible where local tests are more stringent than those of a competent authority. If a product meets the standards of the competent authority, but not that of the localities, the local test is unreasonably prohibitive. The competent authority in that case was the Southern Standard Building Conference, a non-governmental institution. Thus, remedy is available to an individual who, upon securing prequalification approval from NIBS, is denied access to state or local markets. Unfortunately, litigation would proceed on a case by case basis. The costs in time and money may be too high for most innovators.

For the present approach to have any chance of success, cooperation between the various federal agencies and NIBS must take place. The Department of Housing and Urban Development, the National Bureau of Standards, and NIBS, at a minimum, must chart out a common course that builds upon their respective powers and mandates. NIBS has the charter to develop performance-based codes, testing, and training procedures. NIBS has the technical competence to develop these performance criteria, having made a first major exploration under Operation Breakthrough. HUD, in turn, has the program mission of securing a decent home for all American families. For example, the role of NIBS can be enhanced if the Secretary of HUD can establish his own performance standards through NIBS (using **NBS**). He can then use whatever powers he has available to him to implement such standards.

This is particularly germane in the area of mobile home standards, where HUD has the explicit federal mandate. Support should be given NIBS to create performance criteria and standards for mobile homes. In addition, HUD can use performance standards as a back-up to the Minimum Property Standards. NIBS could prequalify building technologies, with HUD providing official qualification relative to the MPS. Thus, there are means of providing some muscle to NIBS activities, but these are contingent upon active cooperation by other federal agencies.

The concept of federal agency cooperation should be extended to embrace other organizations directly involved in construction activity. The Department of Defense, General Services Administration, and the Department of Health, Education, and Welfare are several more that sponsor construction. If they could agree that a NIBS prequalification would automatically qualify the technology for use in their programs, it would be possible to aggregate large volumes of construction demand. Market aggregation, careful procurement practices, and one-stop approvals would stimulate major innovation in the building industry. Proven use in the federal sector might lead to accepted use in the state and local sectors.

We have argued that a pressing national need exists for an effective product approval process. Thus, the effectiveness of NIBS must be carefully monitored and evaluated over the next years to determine whether greater powers must be created to achieve a workable approval system. We have identified points of weakness in the proposed NIBS structure—its nongovernmental standing, lack of enforcement powers, limited budget, and prequalification power. The successes and failures of NIBS will depend, in large measure, upon the extent to which governments at all levels are willing to see it work. If NIBS fails, the reason will probably be that the model was doomed from the beginning. Yet another model exists to take its place, that created by the National Mobile Home Act of 1974.

The major hole in the current approach to reform is the absence of an explicit federal role in the coordination and certification of state building code programs. This was a deliberate slight by Congress, since HUD was given precisely this authority for mobile homes.

Congress has instead authorized federal financing of state activities, with funds available through the Comprehensive Planning (Section 701) program, the National Institute of Building Sciences, and the National Mobile Home Act.

Thus, the current federal role is to encourage and back state efforts with financial resources; action is up to the states.

Congress has gone on record that it will not fail to act if states do not act. Federalizing responsibilities for mobile home standards reflects the political willingness to act. But Congress favors state action and has made funds available in support of state efforts. Whether we move to the second step of a federal building code now seems to be in the hands of the states. Time will tell.

No study of the regulatory system would be complete without observing that periodic reform of the regulatory structure is as essential to the health of the industry as is regulation itself. In our increasingly complex, interdependent, and technical society, there is a growing need for regulation to protect the consumer. Powers can be abused to the detriment of the people they are to serve. Periodic review—and, when necessary, reform—of the rules that govern our lives is essential to a vital economy in a healthy society.

Reform of building code regulations must be approached as a responsible exercise of political power. Recognition of the need for reform is the logical starting point for making building regulations more responsive to the nation's housing needs. We have demonstrated that present building codes burden the consumer with higher housing costs, lower-income families with subtle discrimination, and the economy in general with inefficient use of our natural resources. We have described logical mechanisms to ease that burden. The test now is whether we can follow through on the mandate given the federal bureaucracy and the states by the Congress and reform the building code regulatory system.

Appendix A

Comparative Cost Estimates for Conventional and Industrialized Housing: Four Case Studies

Comparative Cost Estimates for Conventional and Industrialized Housing: Four Case Studies

Study	Type House	Cost Per		Computed at Yearly Production Volume	Computed Profit		Type of Production	Remarks
		Unit	Sq. Ft.					
Institute for Defense Analysis (Neil Weiner) 1968	Single Family 1000 sq. ft.	11,200	11.20	150–200	20%	(1)	Conventional	Excludes land and development costs.
	"	9,515	9.51	5000	15%	(2)	Modular (Factory 1) 275 man hours; 75 skilled, 200 semi-skilled	Factory 1: $3 million plant; $6 million inventory.
		8,540	8.54	3600	15%	(2)	Modular (Factory 2) 150 man hours; 15 skilled, 135 semi-skilled	Factory 2: $2 million plant; $1 million inventory.
Reston Low Income Demonstration Housing Project (Norman Rowland)	Garden type walk-up 1295 sq. ft.	14,584	11.26	12	10%	(1)	Conventional	Excludes land and development costs.
		12,602	9.73	120	7%	(1)	Conventional	
		12,042	9.30	1200	4%	(1)	Conventional	
		13,224	10.21	12	10%	(1)	Modular	
		11,647	8.99	120	8%	(1)	Modular	
		10,391	8.16	1200	6%	(1)	Modular	
Douglas Commission 1968	Single family 1000 sq. ft.	16,791	16.79	12	11%	(1)	Conventional	Excludes land and development costs.
		16,176	16.18		11%	(1)	Panel-walls	
		13,458	13.46		11%	(1)	Sectional	

Douglas Commission (Guy Rothenstein)				
Low rise 2 stories 840 sq. ft./D.V.	11,760	14.00	Conventional Labor $7.80/hr.	Precast and pre-stressed concrete shell
	11,004	13.10	Industrialized Labor $3.80/hr.	Precast walls and partitions
High rise 16 stories 915 sq.ft./D.V.	12,874	14.07	Conventional Labor $7.15/hr.	Masonry and dry wall partitions
	10,779	11.78	Industrialized Factory $3.75 /hr.	Precast walls and partitions

1. Profit as return on gross costs.
2. Profit as return on investment.

Sources:
Weiner, Niel. *Supply Conditions for Low Cost Housing Production* (Washington, D.C.: Clearinghouse for Federal Scientific and Technical Information, 1968).
Rowland, Norman. *Reston Low Income Housing Demonstration Program* (Washington, D.C.: Clearinghouse for Federal Scientific and Technical Information, 1969).
National Commission on Urban Problems. *Building the American City* (Washington, D.C.: U.S. Government Printing Office, 1969).

Appendix B

Housing and Community Development Act of 1974—National Institute of Building Sciences

SEC. 809. (a)(1) The Congress finds (A) that the lack of an authoritative national source to make findings and to advise both the public and private sectors of the economy with respect to the use of building science and technology in achieving nationally acceptable standards and other technical provision for use in Federal, State, and local housing and building regulations is an obstacle to efforts by and imposes severe burdens upon all those who procure, design, construct, use, operate, maintain, and retire physical facilities, and frequently results in the failure to take full advantage of new and useful developments in technology which could improve our living environment; (B) that the establishment of model buildings codes or of a single national building code will not completely resolve the problem because of the difficulty at all levels of government in updating their housing and building regulations to reflect new developments in technology, as well as the irregularities and inconsistencies which arise in applying such requirements to particular localities or special local conditions; (C) that the lack of uniform housing and building regulatory provisions increases the costs of construction and thereby reduces the amount of housing and other community facilities which can be provided; and (D) that the existence of a single authoritative nationally recognized institution to provide for the evaluation of new technology could facilitate introduction of such innovations and their acceptance at the Federal, State, and local levels.

(2) The Congress further finds, however, that while an authoritative source of technical findings is needed, various private organizations and institutions, private industry, labor, and Federal and other governmental agencies and entities are presently engaged in building research, technology development, testing, and evaluation, standards and model code development and promulgation, and information dissemination. These existing activities should be encouraged and these capabilities effectively utilized wherever possible and appropriate to the purposes of this section.

(3) The Congress declares that an authoritative nongovernmental instrument needs to be created to address the problems and issues described in paragraph (1), that the creation of such an instrument should be initiated by the Government, with the advice and assistance of the National Academy of Sciences-National Academy of Engineering-National Research Council (hereinafter referred to as the "Academies-Research Council") and of the various sectors of the building community, including labor and management, technical experts in building science and technology, and the various levels of government.

(b)(1) There is authorized to be established, for the purposes described in subsection (a)(3), an appropriate nonprofit, nongovernmental instrument to be known as the National Institute of Building

Sciences (hereinafter referred to as the "Institute"), which shall not be an agency or establishment of the United States Government. The Institute shall be subject to the provisions of this section and, to the extent consistent with this section, to a charter of the Congress if such a charter is requested and issued or to the District of Columbia Nonprofit Corporation Act if that is deemed preferable.

(2) The Academies-Research Council, along with other agencies and organizations which are knowledgeable in the field of building technology, shall advise and assist in (A) the establishment of the Institute; (B) the development of an organizational framework to encourage and provide for the maximum feasible participation of public and private scientific, technical, and financial organizations, institutions, and agencies now engaged in activities pertinent to the development, promulgation, and maintenance of performance criteria, standards, and other technical provisions for building codes and other regulations; and (C) the promulgation of appropriate organizational rules and procedures including those for the selection and operation of a technical staff, such rules and procedures to be based upon the primary object of promoting the public interest and insuring that the widest possible variety of interests and experience essential to the functions of the Institute are represented in the Institute's operations. Recommendations of the Academies-Research Council shall be based upon consultations with and recommendations from various private organizations and institutions, labor, private industry, and governmental agencies entities operating in the field, and the Consultative Council as provided for under subsection (c) (8).

(3) Nothing in this section shall be construed as expressing the intent of the Congress that the Academies-Research Council itself be required to assume any function or operation vested in the Institute by or under this section.

(c) (1) The Institute shall have a Board of Directors (hereinafter referred to as the "Board") consisting of not less than fifteen nor more than twenty-one members, appointed by the President of the United States by and with the advice and consent of the Senate. The Board shall be representative of the various segments of the building community, of the various regions of the country, and of the consumers who are or would be affected by actions taken in the exercise of the functions and responsibilities of the Institute, and shall include (A) representatives of the construction industry, including representatives of construction labor organizations, product manufacturers, and builders, housing management experts, and experts in building standards, codes, and fire safety, and (B) members representative of the public interest in such numbers as may be necessary to assure that a majority of the members of the Board represent the public interest and that there is adequate consideration by the Institute of consumer interests in the exercise of its functions and responsibilities. Those representing the public interest on the Board shall include architects, professional engineers, officials of Federal, State, and local agencies, and representatives of consumer organizations. Such members of the Board shall hold no financial interest or membership in, nor be employed by, or receive other compensation from, any company, association, or other group associated with the manufacture, distribution, installation, or maintenance of specialized building products, equipment, systems, subsystems, or other construction materials and techniques for which there are available substitutes.

(2) The members of the initial Board shall serve as incorporators and shall take whatever actions are necessary to establish the Institute as provided for under subsection (b)(1).

(3) The term of office of each member of the initial and succeeding Boards shall be three years; except that (A) any member appointed to fill a vacancy occurring prior to the expiration of the term for which his predecessor was appointed shall be appointed for the remainder of such term; and (B) the terms of office of members first taking office shall begin on the date of incorporation and shall expire, as designated at the time of their appointment, one-third at the end of one year, one-third at the end of two years, and one-third at the end of three years. No member shall be eligible to serve in excess of three consecutive terms of three years each. Notwithstanding the preceding provisions of this subsection, a member whose term has expired may serve until his successor has qualified.

(4) Any vacancy in the initial and succeeding Boards shall not affect its power, but shall be filled in the manner in which the original appointments were made, or, after the first five years of operation, as provided for by the organizational rules and procedures of the Institute.

(5) The President shall designate one of the members appointed to the initial Board as Chairman; thereafter, the members of the initial and succeeding Boards shall annually elect one of their number as Chairman. The members of the Board shall also elect one or more of their Members as Vice Chairman. Terms of the Chairman and Vice Chairman shall be for one year and no individual shall serve as Chairman or Vice Chairman for more than two consecutive terms.

(6) The members of the initial or succeeding Boards shall not, by reason of such membership, be deemed to be employees of the United States Government. They shall, while attending meetings of the Board or while engaged in duties related to such meetings or in other activities of the Board pursuant to this section, be entitled to receive compensation at the rate of $100 per day including traveltime, and while away from their homes or regular places of business they may be allowed travel expenses, including per diem in lieu of subsistence, equal to that authorized under section 5703 of title 5, United States Code, for persons in the Government service employed intermittently.

(7) The Institute shall have a president and such other executive officers and employees as may be appointed by the Board at rates of compensation fixed by the Board. No such executive officer or employee may receive any salary or other compensation from any source other than the Institute during the period of his employment by the Institute.

(8) The Institute shall establish, with the advice and assistance of the Academies-Research Council and other agencies and organizations which are knowledgeable in the field of building technology, a Consultative Council, membership in which shall be available to representatives of all appropriate private trade, professional, and labor organizations, private and public standards, code, and testing bodies, public regulatory agencies, and consumer groups, so as to insure a direct line of communication between such groups and the Institute and a vehicle for representative hearings on matters before the Institute.

(d)(1) The Institute shall have no power to issue any shares of stock, or to declare or pay any dividends.

(2) No part of the income or assets of the Institute shall inure to the benefit of any director, officer, employee, or other individual except as salary or reasonable compensation for services.

(3) The Institute shall not contribute to or otherwise support any political party or candidate for elective public office.

(e) (1) The Institute shall exercise its functions and responsibilities in four general areas, relating to building regulations, as follows:

(A) Development, promulgation, and maintenance of nationally recognized performance criteria, standards, and other technical provisions for maintenance of life, safety, health, and public welfare suitable for adoption by building regulating jurisdictions and agencies, including test methods and other evaluative techniques relating to building systems, subsystems, components, products, and materials with due regard for consumer problems.

(B) Evaluation and prequalification of existing and new building technology in accordance with subparagraph (A).

(C) Conduct of needed investigations in direct support of subparagraphs (A) and (B).

(D) Assembly, storage, and dissemination of technical data and other information directly related to subparagraphs (A), (B), and (C).

(2) The Institute in exercising its functions and responsibilities described in paragraph (1) shall assign and delegate, to the maximum extent possible, responsibility for conducting each of the needed activities described in paragraph (1) to one or more of the private organizations, institutions, agencies, and Federal and other governmental entities with a capacity to exercise or contribute to the exercise of such responsibility, monitor the performance achieved through assignment and delegation, and, when deemed necessary, reassign and delegate such responsibility.

(3) The Institute in exercising its functions and responsibilities under paragraphs (1) and (2) shall (A) give particular attention to the development of methods for encouraging all sectors of the economy to cooperate with the Institute and to accept and use its technical findings, and to accept and use the nationally recognized performance criteria, standards, and other technical provisions developed for use in Federal, State, and local building codes and other regulations which result from the program of the Institute; (B) seek to assure that its actions are coordinated with related requirements which are imposed in connection with community and environmental development generally; and (C) consult with the Department of Justice and other agencies of government to the extent necessary to insure that the national interest is protected and promoted in the exercise of its functions and responsibilities.

(f) (1) The Institute is authorized to accept contracts and grants from Federal, State, and local governmental agencies and other entities, and grants and donations from private organizations, institutions, and individuals.

(2) The Institute may, in accordance with rates and schedules established with guidance as provided under subsection (b)(2), establish fees and other charges for services provided by the Institute or under its authorization.

(3) Amounts received by the Institute under this section shall be in addition to any amounts which may be appropriated to provide its initial operating capital under subsection (h).

(g) (1) Every department, agency, and establishment of the Federal Government, in carrying out any building or construction, or any building- or construction-related programs, which involves direct expenditures, and in developing technical requirements for any such building or construction, shall be encouraged to accept the technical findings of the Institute, or any nationally recognized performance criteria, standards, and other technical provisions for building regulations brought about by the Institute, which may be applicable.

(2) All projects and programs involving Federal assistance in the form of loans, grants, guarantees, insurance, or technical aid, or in any other form, shall be encouraged to accept, use, and comply with any of the technical findings of the Institute, or any nationally recognized performance criteria, standards, and other technical provisions for building codes and other regulations brought about by the Institute, which may be applicable to the purposes for which the assistance is to be used.

(3) Every department, agency, and establishment of the Federal Government having responsibility for building or construction, or for building- or construction-related programs, is authorized and encouraged to request authorization and appropriations for grants to the Institute for its general support, and is authorized to contract with and accept contracts from the Institute for specific services where deemed appropriate by the responsible Federal official involved.

(4) The Institute shall establish and carry on a specific and continuing program of cooperation with the States and their political subdivisions designed to encourage their acceptance and its technical findings and of nationally recognized performance criteria, standards, and other technical provisions for building regulations brought about by the Institute. Such program shall include (A) efforts to encourage any changes in existing State and local law to utilize or embody such findings and regulatory provisions; and (B) assistance to States in the development of inservice training programs for building officials, and in the establishment of fully staffed and qualified State technical agencies to advise local officials on questions of technical interpretation.

(h) There is authorized to be appropriated to the Institute not to exceed $5,000,000 for the fiscal year 1975, and $5,000,000 for the fiscal year 1976 (with each appropriation to be available until expended), to provide the Institute with initial capital adequate for the exercise of its functions and responsibilities during such years; and thereafter the Institute shall be financially self-sustaining through the means described in subsection (f).

(i) The Institute shall submit an annual report for the preceding fiscal year to the President for transmittal to the Congress within sixty days of its receipt. The report shall include a comprehensive and detailed report of the Institute's operations, activities, financial condition, and accomplishments under this section and may include such recommendations as the Institute deems appropriate.

TITLE VI—MOBILE HOME CONSTRUCTION AND SAFETY STANDARDS

SHORT TITLE

SEC. 601. This title may be cited as the "National Mobile Home Construction and Safety Standards Act of 1974".

STATEMENT OF PURPOSE

SEC. 602. The Congress declares that the purposes of this title are to reduce the number of personal injuries and deaths and the amount of insurance costs and property damage resulting from mobile home accidents and to improve the quality and durability of mobile homes. Therefore, the Congress determines that it is necessary to establish Federal construction and safety standards for mobile homes and to authorize mobile home safety research and development.

DEFINITIONS

SEC. 603. As used in this title, the term—

(1) "mobile home construction" means all activities relating to the assembly and manufacture of a mobile home including but not limited to those relating to durability, quality, and safety;

(2) "dealer" means any person engaged in the sale, leasing, or distribution of new mobile homes primarily to persons who in good faith purchase or lease a mobile home for purposes other than resale;

(3) "defect" includes any defect in the performance, construction, components, or material of a mobile home that renders the home or any part thereof not fit for the ordinary use for which it was intended;

(4) "distributor" means any person engaged in the sale and distribution of mobile homes for resale;

(5) "manufacturer" means any person engaged in manufacturing or assembling mobile homes, including any person engaged in importing mobile homes for resale;

(6) "mobile home" means a structure, transportable in one or more sections, which is eight body feet or more in width and is thirty-two body feet or more in length, and which is built on a permanent chassis and designed to be used as a dwelling with or without a permanent foundation when connected to the required utilities, and includes the plumbing, heating, air-conditioning, and electrical systems contained therein;

(7) "Federal mobile home construction and safety standard" means a reasonable standard for the construction design, and

performance of a mobile home which meets the needs of the public including the need for quality, durability, and safety;

(8) "mobile home safety" means the performance of a mobile
home in such a manner that the public is protected against any
unreasonable risk of the occurrence of accidents due to the design
or construction of such mobile home, or any unreasonable risk of
death or injury to the user or to the public if such accidents do
occur;

(9) "imminent safety hazard" means an imminent and unreasonable risk of death or severe personal injury;

(10) "purchaser" means the first person purchasing a mobile
home in good faith for purposes other than resale;

(11) "Secretary" means the Secretary of Housing and Urban
Development;

(12) "State" includes each of the several States, the District of
Columbia, the Commonwealth of Puerto Rico, Guam, the Virgin
Islands, the Canal Zone, and American Samoa; and

(13) "United States district courts" means the Federal district
courts of the United States and the United States courts of the
Commonwealth of Puerto Rico, Guam, the Virgin Islands, the
Canal Zone, and American Samoa.

FEDERAL MOBILE HOME CONSTRUCTION AND SAFETY STANDARDS

SEC. 604. (a) The Secretary, after consultation with the Consumer
Product Safety Commission, shall establish by order appropriate Federal mobile home construction and safety standards. Each such Federal mobile home standard shall be reasonable and shall meet the
highest standards of protection, taking into account existing State
and local laws relating to mobile home safety and construction.

(b) All orders issued under this section shall be issued after notice
and an opportunity for interested persons to participate are provided
in accordance with the provisions of section 553 of title 5, United
States Code.

(c) Each order establishing a Federal mobile home construction and
safety standard shall specify the date such standard is to take effect,
which shall not be sooner than one hundred and eighty days or later
than one year after the date such order is issued, unless the Secretary
finds, for good cause shown, that an earlier or later effective date is in
the public interest, and publishes his reasons for such finding.

(d) Whenever a Federal mobile home construction and safety
standard established under this title is in effect, no State or political
subdivision of a State shall have any authority either to establish, or
to continue in effect, with respect to any mobile home covered, any
standard regarding construction or safety applicable to the same
aspect of performance of such mobile home which is not identical to
the Federal mobile home construction and safety standard.

(e) The Secretary may by order amend or revoke any Federal
mobile home construction or safety standard established under this
section. Such order shall specify the date on which such amendment or revocation is to take effect, which shall not be sooner than
one hundred and eighty days or later than one year from the date
the order is issued, unless the Secretary finds, for good cause shown,
than an earlier or later date is in the public interest, and publishes his
reasons for such finding.

(f) In establishing standards under this section, the Secretary
shall—

(1) consider relevant available mobile home construction and safety data, including the results of the research, development, testing, and evaluation activities conducted pursuant to this title, and those activities conducted by private organizations and other governmental agencies to determine how to best protect the public;

(2) consult with such State or interstate agencies (including legislative committees) as he deems appropriate;

(3) consider whether any such proposed standard is reasonable for the particular type of mobile home or for the geographic region for which it is prescribed;

(4) consider the probable effect of such standard on the cost of the mobile home to the public; and

(5) consider the extent to which any such standard will contribute to carrying out the purposes of this title.

(g) The Secretary shall issue an order establishing initial Federal mobile home construction and safety standards not later than one year after the date of enactment of this Act.

NATIONAL MOBILE HOME ADVISORY COUNCIL

SEC. 605. (a) The Secretary shall appoint a National Mobile Home Advisory Council with the following composition: eight members selected from among consumer organizations, community organizations, and recognized consumer leaders; eight members from the mobile home industry and related groups including at least one representative of small business; and eight members selected from government agencies including Federal, State, and local governments. Appointments under this subsection shall be made without regard to the provisions of title 5, United States Code, relating to appointments in the competitive service, classification, and General Schedule pay rates. The Secretary shall publish the names of the members of the Council annually and shall designate which members represent the general public.

(b) The Secretary shall, to the extent feasible, consult with the Advisory Council prior to establishing, amending, or revoking any mobile home construction or safety standard pursuant to the provisions of this title.

(c) Any member of the National Mobile Home Advisory Council who is appointed from outside the Federal Government may be compensated at a rate not to exceed $100 per diem (including travel-time) when engaged in the actual duties of the Advisory Council. Such members, while away from their homes or regular places of business, may be allowed travel expenses, including per diem in lieu of subsistence as authorized by section 5703(b) of title 5, United States Code, for persons in the Government service employed intermittently.

JUDICIAL REVIEW OF ORDERS

SEC. 606. (a) (1) In a case of actual controversy as to the validity of any order under section 604, any person who may be adversely affected by such order when it is effective may at any time prior to the sixtieth day after such order is issued file a petition with the United States court of appeals for the circuit wherein such person resides or has his principal place of business, for judicial review of such order. A copy of the petition shall be forthwith transmitted by the clerk of the court to the Secretary or other officer designated by him for that purpose. The Secretary thereupon shall file in the court the record of the proceedings on which the Secretary based his order, as provided in section 2112 of title 28, United States Code.

(2) If the petitioner applies to the court for leave to adduce additional evidence, and shows to the satisfaction of the court that such additional evidence is material and that there were reasonable grounds for the failure to adduce such evidence in the proceeding before the Secretary, the court may order such additional evidence (and evidence in rebuttal thereof) to be taken before the Secretary, and to be adduced upon the hearing, in such manner and upon such terms and conditions as to the court may seem proper. The Secretary may modify his findings as to the facts, or make new findings, by reason of the additional evidence so taken, and he shall file such modified or new findings, and his recommendation, if any, for the modification or setting aside of his original order, with the return of such additional evidence.

(3) Upon the filing of the petition referred to in paragraph (1) of this subsection, the court shall have jurisdiction to review the order in accordance with the provisions of sections 701 through 706 of title 5, United States Code, and to grant appropriate relief.

(4) The judgment of the court affirming or setting aside, in whole or in part, any such order of the Secretary shall be final, subject to review by the Supreme Court of the United States upon certiorari or certification as provided in section 1254 of title 28, United States Code.

(5) Any action instituted under this subsection shall survive, notwithstanding any change in the person occupying the office of Secretary or any vacancy in such office.

(6) The remedies provided for in this subsection shall be in addition to and not in substitution for any other remedies provided by law.

(b) A certified copy of the transcript of the record and proceedings under this section shall be furnished by the Secretary to any interested party at his request and payment of the costs thereof, and shall be admissible in any criminal, exclusion of imports, or other proceeding arising under or in respect of this title, irrespective of whether proceedings with respect to the order have previously been initiated or become final under subsection (a).

PUBLIC INFORMATION

Sec. 607. (a) Whenever any manufacturer is opposed to any action of the Secretary under section 604 or under any other provision of this title on the grounds of increased cost or for other reasons, the manufacturer shall submit such cost and other information (in such detail as the Secretary may by rule or order prescribe) as may be necessary in order to properly evaluate the manufacturer's statement.

(b) Such information shall be available to the public unless the manufacturer establishes that it contains a trade secret or that disclosure of any portion of such information would put the manufacturer at a substantial competitive disadvantage. Notice of the availability of such information shall be published promptly in the Federal Register. If the Secretary determines that any portion of such information contains a trade secret or that the disclosure of any portion of such information would put the manufacturer at a substantial competitive disadvantage, such portion may be disclosed to the public only in such manner as to preserve the confidentiality of such trade secret or in such combined or summary form so as not to disclose the identity of any individual manufacturer, except that any such information may be disclosed to other officers or employees concerned with carrying out this title or when relevant in any proceeding under this title. Nothing in this subsection shall authorize the withholding of information by the Secretary or any officer or employee under his control from the duly authorized committees of the Congress.

(c) If the Secretary proposes to establish, amend, or revoke a Federal mobile home construction and safety standard under section 604 on the basis of information submitted pursuant to subsection (a), he shall publish a notice of such proposed action, together with the reasons therefor, in the Federal Register at least thirty days in advance of making a final determination, in order to allow interested parties an opportunity to comment.

(d) For purposes of this section, "cost information" means information with respect to alleged cost increases resulting from action by the Secretary, in such a form as to permit the public and the Secretary to make an informed judgment on the validity of the manufacturer's statements. Such term includes both the manufacturer's cost and the cost to retail purchasers.

(e) Nothing in this section shall be construed to restrict the authority of the Secretary to obtain or require submission of information under any other provision of this title.

RESEARCH, TESTING, DEVELOPMENT, AND TRAINING

SEC. 608. (a) The Secretary shall conduct research, testing, development, and training necessary to carry out the purposes of this title, including, but not limited to—

(1) collecting data from any source for the purpose of determining the relationship between mobile home performance characteristics and (A) accidents involving mobile homes, and (B) the occurrence of death, personal injury, or damage resulting from such accidents;

(2) procuring (by negotiation or otherwise) experimental and other mobile homes for research and testing purposes; and

(3) selling or otherwise disposing of test mobile homes and reimbursing the proceeds of such sale or disposal into the current appropriation available for the purpose of carrying out this title.

(b) The Secretary is authorized to conduct research, testing, development, and training as authorized to be carried out by subsection (a) of this section by contracting for or making grants for the conduct of such research, testing, development, and training to States, interstate agencies, and independent institutions.

COOPERATION WITH PUBLIC AND PRIVATE AGENCIES

SEC. 609. The Secretary is authorized to advise, assist, and cooperate with other Federal agencies and with State and other interested public and private agencies, in the planning and development of—

(1) mobile home construction and safety standards; and

(2) methods for inspecting and testing to determine compliance with mobile home standards.

PROHIBITED ACTS

SEC. 610. (a) No person shall—

(1) make use of any means of transportation or communication affecting interstate or foreign commerce or the mails to manufacture for sale, lease, sell, offer for sale or lease, or intro-

duce or deliver, or import into the United States, any mobile
home which is manufactured on or after the effective date of any
applicable Federal mobile home construction and safety standard
under this title and which does not comply with such standard,
except as provided in subsection (b), where such manufacture,
lease, sale, offer for sale or lease, introduction, delivery, or
importation affects commerce;

(2) fail or refuse to permit access to or copying of records, or
fail to make reports or provide information, or fail or refuse to
permit entry or inspection, as required under section 614;

(3) fail to furnish notification of any defect as required by
section 615;

(4) fail to issue a certification required by section 616, or issue
a certification to the effect that a mobile home conforms to all
applicable Federal mobile home construction and safety standards,
if such person in the exercise of due care has reason to know that
such certification is false or misleading in a material respect; or

(5) fail to comply with a final order issued by the Secretary
under this title.

(b) (1) Paragraph (1) of subsection (a) shall not apply to the sale,
the offer for sale, or the introduction or delivery for introduction in
interstate commerce of any mobile home after the first purchase of it
in good faith for purposes other than resale.

(2) For purposes of section 611, paragraph (1) of subsection (a)
shall not apply to any person who establishes that he did not have
reason to know in the exercise of due care that such mobile home is not
in conformity with applicable Federal mobile home construction and
safety standards, or to any person who, prior to such first purchase,
holds a certificate issued by the manufacturer or importer of such
mobile home to the effect that such mobile home conforms to all applicable Federal mobile home construction and safety standards, unless
such person knows that such mobile home does not so conform.

(3) A mobile home offered for importation in violation of paragraph (1) of subsection (a) shall be refused admission into the United
States under joint regulations issued by the Secretary of the Treasury
and the Secretary, except that the Secretary of the Treasury and the
Secretary may, by such regulations, provide for authorizing the
importation of such mobile home into the United States upon such
terms and conditions (including the furnishing of a bond) as may
appear to them appropriate to insure that any such mobile home will
be brought into conformity with any applicable Federal mobile home
construction or safety standard prescribed under this title, or will be
exported from, or forfeited to, the United States.

(4) The Secretary of the Treasury and the Secretary may, by joint
regulations, permit the importation of any mobile home after the first
purchase of it in good faith for purposes other than resale.

(5) Paragraph (1) of subsection (a) shall not apply in the case of
a mobile home intended solely for export, and so labeled or tagged on
the mobile home itself and on the outside of the container, if any,
in which it is to be exported.

(c) Compliance with any Federal mobile home construction or
safety standard issued under this title does not exempt any person
from any liability under common law.

CIVIL AND CRIMINAL PENALTY

SEC. 611. (a) Whoever violates any provision of section 610, or any
regulation or final order issued thereunder, shall be liable to the United

States for a civil penalty of not to exceed $1,000 for each such violation. Each violation of a provision of section 610, or any regulation or order issued thereunder shall constitute, a separate violation with respect to each mobile home or with respect to each failure or refusal to allow or perform an act required thereby, except that the maximum civil penalty may not exceed $1,000,000 for any related series of violations occurring within one year from the date of the first violation.

(b) An individual or a director, officer, or agent of a corporation who knowingly and willfully violates section 610 in a manner which threatens the health or safety of any purchaser shall be fined not more than $1,000 or imprisoned not more than one year, or both.

SEC. 612. (a) The United States district courts shall have jurisdiction, for cause shown and subject to the provisions of rule 65 (a) and (b) of the Federal Rules of Civil Procedure, to restrain violations of this title, or to restrain the sale, offer for sale, or the importation into the United States, of any mobile home which is determined, prior to the first purchase of such mobile home in good faith for purposes other than resale, not to conform to applicable Federal mobile home construction and safety standards prescribed pursuant to this title or to contain a defect which constitutes an imminent safety hazard, upon petition by the appropriate United States attorney or the Attorney General on behalf of the United States. Whenever practicable, the Secretary shall give notice to any person against whom an action for injunctive relief is contemplated and afford him an opportunity to present his views and the failure to give such notice and afford such opportunity shall not preclude the granting of appropriate relief.

(b) In any proceeding for criminal contempt for violation of an injunction or restraining order issued under this section, which violation also constitutes a violation of this title, trial shall be by the court or, upon demand of the accused, by a jury. Such trial shall be conducted in accordance with the practice and procedure applicable in the case of proceedings subject to the provisions of rule 42(b) of the Federal Rules of Criminal Procedure.

(c) Actions under subsection (a) of this section and section 611 may be brought in the district wherein any act or transaction constituting the violation occurred, or in the district wherein the defendant is found or is an inhabitant or transacts business, and process in such cases may be served in any other district of which the defendant is an inhabitant or wherever the defendant may be found.

(d) In any action brought by the United States under subsection (a) of this section or section 611, subpenas by the United States for witnesses who are required to attend at United States district court may run into any other district.

(e) It shall be the duty of every manufacturer offering a mobile home for importation into the United States to designate in writing an agent upon whom service of all administrative and judicial processes, notices, orders, decisions, and requirements may be made for and on behalf of such manufacturer, and to file such designation with the Secretary, which designation may from time to time be changed by like writing, similarly filed. Service of all administrative and judicial processes, notices, orders, decisions, and requirements may be made upon such manufacturer by service upon such designated agent at his office or usual place of residence with like effect as if made personally upon such manufacturer, and in default of such designation of such agent, service of process or any notice, order, requirement, or decision in any proceeding before the Secretary or in any judicial proceeding pursuant to this title may be made by mailing such process, notice, order, requirement, or decision to the Secretary by registered or certified mail.

NONCOMPLIANCE WITH STANDARDS

SEC. 613. (a) If the Secretary or a court of appropriate jurisdiction determines that any mobile home does not conform to applicable Federal mobile home construction and safety standards, or that it contains a defect which constitutes an imminent safety hazard, after the sale of such mobile home by a manufacturer to a distributor or a dealer and prior to the sale of such mobile home by such distributor or dealer to a purchaser—

(1) the manufacturer shall immediately repurchase such mobile home from such distributor or dealer at the price paid by such distributor or dealer, plus all transportation charges involved and a reasonable reimbursement of not less than 1 per centum per month of such price paid prorated from the date of receipt by certified mail of notice of such nonconformance to the date of repurchase by the manufacturer; or

(2) the manufacturer, at his own expense, shall immediately furnish the purchasing distributor or dealer the required conforming part or parts or equipment for installation by the distributor or dealer on or in such mobile home, and for the installation involved the manufacturer shall reimburse such distributor or dealer for the reasonable value of such installation plus a reasonable reimbursement of not less than 1 per centum per month of the manufacturer's or distributor's selling price prorated from the date of receipt by certified mail of notice of such nonconformance to the date such vehicle is brought into conformance with applicable Federal standards, so long as the distributor or dealer proceeds with reasonable diligence with the installation after the required part or equipment is received.

The value of such reasonable reimbursements as specified in paragraphs (1) and (2) of this subsection shall be fixed by mutual agreement of the parties, or, failing such agreement, by the court pursuant to the provisions of subsection (b).

(b) If any manufacturer fails to comply with the requirements of subsection (a), then the distributor or dealer, as the case may be, to whom such mobile home has been sold may bring an action seeking a court injunction compelling compliance with such requirements on the part of such manufacturer. Such action may be brought in any district court in the United States in the district in which such manufacturer resides, or is found, or has an agent, without regard to the amount in controversy, and the person bringing the action shall also be entitled to recover any damage sustained by him, as well as all court costs plus reasonable attorneys' fees. Any action brought pursuant to this section shall be forever barred unless commenced within three years after the cause of action shall have accrued.

INSPECTION OF MOBILE HOMES AND RECORDS

SEC. 614. (a) The Secretary is authorized to conduct such inspections and investigations as may be necessary to promulgate or enforce Federal mobile home construction and safety standards established under this title or otherwise to carry out his duties under this title. He shall furnish the Attorney General and, when appropriate, the Secretary of the Treasury any information obtained indicating noncompliance with such standards for appropriate action.

(b) (1) For purposes of enforcement of this title, persons duly designated by the Secretary, upon presenting appropriate credentials to the owner, operator, or agent in charge, are authorized—

(A) to enter, at reasonable times and without advance notice, any factory, warehouse, or establishment in which mobile homes are manufactured, stored, or held for sale; and

(B) to inspect, at reasonable times and within reasonable limits and in a reasonable manner, any such factory, warehouse, or establishment, and to inspect such books, papers, records, and documents as are set forth in subsection (c). Each such inspection shall be commenced and completed with reasonable promptness.

(2) The Secretary is authorized to contract with State and local governments and private inspection organizations to carry out his functions under this subsection.

(c) For the purpose of carrying out the provisions of this title, the Secretary is authorized—

(1) to hold such hearings, take such testimony, sit and act at such times and places, administer such oaths, and require, by subpena or otherwise, the attendance and testimony of such witnesses and the production of such books, papers, correspondence, memorandums, contracts, agreements, or other records, as the Secretary or such officer or employee deems advisable. Witnesses summoned pursuant to this subsection shall be paid the same fees and mileage that are paid witnesses in the courts of the United States;

(2) to examine and copy any documentary evidence of any person having materials or information relevant to any function of the Secretary under this title;

(3) to require, by general or special orders, any person to file, in such form as the Secretary may prescribe, reports or answers in writing to specific questions relating to any function of the Secretary under this title. Such reports and answers shall be made under oath or otherwise, and shall be filed with the Secretary within such reasonable period as the Secretary may prescribe;

(4) to request from any Federal agency any information he deems necessary to carry out his functions under this title, and each such agency is authorized and directed to cooperate with the Secretary and to furnish such information upon request made by the Secretary, and the head of any Federal agency is authorized to detail, on a reimbursable basis, any personnel of such agency to assist in carrying out the duties of the Secretary under this title; and

(5) to make available to the public any information which may indicate the existence of a defect which relates to mobile home construction or safety or of the failure of a mobile home to comply with applicable mobile home construction and safety standards. The Secretary shall disclose so much of other information obtained under this subsection to the public as he determines will assist in carrying out this title; but he shall not (under the authority of this sentence) make available or disclose to the public any information which contains or relates to a trade secret or any information the disclosure of which would put the person furnish-

ing such information at a substantial competitive disadvantage, unless he determines that it is necessary to carry out the purpose of this title.

(d) Any of the district courts of the United States within the jurisdiction of which an inquiry is carried on may, in the case of contumacy or refusal to obey a subpena or order of the Secretary issued under paragraph (1) or paragraph (3) of subsection (c) of this section, issue an order requiring compliance therewith; and any failure to obey such order of the court may be punished by such court as a contempt thereof.

(e) Each manufacturer of mobile homes shall submit the building plans for every model of such mobile homes to the Secretary or his designee for the purpose of inspection under this section. The manufacturer must certify that each such building plan meets the Federal construction and safety standards in force at that time before the model involved is produced.

(f) Each manufacturer, distributor, and dealer of mobile homes shall establish and maintain such records, make such reports, and provide such information as the Secretary may reasonably require to enable him to determine whether such manufacturer, distributor, or dealer has acted or is acting in compliance with this title and Federal mobile home construction and safety standards prescribed pursuant to this title and shall, upon request of a person duly designated by the Secretary, permit such person to inspect appropriate books, papers, records, and documents relevant to determining whether such manufacturer, distributor, or dealer has acted or is acting in compliance with this title and mobile home construction and safety standards prescribed pursuant to this title.

(g) Each manufacturer of mobile homes shall provide to the Secretary such performance data and other technical data related to performance and safety as may be required to carry out the purposes of this title. These shall include records of tests and test results which the Secretary may require to be performed. The Secretary is authorized to require the manufacturer to give notification of such performance and technical data to—

(1) each prospective purchaser of a mobile home before its first sale for purposes other than resale, at each location where any such manufacturer's mobile homes are offered for sale by a person with whom such manufacturer has a contractual, proprietary, or other legal relationship and in a manner determined by the Secretary to be appropriate, which may include, but is not limited to, printed matter (A) available for retention by such prospective purchaser, and (B) sent by mail to such prospective purchaser upon his request; and

(2) the first person who purchases a mobile home for purposes other than resale, at the time of such purchase or in printed matter placed in the mobile home.

(h) All information reported to or otherwise obtained by the Secretary or his representative pursuant to subsection (b), (c), (f), or (g) which contains or relates to a trade secret, or which, if disclosed, would put the person furnishing such information at a substantial competitive disadvantage, shall be considered confidential, except that such information may be disclosed to other officers or employees concerned with carrying out this title or when relevant in any proceeding under this title. Nothing in this section shall authorize the withholding of information by the Secretary or any officer or employee under his control from the duly authorized committees of the Congress.

NOTIFICATION AND CORRECTION OF DEFECTS

SEC. 615. (a) Every manufacturer of mobile homes shall furnish notification of any defect in any mobile home produced by such manufacturer which he determines, in good faith, relates to a Federal mobile home construction or safety standard or contains a defect which constitutes an imminent safety hazard to the purchaser of such mobile home, within a reasonable time after such manufacturer has discovered such defect.

(b) The notification required by subsection (a) shall be accomplished—

(1) by mail to the first purchaser (not including any dealer or distributor of such manufacturer) of the mobile home containing the defect, and to any subsequent purchaser to whom any warranty on such mobile home has been transferred;

(2) by mail to any other person who is a registered owner of such mobile home and whose name and address has been ascertained pursuant to procedures established under subsection (f); and

(3) by mail or other more expeditious means to the dealer or dealers of such manufacturer to whom such mobile home was delivered.

(c) The notification required by subsection (a) shall contain a clear description of such defect or failure to comply, an evaluation of the risk to mobile home occupants' safety reasonably related to such defect, and a statement of the measures needed to repair the defect. The notification shall also inform the owner whether the defect is a construction or safety defect which the manufacturer will have corrected at no cost to the owner of the mobile home under subsection (g) or otherwise, or is a defect which must be corrected at the expense of the owner.

(d) Every manufacturer of mobile homes shall furnish to the Secretary a true or representative copy of all notices, bulletins, and other communications to the dealers of such manufacturer or purchasers of mobile homes of such manufacturer regarding any defect in any such mobile home produced by such manufacturer. The Secretary shall disclose to the public so much of the information contained in such notices or other information obtained under section 614 as he deems will assist in carrying out the purposes of this title, but he shall not disclose any information which contains or relates to a trade secret, or which, if disclosed, would put such manufacturer at a substantial competitive disadvantage, unless he determines that it is necessary to carry out the purposes of this title.

(e) If the Secretary determines that any mobile home—

(1) does not comply with an applicable Federal mobile home construction and safety standard prescribed pursuant to section 604; or

(2) contains a defect which constitutes an imminent safety hazard,

then he shall immediately notify the manufacturer of such mobile home of such defect or failure to comply. The notice shall contain the findings of the Secretary and shall include all information upon which the findings are based. The Secretary shall afford such manufacturer an opportunity to present his views and evidence in support thereof, to establish that there is no failure of compliance. If after such presentation by the manufacturer the Secretary determines that such mobile home does not comply with applicable Federal mobile home construction or safety standards, or contains a defect which constitutes an imminent safety hazard, the Secretary shall direct the manufacturer to furnish the notification specified in subsections (a) and (b) of this section.

(f) Every manufacturer of mobile homes shall maintain a record of the name and address of the first purchaser of each mobile home (for purposes other than resale), and, to the maximum extent feasible, shall maintain procedures for ascertaining the name and address of any subsequent purchaser thereof and shall maintain a record of names and addresses so ascertained. Such records shall be kept for each home produced by a manufacturer. The Secretary may establish by order procedures to be followed by manufacturers in establishing and maintaining such records, including procedures to be followed by distributors and dealers to assist manufacturers to secure the information required by this subsection. Such procedures shall be reasonable for the particular type of mobile home for which they are prescribed.

(g) A manufacturer required to furnish notification of a defect under subsection (a) or (e) shall also bring the mobile home into compliance with applicable standards and correct the defect or have the defect corrected within a reasonable period of time at no expense to the owner, but only if—

(1) the defect presents an unreasonable risk of injury or death to occupants of the affected mobile home or homes;

(2) the defect can be related to an error in design or assembly of the mobile home by the manufacturer.

The Secretary may direct the manufacturer to make such corrections after providing an opportunity for oral and written presentation of views by interested persons. Nothing in this section shall limit the rights of the purchaser or any other person under any contract or applicable law.

(h) The manufacturer shall submit his plan for notifying owners of the defect and for repairing such defect (if required under subsection (g)) to the Secretary for his approval before implementing such plan. Whenever a manufacturer is required under subsection (g) to correct a defect, the Secretary shall approve with or without modification, after consultation with the manufacturer of the mobile home involved, such manufacturer's remedy plan including the date when, and the method by which, the notification and remedy required pursuant to this section shall be effectuated. Such date shall be the earliest practicable one but shall not be more than sixty days after the date of discovery or determination of the defect or failure to comply, unless the Secretary grants an extension of such period for good cause shown and publishes a notice of such extension in the Federal Register. Such manufacturer is bound to implement such remedy plan as approved by the Secretary.

(i) Where a defect or failure to comply in a mobile home cannot be adequately repaired within sixty days from the date of discovery or determination of the defect, the Secretary may require that the mobile home be replaced with a new or equivalent home without charge, or that the purchase price be refunded in full, less a reasonable allowance for depreciation based on actual use if the home has been in the possession of the owner for more than one year.

CERTIFICATION OF CONFORMITY WITH CONSTRUCTION AND SAFETY STANDARDS

Sec. 616. Every manufacturer of mobile homes shall furnish to the distributor or dealer at the time of delivery of each such mobile home produced by such manufacturer certification that such mobile home conforms to all applicable Federal construction and safety standards. Such certification shall be in the form of a label or tag permanently affixed to each such mobile home.

CONSUMER INFORMATION

SEC. 617. The Secretary shall develop guidelines for a consumer's manual to be provided to mobile home purchasers by the manufacturer. These manuals should identify and explain the purchasers' responsibilities for operation, maintenance, and repair of their mobile homes.

EFFECT UPON ANTITRUST LAWS

SEC. 618. Nothing contained in this title shall be deemed to exempt from the antitrust laws of the United States any conduct that would otherwise be unlawful under such laws, or to prohibit under the antitrust laws of the United States any conduct that would be lawful under such laws. As used in this section, the term "antitrust laws" includes, but is not limited to, the Act of July 2, 1890, as amended; the Act of October 14, 1914, as amended; the Federal Trade Commission Act (15 U.S.C. 41 et seq.); and sections 73 and 74 of the Act of August 27, 1894, as amended.

USE OF RESEARCH AND TESTING FACILITIES OF PUBLIC AGENCIES

SEC. 619. The Secretary, in exercising the authority under this title, shall utilize the services, research and testing facilities of public agencies and independent testing laboratories to the maximum extent practicable in order to avoid duplication.

INSPECTION FEES

SEC. 620. In carrying out the inspections required under this title, the Secretary may establish and impose on mobile home manufacturers, distributors, and dealers such reasonable fees as may be necessary to offset the expenses incurred by him in conducting such inspections, except that this section shall not apply in any State which has in effect a State plan under section 623.

PENALTIES ON INSPECTIONS

SEC. 621. Any person, other than an officer or employee of the United States, or a person exercising inspection functions under a State plan pursuant to section 623, who knowingly and willfully fails to report a violation of any construction or safety standard established under section 604 may be fined up to $1,000 or imprisoned for up to one year, or both.

PROHIBITION ON WAIVER OF RIGHTS

SEC. 622. The rights afforded mobile home purchasers under this title may not be waived, and any provision of a contract or agreement entered into after the enactment of this title to the cor   v shall be void.

STATE JURISDICTION; STATE PLANS

SEC. 623. (a) Nothing in this title shall prevent any State agency or court from asserting jurisdiction under State law over any mobile home construction or safety issue with respect to which no Federal mobile home construction and safety standard has been established pursuant to the provisions of section 604.

(b) Any State which, at any time, desires to assume responsibility for enforcement of mobile home safety and construction standards relating to any issue with respect to which a Federal standard has been established under section 604, shall submit to the Secretary a State plan for enforcement of such standards.

(c) The Secretary shall approve the plan submitted by a State under subsection (b), or any modification thereof, if such plan in his judgment—

(1) designates a State agency or agencies as the agency or agencies responsible for administering the plan throughout the State;

(2) provides for the enforcement of mobile home safety and construction standards promulgated under section 604;

(3) provides for a right of entry and inspection of all factories, warehouses, or establishments in such State in which mobile homes are manufactured and for the review of plans, in a manner which is identical to that provided in section 614;

(4) provides for the imposition of the civil and criminal penalties under section 611;

(5) provides for the notification and correction procedures under section 615;

(6) provides for the payment of inspection fees by manufacturers in amounts adequate to cover the costs of inspections;

(7) contains satisfactory assurances that the State agency or agencies have or will have the legal authority and qualified personnel necessary for the enforcement of such standards;

(8) give satisfactory assurances that such State will devote adequate funds to the administration and enforcement of such standards;

(9) requires manufacturers, distributors, and dealers in such State to make reports to the Secretary in the same manner and to the same extent as if the State plan were not in effect;

(10) provides that the State agency or agencies will make such reports to the Secretary in such form and containing such information as the Secretary shall from time to time require; and

(11) complies with such other requirements as the Secretary may by regulation prescribe for the enforcement of this title.

(d) If the Secretary rejects a plan submitted under subsection (b), he shall afford the State submitting the plan due notice and opportunity for a hearing before so doing.

(e) After the Secretary approves a State plan submitted under subsection (b), he may, but shall not be required to, exercise his authority under this title with respect to enforcement of mobile home construction and safety standards in the State involved.

(f) The Secretary shall, on the basis of reports submitted by the designated State agency and his own inspections, make a continuing evaluation of the manner in which each State having a plan approved under this section is carrying out such plan. Such evaluation shall be made by the Secretary at least annually for each State, and the results of such evaluation and the inspection reports on which it is based shall be promptly submitted to the appropriate committees of the Congress. Whenever the Secretary finds, after affording due notice and opportunity for a hearing, that in the administration of the State plan there is a failure to comply substantially with any provision of the State plan or that the State plan has become inadequate, he shall notify the State agency or agencies of his withdrawal of approval of such plan. Upon receipt of such notice by such State agency or agencies such plan shall cease to be in effect, but the State may retain jurisdiction in any case commenced before the withdrawal of the plan in order to enforce mobile home standards under the plan whenever the issues involved do not relate to the reasons for the withdrawal of the plan.

GRANTS TO STATES

SEC. 624. (a) The Secretary is authorized to make grants to the States which have designated a State agency under section 623 to assist them—

(1) in identifying their needs and responsibilities in the area of mobile home construction and safety standards; or

(2) in developing State plans under section 623.

(b) The Governor of each State shall designate the appropriate State agency for receipt of any grant made by the Secretary under this section.

(c) Any State agency designated by the Governor of a State desiring a grant under this section shall submit an application therefor to the Secretary. The Secretary shall review and either accept or reject such application.

(d) The Federal share for each State grant under subsection (a) of this section may not exceed 90 per centum of the total cost to the State in identifying its needs and developing its plan. In the event the Federal share for all States under such subsection is not the same, the differences among the States shall be established on the basis of objective criteria.

RULES AND REGULATIONS

SEC. 625. The Secretary is authorized to issue, amend, and revoke such rules and regulations as he deems necessary to carry out this title.

ANNUAL REPORT TO CONGRESS

SEC. 626. (a) The Secretary shall prepare and submit to the President for transmittal to the Congress on March 1 of each year a comprehensive report on the administration of this title for the preceding calendar year. Such report shall include but not be restricted to (1) a thorough statistical compilation of the accidents, injuries, deaths, and property losses occurring in or involving mobile homes in such year; (2) a list of Federal mobile home construction and safety standards prescribed or in effect in such year; (3) the level of compliance with all applicable Federal mobile home standards; (4) a summary of all current research grants and contracts together with a description of the problems to be studied in such research; (5) an analysis and evaluation, including relevant policy recommendations, of research activities completed and technological progress achieved during such year; (6) a statement of enforcement actions including judicial decisions, settlements, defect notifications, and pending litigation commenced during the year; and (7) the extent to which technical information was disseminated to the scientific community and consumer-oriented information was made available to mobile home owners and prospective buyers.

(b) The report required by subsection (a) of this section shall contain such recommendations for additional or revised legislation as the Secretary deems necessary to promote the improvement of mobile home construction and safety and to strengthen the national mobile home program.

(c) In order to assure a continuing and effective national mobile home construction and safety program, it is the policy of Congress to encourage the adoption of State inspection of used mobile homes. Therefore, to that end the Secretary shall conduct a thorough study and investigation to determine the adequacy of mobile home construction and safety standards and mobile home inspection requirements and procedures applicable to used mobile homes in each State, and the effect of programs authorized by this title upon such standards, requirements, and procedures for used mobile homes, and report to Congress as soon as practicable, but not later than one year after the date of enactment of this Act, the results of such study, and recommendations for such additional legislation as he deems necessary to carry out the purposes of this title. Such report shall also include recommendations by the Secretary relating to the problems of disposal of used mobile homes.

AUTHORIZATION OF APPROPRIATIONS

SEC. 627. There are authorized to be appropriated such sums as may be necessary to carry out the provisions of this title.

EFFECTIVE DATE

SEC. 628. The provisions of this title shall take effect upon the expiration of 180 days following the date of enactment of this title.

Appendix D
State Building Regulatory Programs
for Mobile Homes and Manufactured
Buildings—A Summary (Excerpts)

Patrick W. Cooke, Hotchand K. Tejuja,
Robert D. Dikkers, and Louis P. Zelenka

Office of Building Standards and Codes Services
Center for Building Technology
Institute for Applied Technology
National Bureau of Standards
Washington, D.C.   20234

U.S. DEPARTMENT OF COMMERCE, Frederick B. Dent, *Secretary*

NATIONAL BUREAU OF STANDARDS, Richard W. Roberts, *Director*

Issued September 1974

Map D–1. Status of Manufactured Building Regulatory Programs in the U.S. as of June 1, 1974.

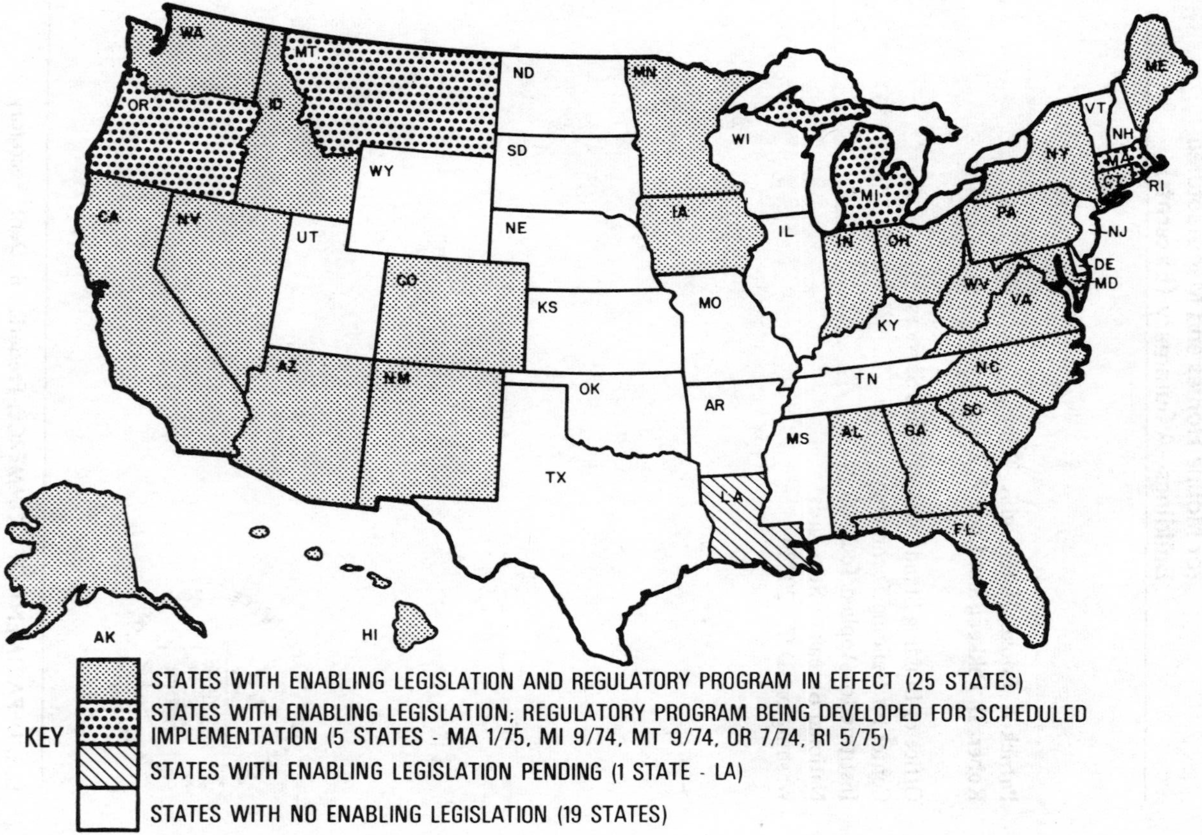
WA
OR
CA
NV
ID
MT
WY
UT
AZ
CO
NM
ND
SD
NE
KS
OK
TX
MN
IA
MO
AR
LA
WI
IL
MI
IN
OH
KY
TN
MS
AL
GA
FL
SC
NC
VA
WV
PA
NY
VT
NH
ME
MA
CT
RI
NJ
DE
MD
AK
HI
KEY
STATES WITH ENABLING LEGISLATION AND REGULATORY PROGRAM IN EFFECT (25 STATES)
STATES WITH ENABLING LEGISLATION; REGULATORY PROGRAM BEING DEVELOPED FOR SCHEDULED IMPLEMENTATION (5 STATES - MA 1/75, MI 9/74, MT 9/74, OR 7/74, RI 5/75)
STATES WITH ENABLING LEGISLATION PENDING (1 STATE - LA)
STATES WITH NO ENABLING LEGISLATION (19 STATES)

TABLE 2.0 STATE MANUFACTURED BUILDING PROGRAMS-ENABLING LEGISLATION

A ST	B IDENTIFICATION OF LAW	C ENAC DATE	D EFF DATE	E AMEN DATE	F	G REPO DATE
AL	FACTORY-BUILT HOUSING ACT,ACT NO.2059.	1071	4 72		X	5 74
AK	FIRE SAFETY CODE.	4 71	4 71			12 73
AZ	TITLE 44,CH.11,ART.7,ARIZONA REVISED STATUTES.	5 72	9 72	1 73	X	11 73
AR	(NO MANUFACTURED BUILDING PROGRAM)					5 74
CA	FACTORY-BUILT HSG.LAW-DIV.13,PART 6,HEALTH & SAF CODE.	9 69	5 70	1 73	X	12 73
CO	SECTION-1,CH-69 COLORADO REVISED STATUTES.		7 71		X	11 73
CT	SECTIONS 401.0,1900.0,1901.0 OF STATE CODE.		107?			5 74
DE	(NO MANUFACTURED BUILDING PROGRAM)					5 74
FL	FACTORY-BUILT HOUSING ACT,SEC.553.35 TO 553.42	6 71	6 71		X	11 73
GA	FACTORY-BUILT HOUSING ACT,H.B.273,ACT H325.	117?	6 72		X	5 74
HI	FACTORY-BUILT HOUSING ACT,ACT 111,LAWS 1970.	6 70	6 70		X	1 74
ID	IDAHO CODE, TITLE 39,CH. 41.	3 72	7 73		X	5 74
IL	(NO MANUFACTURED BUILDING PROGRAM)					5 74
IN	ACT 1393 CODIFIED AMEND.TO IN CODE 1971,TIT.22,ACT-11.	4 71	1072		X	5 74
IA	STATE BUILDING CODE,CH.103A,1973.	7 72	2 73		X	12 73
KS	(NO MANUFACTURED BUILDING PROGRAM)					5 74
KY	(NO MANUFACTURED BUILDING PROGRAM)					5 74
ME	INDUSTRIALIZED HOUSING LAW,TITLE 30MRS,CH.456,ART.7.	6 71	1071	6 74	X	5 74
LA	(LEGISLATION PENDING)					5 74
MD	INDUSTRIALIZED BUILDING & MOBILE HOME ACT.	5 71	7 71		X	1 74
MA	MGLA CH. 143, AMENDMENT C.802, 1972	7 72	1 75		X	1 74
MI	STATE CONSTRUCTION CODE ACT,ACT-230 OF PA-1972.	7 72	0 74		X	12 73
MN	STATE BUILDING CODE-CH.561,MS 16.83-16.86.	7 71	7 72		X	5 74
MS	(NO MANUFACTURED BUILDING PROGRAM)					5 74
MO	(NO MANUFACTURED BUILDING PROGRAM)					5 74
MT	CHAP. 21, TITLE 69, P.C.M, 1947	6 69	9 74			5 74
NE	(NO MANUFACTURED BUILDING PROGRAM)					5 74
NV	FACTORY-BUILT HOUSING LAW-REVISED STATUTES CH.461.	7 71	6 72		X	11 73
NH	(NO MANUFACTURED BUILDING PROGRAM)					5 74
NJ	(NO MANUFACTURED BUILDING PROGRAM)					5 74
NM	NMSA SECTION 67-35-1 THRU 67-35-67	2 67	7 67	73	X	6 74
NY	FACTORY-MANUFACTURED HOMES ACT,ART.18-B.	6 72	1 74	6 73	X	2 74
NC	GENERAL STATUTE 143-139.1.	5 69	6 70	6 71		5 74
ND	(NO MANUFACTURED BUILDING PROGRAM)					5 74
OH	BUILDING STANDARDS,GEN'L PROVISIONS,CH.3781,OH REV.CODE	8 69	1169	9 70	X	11 73
OK	(NO MANUFACTURED BUILDING PROGRAM)					5 74
OR	CHAP. 50, OREGON STRUCTURAL SPECIALTY CODE.	1 74	5 74			5 74
PA	INDUSTRIAL HOUSING ACT NO.70 OF 1972.	5 72	5 72		X	5 74
RI	CHAP. 138, PUBLIC LAWS OF 1973. (SEE TABLE 2.3)	3 73	5 75		X	5 74
SC	FACTORY-BUILT HOUSING ACT,CH.5.1,SEC.36-51 THRU 36-601	5 70	5 70		X	5 74
SD	(NO MANUFACTURED BUILDING PROGRAM)					5 74
TN	(NO MANUFACTURED BUILDING PROGRAM)					5 74
TX	(NO MANUFACTURED BUILDING PROGRAM)					5 74
UT	(NO MANUFACTURED BUILDING PROGRAM)					5 74
VT	(NO MANUFACTURED BUILDING PROGRAM)					5 74
VA	INDUSTRIALIZED BLDG UNIT & MOBILE HOME SAF-LAW,ACT-1970	4 70	7 71	2 71	X	11 73
WA	FACTORY-BUILT HSG-LAW-RCW 43.22.450 THRU RCW 43.22.490	2 70	5 70		X	5 74
WV	H-B,H 1015 (AMEND TO ART. 24), CH.8 OF W.VA.CODE.	3 71	6 71		X	5 74
WI	(NO MANUFACTURED BUILDING PROGRAM)					5 74
WY	(NO MANUFACTURED BUILDING PROGRAM)					5 74
DC	(NO MANUFACTURED BUILDING PROGRAM)					5 74
PR	(NO MANUFACTURED BUILDING PROGRAM)					5 74
VI	(NO MANUFACTURED BUILDING PROGRAM)					5 74

EXPLANATION OF COLUMN HEADINGS

COL.	EXPLANATION
A	STANDARD TWO LETTER ABBREVIATION REPRESENTING THE 50 STATES AND CERTAIN OTHER FIRST ORDER SUBDIVISIONS OF THE UNITED STATES (REFER TO APPENDIX A FOR NAMES OF STATES REPRESENTED BY THESE STANDARD ABBREVIATIONS)
B	TITLE BY WHICH THE ENABLING LEGISLATION (i.e., LAW, ACT, OR SECTION OF STATE BUILDING CODE) FOR THE REGULATION OF MANUFACTURED BUILDINGS MAY BE DESCRIBED AND CONVENIENTLY CITED
C	DATE (MONTH-YEAR) THE ENABLING LEGISLATION IDENTIFIED IN COLUMN B WAS ENACTED
D	EFFECTIVE DATE (MONTH-YEAR) OF THE ENABLING LEGISLATION IDENTIFIED IN COLUMN B
E	IF AMENDED, THE LATEST DATE (MONTH-YEAR) THE ENABLING LEGISLATION IDENTIFIED IN COLUMN B WAS AMENDED
F	"X" INDICATES THAT A COPY OF THE ENABLING LEGISLATION IDENTIFIED IN COLUMN B IS AVAILABLE FOR REVIEW AT THE OFFICE OF BUILDING STANDARDS AND CODES SERVICES, CENTER FOR BUILDING TECHNOLOGY, IAT, NATIONAL BUREAU OF STANDARDS, WASHINGTON, DC 20234
G	DATE (MONTH-YEAR) THE INFORMATION FOR THIS TABLE WAS REPORTED BY AN INDIVIDUAL STATE

EXPLANATION OF COLUMN HEADINGS

COL.	EXPLANATION
A	STANDARD TWO LETTER ABBREVIATION REPRESENTING THE 50 STATES AND CERTAIN OTHER FIRST ORDER SUBDIVISIONS OF THE UNITED STATES (REFER TO APPENDIX A FOR NAMES OF STATES REPRESENTED BY THESE STANDARD ABBREVIATIONS)
B	TYPE OF CONSTRUCTION TO WHICH LEGISLATION IS APPLICABLE. TYPES OF CONSTRUCTION MAY INCLUDE: "MB"--MANUFACTURED BUILDINGS; "MH"--MOBILE HOMES; "BC"--BUILDING COMPONENTS; "BM"--BUILDING MATERIALS
C	STANDARD MCSC OCCUPANCY CLASSIFICATION TO WHICH LEGISLATION IS APPLICABLE. APPLICABLE OCCUPANCY CLASSIFICATIONS MAY INCLUDE: "A"--ASSEMBLY "E"--EDUCATIONAL; "B"--BUSINESS "M"--MERCHANTILE; "I"--INSTITUTIONAL "H"--HAZARDOUS; "F"--FACTORY & INDUSTRIAL "S"--STORAGE; "R-1"--RESIDENTIAL--DORMITORY, HOTEL, MOTEL; "R-2"--RESIDENTIAL--MULTI-FAMILY; "R-3"--RESIDENTIAL--1 OR 2 FAMILY (REFER TO APPENDIX B FOR DESCRIPTIONS OF STANDARD MCSC OCCUPANCY CLASSIFICATIONS)
D	PREEMPTION STATUS OF LAW. PREEMPTION FEATURES OF THE LAW MAY INCLUDE: "PR"--LAW IS MANDATORY AND PREEMPTS LOCAL CODES; "OP"--LAW ALLOWS OPTION FOR MANUFACTURER TO OBTAIN APPROVAL FROM LOCAL JURISDICTIONS
E	PROVISION FOR ESTABLISHMENT OF A STATE ADVISORY COMMITTEE (OR COUNCIL) IN THE LAW AND EXTENT OF ITS RULE-MAKING AUTHORITY: "EST"-- COMMITTEE ESTABLISHED BY LAW; "RMAN"--COMMITTEE RECOMMENDATIONS MANDATORY; "RAD"-- COMMITTEE RECOMMENDATIONS ADVISORY
F	PROVISION FOR ESTABLISHMENT OF APPEAL PROCEDURES IN THE LAW
G	PROVISION FOR ESTABLISHMENT OF INTERSTATE RECIPROCITY IN THE LAW
H	PROVISION IN THE LAW FOR CRIMINAL PENALTIES FOR VIOLATIONS
I	PROVISION FOR WRITTEN MANUFACTURER WARRANTY AND DISCLOSURE REQUIREMENT IN THE LAW
J	DATE (MONTH-YEAR) THE INFORMATION FOR THIS TABLE WAS REPORTED BY AN INDIVIDUAL STATE

LEGEND
X - YES
O - NO

TABLE 2.0.1 STATE MANUFACTURED BUILDING PROGRAMS—ENABLING LEGISLATION

A ST	B APPLICABILITY				C OCCUPANCIES COVERED											D PREEM		E ST ADV COMM			F APP PRO	G INT RFC	H CRM PEN	I W WRW	J RFPA DATE
	MB	MH	BC	BM	A	E	R	M	I	F	H	S	R1	R2	R3	PR	OP	EST	RMAN	RAD					
AL	X	O	X	X	X	X	X	X	X	X	X	X	X	X	X	X	O	X	X		X	X	X		5 74
AK	X	X	X		X	X	X	X	X	X	X	X	X	Y		Y	X				X	O	Y		12 74
AZ	X	X			X	X	X	X	X	X	X	X	Y	C	Y	X		X			X				11 77*
AR	O	O	O	O																					5 74
CA	X	X	X	X	X	X	X		X	X	Y	X	X	X	X	X	O	Y	X		X	X	Y		12 77*
CO	X	X			X	X	X	X	X	X	X	X	X	X	X	X	X				X	X	X		11 77*
CT	X	X			X	X	X	X	X	X	X	X	Y	X	X	X	O	Y	X		X	X	Y		5 74
DE	X				X	X	X						X	X		X	O		C		X	C	X		11 77*
FL	X	O	X		X	X	X	X	X	X	X	X	X	X	X	O	C	X	X		X		X		11 77*
GA	X	O	O				Y		X	X			X	Y	Y	C	C		C		O				5 74
HI	X																								1 74
ID	X	O			X	X	X	X	X	X	X	X	X	X	X	X		X	X		O	O	X		5 74
IL	X				X	X	X	X	X	X	X	X	X	X	X	C	C				X	C	X		11 77*
IN	X	X	X	X	X	X	X	X	X	X	X	X	X	X	Y	C	C	X	X		X	X	X		12 77*
IA	X	X			X	X	X	X	X	X	X	X	X	X	X	C		C			O	X	X		1 74
KS	X	X			X	X	X	X	X	X	X	X	X	X	X										5 74
KY	X	X			X	X	X	X	X	X	X	X	X	X	X										5 74
LA	X	X			X	X	X	X	X	X	X	X	X	X	X										5 74
ME	X	X			X	X	X	X	X	X	X	X	X	X	X			X	X		X	X	X		5 74
MD	X	X	X		X	X	Y	X	X	X	X	X	X	X	X	X	X	Y	X		X	O	X		1 74
MA	X				X	X	X	X	X	X	X	X	X	X	X	X	O	X			X	O	X		5 74
MI	X	X	X		X	X	X	X	X	X	X	X	X	X	Y	O	O	O	C		Y	O	Y		12 77*
MN	X	X	X		X	X	X	X	X	X	X	X	X	X	Y	C	O	C			X	C	X		5 74
MS	X	X	O		X	X	X	X	X	X	X	X	Y	Y	Y	C		X			X	X	X		5 74
MO	X				X	X	X	X	X	X	X	X	X	X											5 74
MT	X	X			X	X	X	X	X	X	X	X	Y	Y	Y	X	X	X	X		Y	X	X		5 74
NE	X				X	X	X	X	X	X				X		O	O	O	Y		X	O	X		5 74
NH	X	X			X	X	X	X	X	X	X	X	X	X	X	X	X	X	X		X	X	X		11 77*
NJ	X				X	X	X	X	X	X	X	X	X	X	X	X		X			X	O	X		5 74
NM	X	X			X	X	X	X	X	X	X	X	X	X	X	X	X	X	O	X	X	X	X		6 74*
NY	X	X			X	X	X	X	X	X	X	X	X	X	X	X	X	O	Y		X	X	Y		2 74
NC	X	X	X		X	X	X	X	X	X	X	X	X	X	X	X	X	O			X	X	X		5 74
ND	X				X	X	X	X	X	X	X	X	X	X	X	X	X	X			X		X		11 77*
OK	X	X			X	X	X	X	X	X	X	X	X	X	X	C	X	C	X		Y	X	Y		5 74
OR	X	O			X	X	X	X	X					X		X		X			Y	X	Y		5 74
PA	X	X			X	X	X	X	X	X	X	X	X	X	X	X	X	X			X	X	X		5 74
RI	X	O			X	X	X	X	X	X	X	X	X	X	X	X	X	X			C	C	C		5 74
SC	X	X				X			X					X		X	X	X			X	X	X		5 74
SD																									5 74
TN																									5 71
TX																									5 74
UT																									5 74
VT																									5 74
VA	X	X			X	X	X	X	X	X	X	X	X	X	X	X	X	C	X		X	X	X		11 77*
WA	X	X			Y	Y	Y	Y	Y	Y	Y	Y	Y	Y	X	X	X	X			X	X	X		5 74
WV	X	X			X	X	X	X	X	X	X	X	X	X	X	X	X	X			X		X		5 74
WI	X					X																			5 74
WY	X																								5 74
DC																									
PR																									
VI																									

EXPLANATION OF COLUMN HEADINGS

COL.	EXPLANATION
A	STANDARD TWO LETTER ABBREVIATION REPRESENTING THE 50 STATES AND CERTAIN OTHER FIRST ORDER SUBDIVISIONS OF THE UNITED STATES (REFER TO APPENDIX A FOR NAMES OF STATES REPRESENTED BY THESE STANDARD ABBREVIATIONS)
B	STATUS OF ADMINISTRATIVE RULES AND REGULATIONS ADOPTED BY STATE "ADOP DATE"—DATE (MONTH-YEAR) THE RULES AND REGULATIONS WERE ADOPTED "EFF DATE"—DATE (MONTH-YEAR) THE RULES AND REGULATIONS BECAME (OR ARE TO BECOME) EFFECTIVE "AMEN DATE"—IF AMENDED, THE LATEST DATE (MONTH-YEAR) THE RULES AND REGULATIONS WERE AMENDED "CA"—COPY OF THE RULES AND REGULATIONS IS AVAILABLE FOR REVIEW AT THE OFFICE OF BUILDING STANDARDS AND CODES SERVICES, CENTER FOR BUILDING TECHNOLOGY, IAT, NATIONAL BUREAU OF STANDARDS, WASHINGTON, D.C. 20234
C	CODES AND STANDARDS (IF ANY) CITED IN THE LAW "CONS CODE"*—CONSTRUCTION/BUILDING CODE "MECH CODE"*—MECHANICAL CODE "PLUM CODE"*—PLUMBING CODE "ELEC CODE"*—ELECTRICAL CODE "1&2F CODE"*—ONE AND TWO FAMILY DWELLING CODE *REFER TO LEGEND BELOW FOR EXPLANATION OF SYMBOLS USED IN THESE COLUMNS
D	CODES AND STANDARDS ACTUALLY ADOPTED BY STATE (NORMALLY IN THE RULES AND REGULATIONS) —COLUMN DESIGNATIONS ARE THE SAME AS THOSE GIVEN ABOVE FOR COLUMN "C" EXCEPT THAT ADDITIONAL COLUMN IS PROVIDED TO INDICATE ANY OTHER CODES ADOPTED TO REGULATE OTHER ASPECTS OF CONSTRUCTION
E	DATE (MONTH-YEAR) THE INFORMATION FOR THIS TABLE WAS REPORTED BY AN INDIVIDUAL STATE

LEGEND
X – YES
0 – NO

CODES AND STANDARDS

M—MODEL CODE (AS PROMULGATED BY A MODEL CODE GROUP)
V—BASIC CODE (BOCA)
U—UNIFORM CODE (ICBO)
S—SOUTHERN CODE (SBCC)
T—STATE CODE
H—HUD/FHA STANDARDS
NF—NFPA STANDARDS (PRIMARILY No.70, "NATIONAL ELECTRICAL CODE")

EDITION OF CODES AND STANDARDS

DIGITS GIVEN AFTER SYMBOLS INDICATE THE EDITION YEAR OF THE CODE OR STANDARD INDICATED, e.g., "73" WOULD BE THE 1973 EDITION OF THE APPLICABLE STATE CODE

TABLE 2.1 STATE MANUFACTURED BUILDING PROGRAMS—RULES AND REGULATIONS

	B RULES–REGULATIONS			C CODES–STDS CITED IN LAW					D CODES–STDS ADOPTED BY RULES						E
A ST	ADOP DATE	EFF DATE	AMEN DATE	CA	CONS CODE	MECH CODE	PLUM CODE	ELEC CODE	1&2F CODE	CONS CODE	MECH CODE	PLUM CODE	ELEC CODE	1&2F CODE	OTHR CODE	REPO DATE
AL	71 4 72			X	M	M	M	V	V	S 71	C 71	S 71	NF71		5 74
AK	4 71	4 71		0	U 70	U 70	V	NF6A	NF6A	U 70	U 70	V 70	NF6A		1277
AZ	9 72	9 72	9 73	X	U 73	U 73	U 73	NF71	NF71	U 73	U 73	U 73	NF71		1173
AR															5 74
CA	3 70	5 70	1 73	X	U 70	U 70	U 70	NF71	NF71	U 70	U 70	U 70	NF71		1277
CO	2 72	4 72	1277	X	M	M	M	V	V	U 70	U 70	V 70	NF71		1177
CT		9 71		X	V	V	V	V	V	U 70	U 70	V 70	NF71		5 74
DE				X	M	M	M	M	M	S 71		S 71	NF71	NF	1177
FL		4 72		X											5 74
GA					M	M	M	M	M						1 74
HI	3 71	6 71		X	U 67	U 67	U 67	NF6A	NF	U 67	U 67	U 67	NF6A		5 77
ID	1 73	7 73		X	U	U	U	NF		U 70	U 70	U 70	NF		5 71
IL										T 69	T 69	T 69	T 71		5 71
IN	1 72	1072		X	M	M	M	M	M	U 70	U 70	U 70	NF71		5 71
IA	2 73	2 73		X	U 70	U 70	U 70	NF71		U 70	U 70	U 70	NF71		1277
KS															5 74
KY															5 74
LA					V 70	V 70	V 70	NF71		V 74	V 74	V 74	NF71		5 74
ME	2 75	7 72	1 74	X	M	M	M	M		V 72	V 72	V 72	NF71		5 74
MD	1 72	7 72	1 74	X	T	T	T	T	T	V 70	NC65	NC65	NF6A		5 74
MA	7 74	7 75		0	V 73	V 73	V 73	NF71		V 73	NC71	NC71	NF71		1277
MI	7 72	7 72		X	T 72	T 72	T 72	NF71		U 73	T 69	T 69	NF71		5 74
MN															5 74
MS															5 74
MO															5 74
MT	9 74			0	U 70	U 70	U 70	NF71	U 71	U 70	U 70	U 70	NF71	U 71	5 74
NE		6 72		X	U	U	U	NF		U 70	U 70	U 70	NF71		1177
NH															5 74
NJ										U 70	U 70	U 70	NF71		6 77
NM		67		X	M	M	M	M	M	T	T	T	NF71		6 77
NY	3 72	2 73	1673	X	T 71	T 71	T 71	T 70	T 70	T 74	T 74	T 74	NF71		5 74
NC	3 71	9 71	1277		T	T	T		M	T 70	T 70	T 70	NF71		5 74
ND					T	T	T	T	T	T 70	T 70	T 70	T 70		5 74
OH	1270	1 71			T	T	T	T	T	T 70	T 70	T 70	T 70		1177
OK		7 74								U 73	U 73	U 73	NF		5 74
OR		7 74			H	H	H	H	H	V 73	V 73	V 73	NF71		5 74
PA		7 74													5 74
RI		5 75			H	H	H	H	H	H	H	H	H		5 74
SC															5 74
SD															5 74
TN															5 74
TX															5 74
UT															1 79
VT															5 74
VA	5 71	9 71	1 73	X	V 70	V 70	S 69	NF6A	NF6A	V 70	S 69	NF6A	NF	1177
WA	1 71	3 71	1 74	X	U 67	U 67	U 67	NF6A	H	U 73	U 73	U 73	NF71		5 74
WV					H	H	H	H		H	H				5 74
WI															5 71
WY															5 71
DC															5 74
PR															5 74
VI															5 71

TABLE 2.1.1 STATE MANUFACTURED BUILDING PROGRAMS—RULES AND REGULATIONS

A ST	C CODE AMENDMENT PROCEDURE	D EVAL PROCESS ST	TP	LO	OT	E APPR PROCESS ST	TP	LO	OT	AP	F RFPO DATE
AL	X	X				X					5 74
AK	X	X				X					12 73
AZ	X					X					11 74
AR											5 74
CA	X	X				X					12 74
CO	X	X				X					11 74
CT	X		X				X				5 74
DE			X				X				5 74
FL	X	O	X			X	O			1	11 73
GA	X	X				X					5 74
HI	X	X				X					1 74
ID	X	X				X					5 74
IL	X										5 78
IN	X	X				X					5 74
IA	X	X		X		X					12 74
KS											5 74
KY	X	X				X					5 74
LA	X	X				X					5 74
ME	X	X				X				1	1 74
MD	X	X				X					12 73
MA	O	X	X			X	X				1 74
MI	X	X	X			X					5 74
MN	X	X	X			X					5 74
MS											5 74
MO											5 74
MT	X	X				X					5 74
NE	X										5 74
NV	X	X				X					11 74
NH											5 74
NJ											5 74
NM	X	X				X					6 74
NY	X	X				X					2 74
NC	X	X				X					5 74
ND											5 74
OH		X				X					11 73
OK											5 74
OR	X	X				X					5 74
PA						X					5 74
RI											5 74
SC	X			X				X			5 74
SD											5 74
TN											5 74
TX											5 74
UT											5 74
VT											1 74
VA	X	X				X	X	X			11 74
WV	X					X					5 74
WI											5 74
WY											5 74
DC											5 74
PR											5 74
VI											5 74

EXPLANATION OF COLUMN HEADINGS

COL. — EXPLANATION

A — STANDARD TWO LETTER ABBREVIATION REPRESENTING THE 50 STATES AND CERTAIN OTHER FIRST ORDER SUBDIVISIONS OF THE UNITED STATES (REFER TO APPENDIX A FOR NAMES OF STATES REPRESENTED BY THESE STANDARD ABBREVIATIONS)

B — AN "X" IN THIS COLUMN IS TO INDICATE THAT A COPY OF THE ADOPTED CODES AND STANDARDS IDENTIFIED IN THE PRECEDING TABLE IS AVAILABLE FOR REVIEW AT THE OFFICE OF BUILDING STANDARDS AND CODES SERVICES, CENTER FOR BUILDING TECHNOLOGY, IAT, NATIONAL BUREAU OF STANDARDS, WASHINGTON, D.C. 20234

C — PROCEDURE (IF ANY) EMPLOYED BY STATE TO ADOPT CODE AMENDMENTS. TABULAR INFORMATION ON SUCH PROCEDURES COULD INCLUDE:
    LEGISLATIVE ACTION
    PUBLIC HEARINGS
    ADMINISTRATIVE PROCEDURE
(NOTE—SPECIFIC INFORMATION ON THIS SUBJECT WAS NOT AVAILABLE FOR ANY STATE AT THE TIME OF PUBLICATION)

D — TYPE OF PROCESS FOLLOWED BY STATE FOR EVALUATION OF MANUFACTURED BUILDING SYSTEMS
    "ST"—STATE AGENCY EVALUATION
    "TP"—THIRD PARTY AGENCY EVALUATION
    "LO"—LOCAL AGENCY EVALUATION
    "OT"—EVALUATION BY AGENCY OTHER THAN STATE, THIRD PARTY OR LOCAL

E — TYPE OF PROCESS FOLLOWED BY STATE FOR APPROVAL OF MANUFACTURED BUILDING SYSTEMS
    "ST"—STATE AGENCY APPROVAL
    "TP"—THIRD PARTY AGENCY APPROVAL
    "LO"—LOCAL AGENCY APPROVAL
    "OT"—APPROVAL BY AGENCY OTHER THAN STATE, THIRD PARTY OR LOCAL
    "AP"—APPROVAL PERIOD (IN YEARS)

F — DATE (MONTH-YEAR) THE INFORMATION FOR THIS TABLE WAS REPORTED BY AN INDIVIDUAL STATE

LEGEND
X - YES
O - NO

TABLE 2.1.2 STATE MANUFACTURED BUILDING PROGRAMS--RULES AND REGULATIONS

A	B — INSPECTION AND CERTIFICATION PROCESS																	C	D	E — TP ACC PROCESS			F
ST	ST	TP	LO	MC	FI	OT	SM	AU	AP	PI	RI	OT	SL	TPL	NL	OT	MD	OI	SF	CE	NAA	AP	REPD DATE
AL	X		X						X				X		X			X	X				5 74
AK	X				X			X	X				O		X	X		X	X				12 77
AZ		X						X	X				X			X			X		3		11 77
AR				X						X			X		X			X	X	X	15		5 74
CA	X							X	X				X				X	X	O				12 77
CO	O	X	O					O	X				X		X	O		X	X	X	5	1	11 77
CT	X	X						X	X				X										5 74
DE													O		X								5 74
FL	O	X	O					O	X	X		O	X		X	O		X	C	X	12	1	11 77
GA	O	X	O						X						X								5 74
HI		X							X						X				C		1		1 74
ID	O								X				X		O	C		C		C			5 74
IL								O	X				X		X				X	O	12	1	5 74
IN	X	X						X	X				X		X	X		X	X	X	12		12 77
IA	X	X						X		X			X										
KS																							5 70
KY																							5 74
LA																							5 74
ME	X	X						X	X				X		X			X	X	O	13	1	5 74
MD	X	X						X	X				X		X			X	X	X			1 74
MA	X	X				O		O	X				X						O				5 74
MI	X	X						X	X				X										5 74
MN	X	X						X	X									X	X	X	7		5 74
MS	X	X								X			X										5 74
MO																							5 74
MT	X	X						X	X				X		X			X	X	O			5 74
NE	X	X						X					X		O			C		X			11 77
NV													C		O			O					5 74
NH																							5 74
NJ																							
NM	X	X						X	X				X	X	X			X	X	X	6		6 73
NY	X	X						X	X				X						X	X	3		2 76
NC								X					X		X			C		O			5 74
ND										X			X		X			X		Y			5 74
OH	X							X					X		X			X	X				11 77
OK	X	X						X	X				X		X				Y				5 74
OR	X	X						X					X									1	5 74
PA																							5 74
RI															C								5 74
SC	X		X											X									5 74
SD																							5 71
TN																							5 71
TX																							5 71
UT																							5 74
VT	X	X						X	X				X										1 74
VA	X	X						X	X				X		X			X	C	X	5	3	11 77
WV	X	X						X	X				X		X			X	X	Y	O		5 74
WI	X	X																					5 74
WY	X	X																					5 74
DC																							5 74
PR																							5 74
VI																							5 74

EXPLANATION OF COLUMN HEADINGS

COL.	EXPLANATION
A	STANDARD TWO LETTER ABBREVIATION REPRESENTING THE 50 STATES AND CERTAIN OTHER FIRST ORDER SUBDIVISIONS OF THE UNITED STATES (REFER TO APPENDIX A FOR NAMES OF STATES REPRESENTED BY THESE STANDARD ABBREVIATIONS)
B	TYPE OF PROCESS FOLLOWED BY STATE FOR INSPECTION AND CERTIFICATION OF MANUFACTURED BUILDINGS o IN-PLANT INSPECTION COVERAGE "ST"--STATE AGENCY INSPECTIONS "TP"--THIRD PARTY AGENCY INSPECTIONS "LO"--LOCAL AGENCY INSPECTIONS "MC"--MANUFACTURER SELF-CERTIFICATION "FI"--EMPLOYMENT OF FEE INSPECTORS "OT"--INSPECTION BY AGENCY OTHER THAN THOSE DESCRIBED ABOVE o IN PLANT INSPECTION MONITORING "SM"--STATE AGENCY MONITORING OF IN-PLANT INSPECTIONS o FREQUENCY OF IN-PLANT INSPECTIONS "AU"--SOME ASPECT OF ALL UNITS INSPECTED "AP"--INITIALLY ALL UNITS INSPECTED FOLLOWED BY PERIODIC INSPECTIONS "PI"--PERIODIC INSPECTIONS (e.g., WEEKLY, BI-WEEKLY, ETC.) "RI"--RANDOM SPOT CHECK INSPECTIONS "OT"--FREQUENCY OF INSPECTION COVERAGE OTHER THAN THOSE DESCRIBED ABOVE o LABELS REQUIRED "SL"--STATE LABEL REQUIRED "TPL"--THIRD PARTY LABEL REQUIRED "NL"--NO LABEL REQUIRED "OT"--LABEL OTHER THAN STATE OR THIRD PARTY REQUIRED "MD"--MANUFACTURER'S DATA PLATE REQUIRED
C	OUT-OF-STATE INSPECTIONS CONDUCTED BY STATE "OI"--STATE INSPECTIONS CROSS STATE LINES TO MAKE IN-PLANT INSPECTIONS
D	STATE EXAMINATION REQUIREMENTS "SF"--STATE INSPECTORS IDENTIFIED IN COLUMN B ARE REQUIRED TO PASS STATE EXAMINATION
E	THIRD PARTY AGENCY APPROVAL PROCEDURES "CE"--APPROVAL CRITERIA ESTABLISHED BY STATE "NAA"--NUMBER OF THIRD PARTY AGENCIES APPROVED BY STATE "AP"--LENGTH OF APPROVAL PERIOD (IN YEARS)
F	DATE (MONTH-YEAR) THE INFORMATION FOR THIS TABLE WAS REPORTED BY AN INDIVIDUAL STATE

LEGEND--X - YES; O - NO

TABLE 2.2 STATE MANUFACTURED BUILDING PROGRAMS-ADMINISTRATION & ENFORCEMENT

A ST	B DEPARTMENT OR AGENCY	C ADDRESS	D RFPO DATE
AL	STATE HOUSING COMMISSION	3866 S. COURT ST.,MONTGOMERY 36104	5 74
AK	FIRE MARSHAL	POUCH N- STATE CAPITOL,JUNEAU 99801	12 73
AZ	DIVISION OF BUILDING CODES	1645 W. JEFFERSON,PHOENIX 85007	11 73
AR	DEPT. OF PLANNING	CAP'L HILL BLDG.,LITTLE ROCK 72201	5 74
CA	DIVISION OF CODES AND STANDARDS	1500 5TH ST.,SACRAMENTO 95814	12 73
CO	DIVISION OF HOUSING	1575 SHERMAN ST.,DENVER 80203	11 73
CT	DEPT. OF PUBLIC WORKS	STATE OFFICE BLDG.,HARTFORD 06115	5 74
DE	DIVISION OF CONSUMER AFFAIRS	201 W. 14TH ST,WILMINGTON 19801	5 74
FL	BUREAU OF CODES & STANDARDS	2711 APALACHEE PKWY.,TALAHASSEE 32301	11 73
GA	STATE BLDG. ADMINISTRATIVE DEPT.	166 PRYOR ST.,ATLANTA 30334	5 74
HI	LABOR & INDUST. RELATIONS DEPT.	825 MILILANI ST.,HONOLULU 96813	5 74
ID	M.H., R&V. & MANIF. HOUSING DIV.	STATEHOUSE ANNEX 4,BOISE 83706	5 74
IL	DEPT. OF LOCAL GOV'T.,HOUSING OFF	325 W. ADAMS,SPRINGFIELD 62704	5 74
IN	ADMINISTRATIVE BUILDING COUNCIL	215 N. SENATE AVE.,INDIANAPOLIS 46204	5 74
IA	BUILDING CODE COMMISSION	523 E. 12TH ST.,DES MOINES 50319	12 73
KS	DIV. OF ARCHITECTURAL SERVICES	STATE OFFICE BUILDING,TOPEKA 66612	5 74
KY	OFFICE OF LOCAL GOVERNMENT	FRANKFORT 40601	5 74
LA	STATE FIRE MARSHAL	106 ST. OFF. BLDG.,NEW ORLEANS 70112	5 74
ME	STATE HOUSING AUTH., INSP. DIV.	P.O. BOX 1450,PORTLAND 04104	1 74
MD	DEPT. OF ECONOMIC & COMMUNITY DEV	2525 RIVA RD.,ANNAPOLIS 21401	5 74
MA	STATE BLDG. CODE COMMISSION	141 MILK ST.,BOSTON 02109	1 74
MI	CONST. CODE COMM.,DEPT. OF LABOR	414 N. LARCH,LANSING 48926	12 73
MN	BUILDING CODE DIVISION	408 METRO SQ. BLDG.,ST. PAUL 55101	5 74
MS	STATE MUNICIPAL ASSOCIATION	230 S A S BLDG.,JACKSON 39202	5 74
MO	DIV. OF DESIGN & CONSTRUCTION	P.O. BOX 809,JEFFERSON CITY 65101	5 74
MT	ADMIN. DEPT.,BLDG. CODE STD. SEC.	CAPITOL STA.,HELENA 59601	5 74
NE	STATE HOUSING ADVISORY COUNCIL	231 S 14TH ST.,LINCOLN 68509	5 74
NV	STATE FIRE MARSHAL	A13 N. PLAZA ST.,CARSON CITY 89701	11 73
NH	OFFICE OF COMPREHENSIVE PLANNING	STATE HOUSE ANNEX,CONCORD 03301	5 74
NJ	DEPT. OF COMMUNITY AFFAIRS	363 W. STATE ST.,TRENTON 08625	5 74
NM	GENERAL CONSTRUCTION BOARD	P.O. BOX 5155,SANTA FE 87501	6 73
NY	STATE BUILDING CODE BUREAU	2 WORLD TRADE CENTER,NEW YORK 10047	2 74
NC	STATE FIRE MARSHAL	P.O. BOX 26387,RALEIGH 27611	5 74
ND	EXECUTIVE OFFICE	BISMARCK 58501	5 74
OH	BOARD OF BUILDING STANDARDS	220 S. PARSONS AVE.,COLUMBUS 43215	11 73
OK	ENGINEERING DEPT.	CAPITOL BLDG.,OKLAHOMA CITY 73105	5 74
OR	DEPT. OF COMMERCE	617 CHEMEKETA ST N.E.,SALEM 97310	5 74
PA	DIV. OF INDUSTRIAL & MOBILE HSG.	P.O. BOX 155,HARRISBURG 17120	5 74
RI	DEPT. OF COMMUNITY AFFAIRS	150 WASHINGTON ST.,PROVIDENCE 02903	5 74
SC	STATE HOUSING AUTHORITY	1122 LADY ST.,COLUMBIA 29201	5 74
SD	STATE OFFICE	STATE OFFICE BLDG NO. 2,PIERRE 57501	11 73
TN	DEPT. OF INSURANCE,FIRE PREV.DIV.	202 CAP'L TOWERS BLDG,NASHVILLE 37219	5 74
TX	DIV. OF HOUSING	P.O. BOX 13166,AUSTIN 78711	5 74
UT	STATE BUILDING BOARD	RM. 124,ST. CAP'L,SALT LAKE CITY 84114	5 74
VT	DEVELOPMENT & COMM. AFFAIR AGENCY	MONTPELIER 05602	5 74
VA	STATE CORPORATION COMMISSION	P.O. BOX 1157,RICHMOND 23209	11 73
WA	FACT. BLT. HSG., M.H. & R.V. SEC.	300 W. HARRISON ST.,SEATTLE 98119	5 74
WV	FIRE MARSHAL'S OFFICE	1800 WASHINGTON ST.,CHARLESTON 25305	5 74
WI	DIV. OF IND. SAFETY & BUILDINGS	P.O. BOX 2209,MADISON 53701	5 74
WY	STATE FIRE MARSHAL	2015 CENTRAL AVE.,CHEYENNE 82002	5 74
DC	BUR. OF BLDG. HOUSING & ZONING	614 H ST. N.W.,WASHINGTON D.C. 20001	5 74
PR	PLANNING BOARD	P.O. BOX 9447,SAN JUAN 00908	5 74
VI	DEPT. OF PUBLIC WORKS	ST. THOMAS 00802	5 74

EXPLANATION OF COLUMN HEADINGS

COL.	EXPLANATION
A	STANDARD TWO LETTER ABBREVIATION REPRESENTING THE 50 STATES AND CERTAIN OTHER FIRST ORDER SUBDIVISIONS OF THE UNITED STATES (REFER TO APPENDIX A FOR NAMES OF STATES REPRESENTED BY THESE STANDARD ABBREVIATIONS)
B	NAME OF DEPARTMENT OR AGENCY RESPONSIBLE FOR THE ADMINISTRATION AND ENFORCEMENT OF THE MANUFACTURED BUILDING REGULATORY PROGRAM (SEE NOTE, TABLE 2.2.1)
C	ADDRESS OF THE DEPARTMENT OR AGENCY IDENTIFIED IN COLUMN B
D	DATE (MONTH-YEAR) THE INFORMATION FOR THIS TABLE WAS REPORTED BY AN INDIVIDUAL STATE

TABLE 2.2.1 STATE MANUFACTURED BUILDING PROGRAMS-ADMINISTRATION & ENFORCEMENT

A ST	B CONTACT	C TITLE	TELEPHONE	F REPO DATE
AL	H.HENDRIX	DIRECTOR	205-269-7913	5 74
AK	R.HENDRIE	FIRE MARSHAL	907-586-2946	1273
AZ	E.V.THORNE	DIRECTOR	602-271-4072	1173
AR	C.T.CROW	DIRECTOR	501-371-1211	5 74
CA	R.BAHR	CHIEF	916-445-9471	1273
CO	J.FRESQUES	DIRECTOR	303-892-2776	1173
CT	B.E.CABELUS	STATE INSPECTOR	203-566-4036	5 74
DE	F.M.WEST	DIRECTOR	302-571-3253	5 74
FL	J.H.HASLAM	CHIEF	904-488-7956	1173
GA	A.KELLY	EXECUTIVE DIR.	404-656-3931	5 74
HI	R.K.HASEGAWA	DIRECTOR	808-548-3150	1 74
ID	C.LIKES	DIRECTOR	208-384-3896	5 7?
IL	J.STERNSTEIN	CHIEF	217-782-3555	5 74
IN	C.J.BETTS	COMMISSIONER	317-633-5433	5 74
IA	K.C.HENKE,JR.	COMMISSIONER	515-281-3861	1273
KS	C.BEARDMORE	CHIEF	913-296-3811	5 74
KY	A.SPADER	DIRECTOR	502-564-4430	5 74
LA	R.B.OLIVER	FIRE MARSHAL	504-527-5956	5 74
ME	J.D.BROWNRIGG	MANAGER	207-781-3350	5 74
MD	W.BRYANT	ADMINISTRATOR	301-267-5162	1 74
MA	C.J.DINEZIO	EXECUTIVE SECRETARY	617-727-6916	5 74
MI	R.C.HILPRECHT	EXECUTIVE DIRECTOR	517-373-8187	1273
MN	H.W.MEYER	DIRECTOR	612-296-4626	5 74
MS	W.J.CARAWAY	EXECUTIVE V.P.	601-353-5454	5 74
MO	J.A.COOPER	DIRECTOR	314-751-4174	5 74
MT	W.J.KEMREL	SUPERVISOR	406-449-3104	5 74
NE	C.L.BRAZIE	CHAIRMAN	402-477-8984	5 74
NV	D.J.GUINAN	FIRE MARSHAL	702-885-4290	1173
NH	W.W.HOFFMAN	PRINCIPAL PLANNER	603-271-2350	5 74
NJ	J.G.FEINBERG	DIRECTOR	609-292-7898	5 74
NM	D.MCNEILL	ADMINISTRATOR	505-827-2085	6 73
NY	L.S.NIELSEN	DIRECTOR	212-488-7040	2 74
NC	K.E.CHURCH	SECRETARY	919-829-3901	5 74
ND	B.MEIER	SECRETARY OF STATE	701-224-2900	5 74
OH	M.J.HUGHES	CHAIRMAN	614-466-3316	1173
OK	A.TSOM	DIRECTOR	405-521-2111	5 74
OR	N.G.PETERSON	CHIEF	503-378-3986	5 74
PA	C.M.EDWARDS	CHIEF	717-787-9683	5 74
RI	F.TURANO	ACT. SECRETARY	401-277-2802	5 74
SC	S.MAYFIELD	EXECUTIVE DIRECTOR	803-758-2894	5 74
SD	E.N.GUAM	STATE ENGINEER	605-224-3466	5 74
TN	E.W.KIMSEY	DIRECTOR	615-741-2981	5 74
TX	C.TALMAGE	DIRECTOR	512-475-3383	5 74
UT	G.R.SWENSON	DIRECTOR	801-328-5561	5 74
VT	P.DONNEI	DIRECTOR	802-823-3231	1 74
VA	C.S.MULLEN,JP.	FIRE MARSHAL	804-770-4751	1173
WA	W.E.DELL	CHIEF	206-464-5300	5 74
WV	M.SMITTLE	FIRE MARSHAL	304-348-2191	5 74
WI	J.WENNING	ADMINISTRATION	608-266-1817	5 74
WY	E.BRADLEY	FIRE MARSHAL	307-777-7288	5 74
DC	W.N.DRIPPS	CHIEF	202-629-5050	5 74
PR	R.A.ALONSO	CHAIRMAN		5 74
VI	J.E.HARDING	DIRECTOR		5 74

EXPLANATION OF COLUMN HEADINGS

COL.	EXPLANATION
A	STANDARD TWO LETTER ABBREVIATION REPRESENTING THE 50 STATES AND CERTAIN OTHER FIRST ORDER SUBDIVISIONS OF THE UNITED STATES (REFER TO APPENDIX A FOR NAMES OF STATES REPRESENTED BY THESE STANDARD ABBREVIATIONS)
B	NAME OF PERSON RESPONSIBLE FOR THE ADMINISTRATION AND ENFORCEMENT OF THE MANUFACTURED BUILDING REGULATORY PROGRAM* (SEE NOTE BELOW)
C	TITLE OF THE PERSON IDENTIFIED IN COLUMN B
D	TELEPHONE NUMBER OF THE PERSON IDENTIFIED IN COLUMN B
E	DATE (MONTH-YEAR) THE INFORMATION FOR THIS TABLE WAS REPORTED BY AN INDIVIDUAL STATE

*NOTE: FOR THOSE STATES WITH NO REGULATORY PROGRAM AS REPORTED IN TABLE 2.0, THE NAME AND ADDRESS OF THE NCSBCS DELEGATE OR OTHER STATE OFFICIAL IS GIVEN

TABLE 2.2.2 STATE MANUFACTURED BUILDING PROGRAMS—ADMINISTRATION & ENFORCEMENT

ST	BUDGET AND FEES					STATE STAFF (M-YRS)			PROGRAM STATUS			RFPO
	CAOB	CAPC	FRGF	FRBA	FCPC	PROF	INSP	CLER	INST	OUTST	ANCU	DATE
AL					X	2	4	1	5	*		5 74
AK			X									12 74
AZ			X		X	4	8	6				11 74
AR												12 74
CA	130				X	2	3	2			866	11 73
CO			X		X	2	3	3	11	13	1,200	5 74
CT			X		X	2		3				5 74
DE			0	X	X	2	0	1				5 74
FL	95	95	0						23	7	3,160	11 73
GA			X		X	<1		<1	3	6	535	5 74
HI			X		X							1 74
ID												5 73
IL												5 74
IN	120	140	X	X	X	3	11	3	21	22	250	5 74
IA						5		1	7	5		12 73
KS												5 74
KY												5 74
LA			X	X		3		1				5 74
ME			X	X		3		2				5 74
MD												1 74
MA	1		X	X		6	39	11	8	82	876	1 74
MI			X	X		1	1	1	2	15	1,500	12 73
MN												5 74
MS												5 74
MO												5 74
MT			X	X		1						5 74
NE			X									5 74
NV			X									11 73
NH												5 70
NJ												5 74
NM			X	0		5	0	3	12	13		6 73
NY	250		0		X	2		1	6	13		2 74
NC						3	3	1	5	20	111	5 74
ND			X		X							5 74
OH			X		X	3		1	5		60	11 73
OK												5 74
OR												5 74
PA			X		X	3						5 74
RI												5 74
SC												5 74
SD												5 74
TN												5 74
TX												5 74
UT												5 74
VT												1 74
VA	85	50	X		X	4	1	1	11	169	25	11 73
WA		37	X		X	2	1	1	31	4	614	5 74
WV												5 74
WI												5 74
WY												5 74
DC												5 74
PR												5 74
VI												5 74

EXPLANATION OF COLUMN HEADINGS

COL.   EXPLANATION

A   STANDARD TWO LETTER ABBREVIATION REPRESENTING THE 50 STATES AND CERTAIN OTHER FIRST SUBDIVISIONS OF THE UNITED STATES (REFER TO APPENDIX A FOR NAMES OF STATES REPRESENTED BY THESE STANDARD ABBREVIATIONS)

B   FISCAL DATA—BUDGET AND FEES FOR ADMINISTRATION AND ENFORCEMENT
    "CAOB"—CURRENT ANNUAL OPERATING BUDGET (IN UNITS OF $1,000)
    "CAPC"—CURRENT ANNUAL PROGRAM COSTS (IN UNITS OF $1,000)
    "FRGF"—FEES RETURNED TO GENERAL FUND
    "FRBA"—FEES RETAINED BY AGENCY
    "FCPC"—FEES COVER PROGRAM COSTS

C   STATE AGENCY STAFFING LEVELS ASSIGNED TO ADMINISTER AND ENFORCE THE MANUFACTURED BUILDING REGULATORY PROGRAM
    "PROF"—NUMBER OF PROFESSIONAL MAN-YEARS
    "INSP"—NUMBER OF INSPECTOR MAN-YEARS
    "CLER"—NUMBER OF CLERICAL MAN-YEARS

D   OPERATIONAL STATUS OF MANUFACTURED BUILDING REGULATORY PROGRAM
    o NUMBER OF APPROVED FACTORIES
       "INST"—IN-STATE
       "OUTST"—OUT-OF-STATE
    o LEVEL OF ACTIVITY
       "ANCU"—ANNUAL NUMBER OF CERTIFIED UNITS

E   DATE (MONTH-YEAR) THE INFORMATION FOR THIS TABLE WAS REPORTED BY AN INDIVIDUAL STATE

LEGEND
X - YES
0 - NO

TABLE 2.2.3 STATE MANUFACTURED BUILDING PROGRAMS—ADMINISTRATION & ENFORCEMENT

A	B			C					D			E
ST	RECIPROCITY		MECH UTILIZED	CES DOC UTILIZED					INFO SYS UTIL			REPO
	EST	NO. STATES		S	E	A	CA	LEA	MTC	COMP	OT	DATE
AL	X	1 IN	AGREEMENT									12 74
AK												11 74
AZ	X	3 IA, IN, NV	AGREEMENTS									11 74
AR	X											5 74
CA	X	1 WA	AGREEMENT							X	X	12 73
CO	O											11 73
CT	O											5 74
DE												5 74
FL	O									O	X	11 73
GA	O											5 74
HI	O											1 74
ID	O											5 74
IL	X	6 AL, AZ, IA, MN, NJ, WA	AGREEMENTS									5 74
IN	X		AGREEMENTS									5 74
IA	X	2 AZ, IN										12 73
KS	O											5 74
KY												5 74
LA												5 74
ME	O											5 74
MD	O											1 74
MA	O											1 74
MI	O	1 IN	PUBLIC HEARING									12 73
MN	X											5 74
MS												5 74
MO												5 74
MT	O											11 74
NE	X	1 AZ	AGREEMENT									11 73
NV	X											5 74
NH	X	1 IN										5 74
NJ	X											5 74
NM	O									O	C	6 74
NY	O									O	C	2 74
NC	X	18 (ANY FACTORY WITH ACCREDITED AGENCY)				X	X					5 74
ND	O											11 73
OH	O											5 74
OK												5 74
OR												5 74
PA										X		5 74
RI												5 74
SC	O											5 74
SD												5 74
TN												5 74
TX												5 74
UT	O											5 74
VT												1 74
VA	X	18 (ANY FACTORY WITH ACCREDITED AGENCY)				X	X			X		5 74
WA	X	2 CA, IN	AGREEMENTS									5 74
WV												5 74
WI												5 74
WY												
DC										X		5 74
PR										X		5 74
VI												5 74

EXPLANATION OF COLUMN HEADINGS

COL.	EXPLANATION
A	STANDARD TWO LETTER ABBREVIATION REPRESENTING THE 50 STATES AND CERTAIN OTHER FIRST ORDER SUBDIVISIONS OF THE UNITED STATES (REFER TO APPENDIX A FOR NAMES OF STATES REPRESENTED BY THESE STANDARD ABBREVIATIONS)
B	STATUS OF INTERSTATE RECIPROCITY ACTIVITIES "EST"--RECIPROCITY ESTABLISHED WITH ANOTHER STATE OR STATES "NO"--NUMBER OF STATES WITH WHICH RECIPROCITY HAS BEEN ESTABLISHED "STATES"--INDIVIDUAL STATES WITH WHICH RECIPROCITY HAS BEEN ESTABLISHED "MECH UTILIZED"--MECHANISM UTILIZED FOR ACCOMPLISHING INTERSTATE RECIPROCITY
C	MODEL DOCUMENTS UTILIZED AS DEVELOPED BY THE CES (COORDINATED EVALUATION SYSTEM) PROJECT "S" --SUBMISSION DOCUMENTS "E" --EVALUATION DOCUMENTS "A" --APPROVAL DOCUMENTS "CA" --COMPLIANCE ASSURANCE (INSPECTION) DOCUMENTS "LEA"--LOCAL ENFORCEMENT AGENCY DOCUMENTS
D	INFORMATION PROCESSING SYSTEMS UTILIZED IN STATE'S ADMINISTRATION AND ENFORCEMENT PROGRAM "MIC" --MICROFORM SYSTEMS "COMP"--COMPUTER SYSTEMS "OT" --OTHER TYPE OF INFORMATION PROCESSING SYSTEM
E	DATE (MONTH-YEAR) THE INFORMATION FOR THIS TABLE WAS REPORTED BY AN INDIVIDUAL STATE

ST	TABLE 2.3 STATE MANUFACTURED BUILDING PROGRAMS-GENERAL REMARKS	REPO DATE
AL		5 74
AK		1273
AZ	CONTRACT AGENT PERFORMS IN-PLANT INSPECTIONS.	1173
AR		5 74
CA		1273
CO		1173
CT		5 74
DE		5 74
FL	STATE ADOPTS S GAS CODE & NEPA 54 & 58 FOR LP GAS.	1173
GA	PROGRAM NOT IMPLEMENTED, RULES BEING DEVELOPED	5 74
HI	ACT 100, SL 1973 AMENDS LAW TO PROVIDE FOR INTERSTATE APPROVALS.	1 74
ID		5 73
IL		5 74
IN		5 74
IA	ADOPTS ANSI A17.1 FOR REGULATION OF ELEVATORS.	1273
KS		5 74
KY		5 74
LA		5 74
ME	ADOPTS BOCA CODES WITH TECHNICAL AMENDMENTS BY STATE	5 74
MD	STATE RECEIVES DEFICIENCY REPORTS FROM LOCAL AGENCIES.	1 74
MA	MANDATORY STATE CODE TO BE EFFECTIVE JAN.1,1975.	1 74
MI	PROGRAM NOT FULLY IMPLEMENTED.	1273
MN		5 74
MS		5 74
MO		5 74
MT	PROGRAM NOT FULLY IMPLEMENTED	5 74
NE		5 74
NV		1173
NH		5 74
NJ		5 74
NM	CODES NOT CITED IN AMENDED ACT.	6 73
NY		2 74
NC	DEPT. HAS LIMITED COVERAGE TO SINGLE FAMILY DWELLINGS.	5 74
ND		5 74
OH		1173
OK		5 74
OR		5 74
PA		5 74
RI	MANDATORY STATE CODE TO BE EFFECTIVE 5-75	5 74
SC	ACCEPTS UNITS MEETING HUD CRITERIA.	5 74
SD	PLUMBING AND ELECTRICAL ASPECTS REGULATED BY STATE BOARDS	5 74
TN		5 74
TX		5 74
UT	STATE OWNED MANUFACTURED BLDGS. REGULATED PER UBC.	5 74
VT		1 74
VA	STATE ADOPTS NFPA 54 FOR GAS APPLIANCES.	1173
WA	FACTORY-BUILT COMMERCIAL STRUCTURES LAW TO BE EFFECTIVE 6-74.	5 74
WV	PROGRAM NOT IMPLEMENTED.	5 74
WI		5 74
WY		5 74
DC		5 74
PR		5 74
VI		5 74

MOBILE HOME PROGRAMS	No.	PROGRAM ELEMENT	No.	MANUFACTURED BUILDING PROGRAM
XXXXXXXXXXXXXXXXXXXXXXXXXXXXXXXXXXX	35	STATES WITH PREEMPTIVE LAWS	25	XXXXXXXXXXXXXXXXXXXXXXXXX
XXXXXXXXXXXXXXXXXXXXXXXXXXXXXXXXXX	34	STATES ADOPTING MODEL CODES	18	XXXXXXXXXXXXXXXXXX
XXXXXXXXXXXXXXXXXXXXXXXXXXXXXXXX	32	STATES REQUIRING LABELS	19	XXXXXXXXXXXXXXXXXXX
XXXXXXXXXXXXXXXXXXXXXXXXXX	26	STATES REQUIRING MANUFACTURERS DATA PLATE	16	XXXXXXXXXXXXXXXX
XXXXXXXXXXXXXXXXXXXXXXXX	24	STATE INSPECTORS MAKE OUT-OF-STATE INSPECTIONS	15	XXXXXXXXXXXXXXX
XXXXXXXXXXXXXXX	15	STATES WITH ESTABLISHED THIRD PARTY ACCREDITATION CRITERIA	14	XXXXXXXXXXXXXX
XXXXXXXXXXXXXXX	15	STATES HAVING ESTABLISHED RECIPROCITY WITH ONE OR MORE STATES	11	XXXXXXXXXXX
XXXXXXXXXXX	11	STATE EXAMINATIONS REQUIRED FOR INSPECTORS	8	XXXXXXXX
XXXXXX	6	STATES HAVING MANUFACTURER WARRANTY AND DISCLOSURE REQUIREMENTS	0	

FIGURE 3—Histogram of Status of Various Program Elements in Existing Mobile Home and Manufactured Building Regulatory Programs

MOBILE HOME PROGRAMS	No.	MANUFACTURED BUILDING PROGRAMS	No.	AGENCY
EVALUATION PROCESS				
XXXXXXXXXXXXXXXXXX	18	XXXXXXXXX	9	STATE AGENCY
XXXXXX	6	XXX	3	THIRD PARTY AGENCY
XXXXX	5	XXXXX	5	STATE AND/OR THIRD PARTY AGENCY
X	1	XX	2	STATE AND/OR LOCAL AGENCY
X	1	XX	2	STATE, THIRD PARTY AND/OR LOCAL AGENCY
APPROVAL PROCESS				
XXXXXXXXXXXXXXXXXXXXX	21	XXXXXXXXXXXXX	13	STATE AGENCY
XXXXXX	6	XX	2	THIRD PARTY AGENCY
XXX	3	XXXXX	5	STATE AND/OR THIRD PARTY AGENCY
X	1	X	1	STATE AND/OR LOCAL AGENCY
	0	X	1	STATE, THIRD PARTY AND/OR LOCAL AGENCY
IN-PLANT INSPECTION PROCESS				
XXXXXXXXXXXXXXXX	16	XXXX	4	STATE AGENCY
XXXXXXXX	8	XXXXXXX	7	THIRD PARTY AGENCY
XXXXXXXX	8	XXXX	4	STATE AND/OR THIRD PARTY AGENCY
X	1	XX	2	STATE AND/OR LOCAL AGENCY
	0	XXXX	4	STATE, THIRD PARTY AND/OR LOCAL AGENCY

FIGURE 4—Histogram of Type of Agency Involved in Evaluation, Approval, and In-Plant Inspection Functions for Existing Mobile Home and Manufactured Building Regulatory Programs

APPENDIX A

STATES OF THE UNITED STATES (INCLUDING CERTAIN OTHER FIRST ORDER SUBDIVISIONS)
WITH THEIR ASSIGNED STANDARD ABBREVIATIONS

NAME	ABBREVIATION	NAME	ABBREVIATION
ALABAMA	AL	MONTANA	MT
ALASKA	AK	NEBRASKA	NE
ARIZONA	AZ	NEVADA	NV
ARKANSAS	AR	NEW HAMPSHIRE	NH
CALIFORNIA	CA	NEW JERSEY	NJ
COLORADO	CO	NEW MEXICO	NM
CONNECTICUT	CT	NEW YORK	NY
DELAWARE	DE	NORTH CAROLINA	NC
FLORIDA	FL	NORTH DAKOTA	ND
GEORGIA	GA	OHIO	OH
HAWAII	HI	OKLAHOMA	OK
IDAHO	ID	OREGON	OR
ILLINOIS	IL	PENNSYLVANIA	PA
INDIANA	IN	RHODE ISLAND	RI
IOWA	IA	SOUTH CAROLINA	SC
KANSAS	KS	SOUTH DAKOTA	SD
KENTUCKY	KY	TENNESSEE	TN
LOUISIANA	LA	TEXAS	TX
MAINE	ME	UTAH	UT
MARYLAND	MD	VERMONT	VT
MASSACHUSETTS	MA	VIRGINIA	VA
MICHIGAN	MI	WASHINGTON	WA
MINNESOTA	MN	WAST VIRGINIA	WV
MISSISSIPPI	MS	WISCONSIN	WI
MISSOURI	MO	WYOMING	WY
DISTRICT OF COLUMBIA		DC	
PUERTO RICO		PR	
VIRGIN ISLANDS		VI	

Notes

Chapter 1

1. *America's Housing Needs: 1970 to 1980* (Cambridge, Mass.: Joint Center for Urban Studies, 1973) pp. 4–7.
2. *Housing in the Seventies* (Washington, D.C.: Department of Housing and Urban Development, 1973), pp. 8–28.
3. Joint Committee on Atomic Energy, *Understanding the "National Energy Dilemma"* (Washington, D.C.: U.S. Government Printing Office, 1975). See Tables C and E.
4. Christopher A. Sims, "Efficiency in the Construction Industry" in the *Report of the President's Committee on Urban Housing, Technical Studies, Vol. II* (Washington, D.C.: U.S. Government Printing Office, 1969).
5. Campbell R. McConnell, "Prefabricated Housing: Problems and Prospects," *Current Economic Comment*, Vol. SVIII, No. 2 (May, 1956), pp. 23–41.
6. Survey of Home Manufacturers conducted in 1970 by Charles G. Field.
7. NAHB Research Foundation, *Constraints to Builders' Use of Cost Saving Innovations* (Report done for the U.S. Department of Housing and Urban Development, 1971).
8. National Commission on Technology, Automation, and Economic Progress, *Applying Technology to Unmet Needs* (Washingtin, D.C.: U.S. Government Printing Office, 1966).
9. National Commission on Mortgage Interest Rates. *Report of the Commission on Mortgage Interest Rates for the President of the United States and to the Congress* (Washington, D.C.: U.S. Government Printing Office, 1969), p. 52.
10. National Commission on Urban Problems *Building the American City* (Washington, D.C.: U.S. Government Printing Office, 1968).

Chapter 2

1. Telephone interview with Dr. George Sternlieb (Rutgers University), August 30, 1974.
2. Leland S. Burns and Frank G. Mittelbach, "Efficiency on the Housing Industry" in the *Report of the President's Committee on Urban Housing, Technical Studies, Volume II* (Washington, D.C.: U.S. Government Printing Office, 1969), p. 79.

3. *Industrialized Building—A Comparative Analysis of European Experience* (Washington, D.C., Department of Housing and Urban Development, 1968).

4. One of the earliest recorded cases of prefabrication occurred in 1624, when Edward Winslow brought the "Great House" to Cape Ann Massachusetts (see Rita Robinson, "Prefabs: An Odd Technique," *Architectural and Engineering News*, IX, No. 6 (June 1967), pp. 64–69). This panelized wooden house was built by the English for use by their fishing fleets. It was dismantled, moved, and reassembled several times. A few years later, in 1633, a trading post was shipped upriver from Plymouth to Windsor, Massachusetts (see Robinson, *op. cit.*).

   More than a century later, Americans exported prefabricated structures to the West Indies (*ibid.*). One interesting record is that of shipbuilder Jonathan Trumbull of East Hamden, Connecticut. In 1764, a London doctor commissioned him to build and ship a house, size 50 by 20 feet, to Grenada. The doctor sent Trumbull specifications for the house, but failed to pay for it. We are not sure whether Trumbull was the first recorded prefabrication bankruptcy, but he left the business to go into politics, later to become the governor of Connecticut (*ibid.*).

5. The role of material shortages is most vividly illustrated by the early settlers of the prairie lands. Many homesteaders took prefabricated homes with them. The home in the back of the wagon was vital to them because of the scarcity of both lumber and labor in the prairie lands (*ibid.*, p. 69). One of the best illustrations of the missing construction industry came at the time of the 1849 California Gold Rush. The immediate need for sheltering the influx of people to California were met by shipments of panelized housing from the East Coast and Europe (see Kelly, *op. cit.*, p. 7) and from as far as Canton and Hong Kong in China, and New Zealand (see Robinson, *op. cit.*, pp. 65–66).

   In 1849, Peter Naylor, a metal roofer, advertised in the New York *Journal of Commerce*:

   Portable Iron Houses for California
   The Galvanized Iron Houses constructed by me for California having met with so much approval, I am thus induced to call the attention of those going to California to an examination of them. The iron is gro(o)ved in such a manner that all parts of the house, roof and sides slide together, and a house 20 X 15 can be put up in less than a day. They are far cheaper than wood, are fireproof and much more comfortable than tents. A house of the above size can be shipped in two boxes 12 feet long and 2 feet wide and 8 inches deep, the freight on which would be about $14 to San Francisco. (*ibid.*).

   The iron house proved to be unsatisfactory; in the winter it was too cold and in the summer too hot. In addition, the house was not fireproof (*ibid.*, p. 30). Not all prefabricated units were houses. The need for shelter in California extended to hotels, hospitals, and warehouses. One historian notes that a 62 X 100 foot, 4½ story hotel was shipped from Baltimore to California (*ibid*, p. 65).

Prefabrication evidently fulfilled a shelter requirement when the local homebuilding industry was either nonexistent or lacked the capacity to meet demand. Unsatisfied demand found expression in high prices—a house costing $400 to produce sold for $5,000 in California (see Kelly, *op. cit.*, p. 7)—which in turn spurred prefabricators in distant locations to enter the market. We can only conjecture that as soon as the local homebuilding industry developed in the West, the supply of locally-built houses increased and the price of such housing declined. In time, as well, the costs of shipping a prefabricated house thousands of miles became prohibitively expensive.

6. In 1907, Grosvenor Atterbury, A New York architect, built a prototype concrete house (see Alfred Bruce and Harold Sandbank *A History of Prefabrication* (New York, John B. Pierce Foundation, 1943), p. 31)). The house was made of hollow-cored, precast elements, which included floors, walls, and roofs. Between 1913–1918, several hundred units were built in Forest Hills Gardens, New York (see Kelly, *op. cit.*, p. 12). The project, while technically reputed an unqualified success, was disadvantaged by high transportation costs and huge frontend investment requirements for plant and equipment.

While Atterbury experimented with concrete panels, Thomas Edison in 1908 took a more radical approach and designed a monolithic process for pouring a 2–3 story house in a single operation.

7. Experimentation extended to steel houses. The Naugle House of 1907 was built for the Tuxedo Park Association (see Bruce, *op. cit.*, p. 42). By the late 1920s, the Steel Frame House Company, a subsidiary of McClintic-Marshall Corporation, experimented with steel studs as structural components (*ibid.*). In 1932, American Houses, Inc. built steel-framed homes in Hazelton, Pennsylvania. Twenty-one homes were constructed and sold for $3500–7200 excluding the costs of land and erection (*ibid.*, p. 45). Buckminster Fuller's Dymaxion House (1927), a hexagonal house, was suspended on a central core or mast and functionally designed to be used in any climate. According to Fuller, the dymaxion objective, an early statement of building systems, was to maximize the performance of the house per pound of house.

8. The Albert Farwell Bemis Foundation, founded in 1921 and active at the Massachusetts Institute of Technology, sought to find new uses for steel, composite gypsum blocks and precast slabs (*ibid.*, p. 10). During 1923–24, several houses were built in Wellesley, Massachusetts. One of Albert Bemis' major contributions was his advocacy of the 4-inch module as the basis of dimensional coordination (see Kelly, *op. cit.,* p. 8).

Concomitantly, the Pierce Foundation undertook investigations into the uses of steel housing and the development of mechanical subsystems. In addition to focusing upon the technological dimensions of prefabrication, the Pierce Foundation extended their studies into the physiological aspects of housing. Twenty experimental housing units, some of which were steel

framed, were constructed in Pierce Heights in Highbridge, New Jersey
(see Bruce, *op. cit.*, p. 12). As part of their technological research designs,
the Foundation experimented with integrated mechanical cores. (see Kelly,
op. cit., p. 31). Mechanical cores contain elements of the utility functions
of toilet-bath, hot water, heating, kitchen, and electrical distribution systems. Interest in mechanical cores was not their sole property. Buckminster
Fuller, in the 1920s, also experimented with mechanical cores, designing an
all-steel bathroom for use in Dymaxion (see Bruce, *op. cit.,* p. 19).

9. The U.S. Forest Products Laboratory sought to find more efficient means
    of utilizing our forest resources and in the process developed the first
    stressed-skin plywood house (see Kelly, *op. cit.*, p. 33). Another federal
    agency, the National Bureau of Standards, was founded in 1937 to conduct
    research on the utilization of materials and development of structures. A
    considerable amount of their time was to be spent on developing testing
    procedures to evaluate uses of materials (see *ibid.*, p. 13; Bruce, *op. cit.*,
    p. 13). Although these various private and public research efforts were of
    limited size, they did mark the beginnings of a sustained interest in industri-
    alization of the housing product.

10. The prewar period was not devoid of successful efforts. Hundreds of thou-
    sands of precut homes were manufactured and sold by companies like Sears
    and Roebuck, and Alladin Company.

Shipment of Precut Homes: 1900–1942

Sears Roebuck	100,000	1900–1940
Alladin Company	100,000	1906–1942
Lewis Manufacturing	14,000	1911–1942
Pacific System of L.A.	38,000	1908–1942
Gordon-Van Line Co.	25,000	1910–1942

Source: *Ibid.*, p. 57.

Sears and Roebuck offered free building plans, valued at $100.00 apiece,
to people interested in buying their precut homes. In their 1908 catalogue,
the company stated that they would send prospective customers complete
plans and specifications to include a complete listing of material and labor
requirements. The company also stated that it made its profit from the sale
of material items and explained their business as follows:

"we realize that we cannot secure your patronage unless we are able to
show you that it is very decidedly to your advantage in dollars and
cents to purchase this material from us. We do the largest mill work
business in the world, we own our own plumbing goods factory, we
manufacture hot air furnaces, steam and hot water boilers, radiators,
and all the materials which enter into plumbing, steam, hot water and
gas fitting. We handle more building hardware than any retail concern
in the world, and our business in all these lines is so enormous and our
policy of selling at the mere cost of material, which in this case means

manufacturing cost, with just one small margin of profit added, that
the prices we name on everything which enters into the construction
of a building are so much lower than the prices asked by local dealers
who sell you goods which have passed through manufacturers', job-
bers', and retailers' hands and therefore paid a profit to several individuals, that we can show you a very large saving. We are the only
concern in the world which can furnish you all the articles you need
in the construction of a house or barn in the finest quality of goods
at such wonderfully low prices, and we know that if we can just have
your interest you would be glad to send us your order when you build."

Sears' great strength and perhaps key to success was its ready-made mass
market. The precut home was only part of a much larger mail-order
business. Not only did the publicity on the Sears home reach thousands
of potential customers; the mail order was a very effective distributing
and marketing system.

11. Military demands for shelter frequently stimulated new approaches to
production. During the Civil War, the Union Army used prefabricated structures as portable buildings to be moved with the troops (see Robinson,
op. cit., p. 69). A half-century later, defense housing needs were met by the
construction of Nissen Huts, more commonly known as Quonset huts.
Soon thereafter, the Tennessee Valley Authority, to meet the special
housing requirements for workers at hydroelectric projects, developed
truckable, demountable, sectional housing. The first houses, built in 1940,
were wooden-framed units weighing three tons and fully equipped with
electric heating, and plumbing equipment. These units, hauled over 600
miles from factory to site, were the forerunners of today's trailer and
mobile home (see Bruce, *op. cit.*, p. 14; Kelly, *op. cit.*, p. 37).

The other notable success came under the aegis of the federal government.
Projects for mobile structures for migratory workers, low-cost wooden
farmsteads and rural communities were initiated under the direction of the
Farm Security Administration (FSA). FSA stressed the need for low-cost
housing by using mass production techniques and unskilled labor (see
Bruce, *op. cit.*, p. 14). By 1938, 100 farmsteads made of prefabricated wall
and roof sections were built under FSA auspices. In a parallel effort, FSA
researched and built several thousand steel units for migratory workers and
by 1940 was responsible for an estimated production of 26,000 units (see
Kelly, *op. cit.*, pp. 35–36).

12. Corporate giants entered the home manufacturing business in the 1930s
primarily to extend their own product lines and/or utilize excess plant
capacity. Included among them were such giants as U.S. Steel, Pullman
Standard Car Manufacturing, Johns-Manville, U.S. Gypsum, and General
Electric (see *ibid.,* p. 38). But very little production took place; only an
estimated 10,000 units were produced in the 1930s (see *Fortune*, XXXIII,
No. 4 (April 1946) p. 127). By 1940, fewer than 30 companies were manufacturing and marketing prefabricated housing (see Kelly, *op. cit.*, p. 50).
Although major corporations expressed a definite interest in prefabrication,

the economic climate of the 1920s and 1930s was not yet conducive to a full involvement.

Burnham Kelly offered some reasons for the lack of progress. The first reason was the inertia of big business. Second was the fragmentation of the market, which discouraged extensive research and development. No one company could command a sufficiently large piece of the action to warrant extensive expenditures of high-risk capital into R & D. The third reason was the fear that the outlets for prefabricated homes would be in direct conflict with a firm's normal market outlets. The perceived possibility of limited profits through prefabricated housing was not sufficient to risk the disruption of the normal distribution channels. Finally, large corporations were unsure of the saleability of prefabricated homes. Fear that consumers would reject prefabrication acted as a brake upon corporate commitment to this business.

According to Kelly:

There has been no element in the housebuilding industry with sufficient power and means of control to initiate fundamental changes in the fabrication and construction processes and carry them through to the final product. . . . (*Ibid.*, pp. 44–45).

These were not the only problems confronting the potential prefab producer. Opposition by local material dealers who stood to lose large quantities of business, opposition by unions, as illustrated in the Fort Wayne Experiment, hesitation by local lending institutions to provide mortgage financing, stiff restrictions imposed by building codes, and depressed economic conditions all acted to dampen any enthusiasm for prefabrication.

13. In 1938, the Federal Housing Administration joined with the Fort Wayne Housing Authority and the Projects Works Administration in sponsoring the Fort Wayne Experiment. Fifty units of stressed-skin paneled single-family housing were built and rented for $2.50 per week. The units, built in a factory rented and equipped by the Fort Wayne Housing Authority, used WPA labor. The houses were only 480 square feet and were demountable. They were placed in blighted areas of the city on land purchased for $1.00 per site. If the former owners decided to repurchase the land, an option extended to the owner under the purchase agreement, the house, due to its demountable quality, could be moved to another location (*ibid.*, pp. 36–37). This plan had strong opposition from the American Federation of Labor, opposition primarily based upon job preservation and fear that skilled tradesmen would be replaced by unskilled WPA labor.

Although the AFL was unsuccessful in blocking the Fort Wayne Experiment, similar projects were not attempted elsewhere (*ibid.*). FHA's role must be considered negligible, during this time, when compared to its major responsibilities for shoring up the sagging real estate market, but its involvement did illustrate a limited willingness to become involved in nonconventional homebuilding.

14. (*Ibid.*, p. 60).

15. Defense housing was to be demountable in anticipation that, upon successful completion of the war, workers would leave war plant locations and return to home areas. Reductions of on-site labor obviously was linked to the manpower drain of both military and wartime industries. Had enough laborers been available, conventional builders might have been called upon to produce the required housing.

16. Expectations for prefabricated housing ran high. The industry, at last, had the opportunity to demonstrate its effectiveness; a market existed. According to *Architectural Forum* in 1942:

   . . . the principal effect of the program [defense housing], assuming that it is relatively successful and continues, will be the creation of a highly efficient, well-equipped, and well-heeled agency for post-war home building. (See "Prefabrication Gets its Chance as FWA Allocates $153 Million for Demountable Houses, Offers to Buy Them F.O.B. for Assembly by Others," *Architectural Forum* LXXVI (February 1942), p. 28).

   Wilson Wyatt, President Truman's Housing Expeditor, projected a prosperous and strong prefabrication future of 250,000 units in 1946 and 600,000 units in 1947 (see Kelly, *op. cit.*, p. 69), with many home manufacturers sharing his dreams.

   Of 200 firms surveyed in 1946, 37 estimated their combined 1946 production at 131, 175 units. Thirty-three firms estimated a 1947 level of 165, 275 units (see "1946 and after—Prefabrication Looks Ahead," *Prefabricated Homes* VI, No. 3 (January 1946), p. 10), somewhat more conservative projections than Wyatt's. Eight firms forecasted production at over 2500 in 1946, fourteen expecting to reach that level by 1947. At least three firms anticipated producing more than 5000 units in 1947.

17. Total housing construction jumped from approximately 325,000 units in 1945 to over 1 million in 1946 and 1.2 million in 1947 (see U.S. Department of Housing and Urban Development, *1967 Statistical Yearbook* (Washington, D.C.: U.S. Government Printing Office, 1967, p. 52). But industrial production of prefabricated housing in 1946 was approximately 38,000 units and 37,000 the next year. These were volume decreases from average war year production runs of 40,000 units (see Kelly, *op. cit.*, p. 60).

18. Many people thought of prefabricated housing as temporary war housing, housing built to minimum standards (*ibid.*, pp. 90, 168–169). Because the government sought performance and not design, there was little incentive for manufacturers to promote a public image of quality during the war years.

   In 1946, *Fortune* conducted a survey on home manufacturing. In response to one *Fortune* question: "What don't you like about prefabricated houses?", people who answered the question said:

Unsatisfactory construction (included "not substantial enough," "not strong enough," "not permanent, not warm enough")	67.4%
Lack individuality	13.4%
Too small	4.6%
All other	18.4%
Don't know	9.6%

Source: *Fortune* XXXIII, No. 4 (April 1946) p. 275.

Quite contrary to popoular opinion, prefabricated housing was often superior in quality to conventional housing (see Kelly, *op. cit.*, p. 90). Unfortunately, this unfavorable image was to persist as a major marketing obstacle throughout the 1940s and into the 1950s.

Many manufacturers attacked the problem of the "staple gun house" image of the product by hiring prominent architects as prestige designers (see Glenn Beyer, *Housing: A Factual Analysis* New York: Macmillan, 1958), p. 112). In a 1956 survey of prefabricators, 76 percent said they used architects (see Irvin Kuper, "Getting Uniform Building Codes," *National Real Estate and Building Journal*, LVII, No. 11 (November 1956), p. 135). Upgrading was also sought by increasing the amount of usable floor space, by introducing greater flexibility into plans, and by increasing the variety of designs offered the buyer (see "Fourth Annual Prefab Report," *National Real Estate and Building Journal*, LVII, No. 11 (November 1956) p. 17).

The results of upgrading were best reflected in the selling price of the manufactured home. The 1950s were a time of a conscious shift in production from lower-income to middle-income housing. Whereas in 1950 most manufactured housing was at first priced below the average-priced, single-family home, six years later the pattern had reversed, with more than half of production exceeding the national average.

The Prefabricated Home Manufacturers Institute (PHMI) estimated that, in 1950, 80 percent of its members sold homes priced $6,000–$9,000, *including* land (see Richard Koyer, "The Case for Prefabs," *National Real Estate and Building Journal*, LII, No. 8 (August 1951), p. 23). The average construction cost, *excluding* land, of all new privately owned non-farm, single-family homes was $8,676 (*Statistical Abstract of the United States*, 1961, p. 761). The average home would have exceeded $9,000–$10,000 if land were included. Six years later, the pattern had changed. The average price of a prefabricated house, according to PHMI, was $12,500 including land (*ibid.*) compared to the $12,225 cost of the average non-farm, single-family home exclusive of land. By the mid–1950s, prefabrication was firmly in the middle-income market.

The marketing strategy of the 1950s is best illustrated by the minimum-priced homes offered by companies. Decided upward shifts in price distributions took place between 1954 and 1958, years for which we have price data. Whereas 46 percent of the firms offered houses priced under $7,000 (excludes land) in 1954, only 10 percent offered this price range in 1958. This pattern is shown in the following table.

Distribution of Lowest Priced Manufactured Homes, 1954 and 1958

	1954	*1958*
Less $5000	10.6	2.3
$5000–$6000	21.2	2.3
$6000–$7000	15.1	5.7
$7000–$8000	16.6	21.6
$8000–$9000	4.5	21.6
$9000–$10,000	21.2	27.0
$10,000–$11,000	7.6	4.5
$11,000–$12,000	1.5	10.2
$12,000–$15,000	1.5	2.3
Over $15,000	–	2.3
	100.0%	100.0%

Sources: *House and Home,* Vol. VI, No. 6 (December 1954) and Vol. XIV, No. 6 (December 1958).

The pattern of price changes by individual firms was not random, rather a pattern of readjustments to middle-income markets. It was possible to trace price changes for 29 firms between the two surveys; 17 increased and 12 decreased their lowest price lines. Most of the firms that introduced lower priced lines came down from high-priced models, $9,400–$11,600, and dropped in the $7,000–$9,000 market. Most firms who upgraded their price lines began with low prices, $5,000–$7,600, and increased to the $8,000–$12,500 market. Remembering that these figures *exclude* the costs of land, the sales price of the house would be in the middle-income market.

At the same time, there was a decided upswing in the highest priced homes. The pattern of change, shown below, clearly indicates an attempt to enter the prestige market.

Distribution of Highest Priced Manufactured Homes, 1954 and 1958

Package Price	*1954*	*1958*
Less $10,000	9	–
$10,000–$20,000	59	28
$20,000–$30,000	23	37
$30,000–$40,000	9	19
$40,000–$50,000	–	2
$50,000–$60,000	–	4
Over $60,000	–	2
	100%	100%

Sources: *House and Home,* Vol. VI, No. 6 (December 1954) and Vol. XIV, No. 6 (December 1958).

19. Manufacturers were forced to seek dealers as market outlets for prefab homes (see Beyer, *Practices and Precepts . . . ,* p. 27). This difficult task was complicated by governmental price controls. The Office of Price Administration (OPA) limited the level of profit realizable by both the

manufacturer and dealer. The manufacturer was allowed a 36 percent mark-up in price. The dealer was restricted to 10 percent. Manufacturers felt their mark-up was reasonable, but claimed that the dealer mark-up was highly restrictive since it limited real profits to 2 percent before taxes.

The 10 percent OPA limit, manufacturers claimed, was equivalent to a 9 percent mark-up on gross profits. Experience showed that dealers incurred overhead expenses equal to 7 percent of gross profits—1½ percent general management plus 1½ percent advertising. This left the dealer with a 2 percent profit before taxes. Builders, unfamiliar with prefabrication, would be reluctant to handle it at a time when they could be building conventional homes, which were in plentiful demand in the postwar years. A 2 percent profit was no incentive to overcome the risks of prefabrication.

Prefabricated Homes, the official journal of the Prefabricated Home Manufacturers Institute, editorialized in May 1946:

One serious obstacle remains, namely, the inadequate 10 percent mark-up for dealers in prefabricated houses which is permitted by OPA. *This may seem to be a small matter, but it is not small.* It discourages the entry of dealers into this industry and *dealers are essential to the sale of prefabricated houses through the natural private channels of distribution*, as called for in the Wyatt program." (*Ibid.*, p. 3).

Manufacturers at first pursued large tract developers to act as local dealers (see "Fourth Annual Prefab. Issue," *National Real Estate and Building Journal* LVII, No. 11 (November 1956), p. 26), but they shifted their emphasis to the development of small builders as dealers (*Building the City . . .* , p. 434). Although the home manufacturer could claim cost savings, large tract builders like Levitt could achieve their own economies of scale, bringing costs down to or lower than a manufacturer's cost. Given the questionable marketability of manufactured homes in the immediate postwar years, large tract developers were hesitant to risk their investment for a zero or negligible cost savings by using prefabricated homes. Small builders, however, could not be cost competitors with the large tract builders. Therefore, any cost savings passed on to them by the manufacturer could be used by the small builder to become competitive with larger builders. By 1964 the typical builder-dealer bought between 10–20 manufactured homes from the manufacturer.

20. Few prefabricators could look back upon the war years, as did James Price of National Homes Corporation, and state:

These war-time experiences developed to a high degree our Company's knowhow in industrialized housing. They were unforgettable lessons in mass production technology, telescoped into a relatively few years. They led to the highly successful way of building developed by National Homes in the postwar years (U.S. Congress, Joint Committee Subcommittee on Urban Affairs. *Hearings on Industrialized Housing*, 91st Cong., 1st Sess., July 1969, p. 278.)

National Homes Corporation, an exception, developed a dealership pattern of distribution during the war. Most dealers were established in the immediate vicinity of the Lafayette, Indiana, plant as market outlets to the general public. After the war, this distribution system was rapidly expanded to other communities.

21. Financing was both a sales and a working capital problem. Without mortgage commitment from local banks. the financing of manufactured housing was an acute problem.

Government-insured mortgages were one method of encouraging lending institutions to issue permanent mortgages on factory housing, the theory being that banks would extend permanent financing on manufactured homes if the mortgage was eligible for FHA–VA insurance. Although FHA–VA programs were not designed to fit the need of manufactured housing, the effect was to reduce some of the risks inherent in this type of production. First, prehabs had been billed as demountable, relocatable shelter. In case of default, what would prevent an owner from collapsing his home and moving it elsewhere, leaving the banker with a bad note? Second, in case of default and foreclosure, what was the probability of reselling the house to a public unreceptive to prefabricated housing? Third, the banker had to consider his relationship to local builders, general and specialty contractors, material suppliers and realtors who used his bank. What would be their reactions to prefabricated units built outside of the community without use of local labor and materials? Insured mortgages offered a means of avoiding the first two lending risks, but not the third.

Although the national intent of FHA–VA insured mortgages was to reduce localism and conservatism in lending practices, this was not the practice in some local FHA–VA offices back in the late 1940s and early 1950s. According to Walter Creese, who had served as city planning director of Louisville, Kentucky in the late 1940s (Interview, December 7, 1969), mortgage practices in the Midwest showed a marked preference for conventional construction. While conventional mortgages were insured up to 90 percent of value, prefabricated homes were insured only up to 70 percent of value. On a $15,000 home, minimum down payment on the conventional home would be $1,500, while that on a prefab would be $4,500, a distinct advantage to conventional construction.

Yet banks were slow to take up the prefabricated home. Because banks considered the prefabricated housing package as chattel—any tangible, movable property—few banks would extend permanent mortgage financing before the house was affixed to the site. Therefore, either the dealer or the manufacturer had to carry the financing of the housing package in the form of working capital. Most dealers were small operators and could not produce equity financing sufficient to cover several units, and few manufacturers had the financial capability to extend so much credit (see Kelly, *op. cit.*, pp. 92–94).

According to Thomas' *Register of American Manufacturers* (December 1947), of 126 prefabricators listed only 44.5 percent had capital ratings in excess of $1,000,000 (*ibid.*, p. 158). If a manufacturer sold 250 homes at

$4,000 each and he were to carry the burden of financing up to the time of on-site erection, he would require $1,000,000 in working capital (*ibid.*, p. 163). Thus, working capital became an acute problem to this infant industry.

In 1947, the government attempted to ease this burden by offering federal insurance on working capital (section 609 of the National Housing Act as amended in 1947). The insurance covered up to 90 percent of the cost of goods sold, excluding profits, but it was only usable where banks held permanent take-out commitments on the homes. Because of a generally negative image of prefabrication, banks were hesitant to issue advanced commitments (*ibid.*, p. 166), making it difficult to obtain take-out commitments and thereby defeating the purpose of the act.

Some manufacturers attacked the financing problem by establishing acceptance corporations as financing vehicles for both the local dealer and final buyer. In the mid–1950s, 75 percent of 110 firms surveyed reported giving some form of financial assistance to dealers either through acceptance corporations or otherwise. Close to 62 percent of these manufacturers gave aid in purchasing land. By 1962, 33 percent of the firms interviewed by *House and Home* had some type of mortgage corporation ("Manufactured Houses," *House and Home* XXII, No. 5 (November 1962), p. 100). A company source of funding was also important, for many dealers who marketed the small urban and rural towns for small-town bankers were often conservative in lending practices ("Fifth Annual Special Report on Prefabrication," *National Real Estate and Building Journal* LXIII, No. 11 (November 1957) p. 44).

Use of a financial subsidiary greatly increased the growth potential of a home manufacturer by placing at his disposal sources of mortgage and construction financing, this combination often being synergistic. Because almost all permanent financing was FHA or VA insured, acceptance corporations could turn over portfolios by selling the insured mortgages on the secondary mortgage market. Thus, there was a stream of mortgage money into the acceptance corporation for the financing of new prefabricated homes. The success of National Homes Corporation's Acceptance Corporation was its continuous source of mortgage money for NHC homes. It accepted over $2.5 billion in FHA-VA mortgages and currently services a $780 million portfolio. Because of its size, NHAC could better negotiate FHA–VA commitments and sell these mortgages on the secondary market. In times of tight money, buyers of NHC homes were provided a source of financing not readily available elsewhere. Loans were not restricted to residential mortgages. The Commercial Loan Department, in 1968, made construction loans and mortgages totaling $8.6 million (Annual Report of National Homes Corporation, 1969).

22. See Kelly, *op. cit.*, p. 92; Hans Heineman, "The Mobilization of House-building for Mass-Production and Mass-Sales," *Prefabricated Homes* VI, No. 5 (April 1946), p. 32.

23. Konrad Wachsmann, "The Turning Point of Building" (New York: Reinhold, 1961).

24. Kelly, *op. cit.*, p. 338.
25. "That Lustron Affair: Its What Happens When Government Starts Handing Out 'Risk' Capital," *Fortune* XXXX, No. 5 November 1949), p. 94.
26. Kelly, *op. cit.*, p. 390; *That Lustron Affair. . . . , op. cit.*, p. 94.
27. *Ibid.*, p. 92.
28. *Ibid.*, p. 93.
29. The story begins with Carl Gunnard Strandlund, general manager of Chicago Vitreous Enamel Products Company, a producer of easy-to-clean procelain-enameled steel wall panels. The company built service stations from these panels for Standard Oil (Indiana). In 1946, he visited Wilson Wyatt, President Truman's Housing Expeditor, to interest him in the proposed industrialized system. Wyatt's enthusiasm was to be crucial to the Lustron dream. Wyatt arranged, through the War Assets Administration (the Veteran's Housing Act, Public Law 388, 79th Congress empowered the Housing Expeditor to sell or lease surplus war plants to housing prefabricators. (see Kelly, *op. cit.*, p. 159)) to lease the Curtiss-Wright aircraft plant in Columbus, Ohio to Lustron for $428,000 per year (see *That Lustron Affair. . .*, p. 92). Wyatt also introduced Strandlund to George Allen, then head of the Reconstruction Finance Corporation (RFC). Strandlund told Allen that $52,000,000 was needed to capitalize the Lustron effort. Allen reluctantly agreed to extend a RFC loan on the condition Strandlund raise $3,600,000 in equity. Hornblower and Weeks of Chicago was engaged to raise the required equity, but the firm sold only $840,000 in stock, primarily to material suppliers (*ibid.*, p. 93). Thus, the first attempt at a RFC loan failed to materialize.

    Strandlund, during this time, had built political support in the banking committees of both House and Senate for a loan program to prefabricators. The result was an amending of the RFC legislation in 1947 to allow issuance of up to $50,000,000 in loans to prefabricated housing manufacturers. About the same time, Allen resigned from RFC, thus eliminating one of the obstacles to the project.
30. *Ibid.*, p. 93; "Is Mass Production of Homes or Home Parts, the Answer to High Building Costs?" *Journal of Housing* XVIII, No. 1 (January 1961), p. 30.
31. "Lustron Under Study by RFC; Rumor Management Changes," *Journal of Housing*, VI, No. 11 (November 1949), p. 242.
32. "Foreclosure of Lustron Ordered, " *Journal of Housing* VII, No. 3, (March 1950), p. 51.
33. "Lustron's Tangled Affairs," *Journal of Housing* VII, No. 7, (July 1950), p. 237.
34. "Foreclosure of Lustron. . . , p. 83.
35. Kelly, *op. cit.*, p. 414; G.H. Dietz, N. Day Castle, and Burnham Kelly (ed.) *Design and the Production of Houses* (New York: McGraw–Hill Book Co. Inc., 1959), pp. 160–174.
36. *Ibid.*; "That Lustron Affiar . . . ," p. 94.
37. *Ibid.*
38. Carl Koch, "Component Design for the Urban Environment," *Building Research* VI, No. 1 (January–March, 1969), p. 13.

39. "Housing As a Process," *Architectural and Engineering News* X, No. 8 (August 1968), p. 20.

40. The war experience had not clearly demonstrated that prefabrication efforts resulted in substantial overall cost reductions. A British Housing Mission, having come over to the U.S. in 1944 to evaluate the American prefabrication experience, reported no appreciable savings.

   While we could find no evidence that factory production of entire houses or parts of houses during the war has effected a saving in cost as compared with site construction, we were assured that there should be a measurable saving once quantity production is in full swing. We heard this forecast made more particularly in respect of houses of steel frame construction with steel cladding. (See Ministry of Works, *Methods of Building in the U.S.A.* The Report of a Mission Appointed By the Minister of Works, (London: His Majesty's Stationary Office, 1944), p. 17).

   Another study, this one of 24 war housing projects, indicated savings in labor requirements. Standard panel construction commonly used during the war years (and after the war) resulted in only a 1.5 percent savings in total labor hours, whereas the most radical form, a stressed-skin panel technology, produced a 25 percent savings (see Alexander C. Findlay, "Construction of Prefabricated and Conventional War Housing Project," *Monthly Labor Review*, (November 1946), p. 726.)

41. Organized labor, not included among our five major problems, was often cited in popular literature as a deterrent to prefabrication. It was thought that unions would oppose prefabrication in order to preserve their jobs, yet the extent to which organized labor inhibited the development of prefabrication is not clear. In fact, unions were involved in prefabrication— the United Brotherhood of Carpenters and Joiners of America were early organizers of prefabrication plants. The United Automobile Workers Union were interested in prefabrication. In a 1946 report, UAW boosted efforts of prefabrication by stating:

   To keep . . . . costs down will require large-scale, scientific operations using modern building materials and mass-production techniques. . . . (See Heineman, *op. cit.*, p. 20.)

   At this time, construction jobs were plentiful, contributing to the Union's relatively unobstructive position on innovation. Although union resistance was highly visible in such cases as the Fort Wayne experiment, few prefabricators of this period found unions to be a major problem. Burnham Kelly concluded in 1951 that:

   Generally speaking, union efforts to restrict plant prefabrication have been minor in extent, and there is evidence that they are becoming steadily even less important. (See Kelly, *op. cit.*, p. 155).

This position was confirmed by the home manufacturers surveyed in 1955, when they listed the opposition of unions as their 12th out of 13 possible problem areas (see McConnell, *op. cit.*, p. 27).

The attack on organized labor has continued to the present time, labor being criticized for imposing restrictive work practices that prevent the use of prefabricated components and impeded the introduction of innovative techniques. Critics often point to the Philadelphia Door Case (*National Woodwork Manufacturers Assocition* v. *NLRB* 386 U.S. 612 [1967]), in which the Supreme Court upheld the right of unions to negotiate restrictive work practices when work preservation is the issue. Less frequently cited are the National Labor Relations Board decisions that soften the Supreme Court ruling by giving strict interpretation of what constitutes work preservation.

Again, as in the 1940s, the degree of union opposition is difficult to determine. The Douglas Commission in its report *Building of the American City*, chastised unions for restrictive practices, citing numerous incidents of obstruction by the United Association of Journeymen and Apprentices of the Plumbing and Pipe Fitting Industry, the United Brotherhood of Carpenters and Joiners of America, the International Brotherhood of Electrical Workers, and the Brotherhood of Painters, Decorators and Paperhangers (see *Building the American City*, pp. 465–475). Although the Commission reported that unions have participated in "breakthroughs involving new products and methods" (*ibid.*, p. 465), the bulk of the reporting illustrated the variety of restrictive practices by the construction trade unions.

Union resistance is not as negative as it appears. Recent agreements between producers and unions show signs of union accommodation to prefabrication. The Sterling Homes Agreement was signed by the carpenters, who agreed to provide competent labor "whenever and where ever needed to erect and complete Sterling housing units" (see "Union Backs Instant Housing," *Engineering News Record* CLXXXII, No. 26 (June 26 1969), p. 22). Carpenters had traditionally organized prefabrication. Sterling, in turn, agreed not to subcontract on-site work falling under the carpenters' jurisdiction. In addition, Sterling would recognize the jurisdiction of other building trade unions. More recently, an agreement involving the carpenters, electricians, and plumbers was concluded with VTR, Inc., a New York producer of modular housing. Part of the agreement established procedures for resolving jurisdictional disputes between the signing unions (see *New York Times*, November 7, 1969).

42. McConnell, *op, cit.,* p. 31.
43. Interview with John Bemis, President, Acorn Homes, November 25, 1970.
44. Statistics are not available as to the frequency of home manufacturers' being their own developers. National Homes Corporation began to switch over to development as it entered the low-rise cluster development business. For their single-family business, however, they have stayed with dealers. A modification of this situation is the Levitt and Sons modular housing operation. The plant was, in part, justified as a means of supplying the conventional Levitt projects with housing units. (Interview with Charles F.

Biederman, President of Levitt Building Systems Inc., November 4, 1971 and Alan Dibble, Marketing Director, National Homes Corporation, August 10, 1969.)

45. *Department of Housing and Urban Development—Trends* (Washington, D.C.: Department of Housing and Urban Development, October 1970), p. 2.

46. *Ibid.*, p. 7.

47. U.S. Senate, Joint Economic Committee, *Hearings before the Subcommittee on Urban Affairs of the Joint Economic Committee*, 91st Congress 1st session, Part 1, July 9, 1969, p. 4.

48. U.S. Senate, Committee on Appropriations, *Department of Housing and Urban Development, Space, Science, Veterans, and Certain Other Independent Agencies Appropriations, Fiscal Year 1975.* Part 2. 93rd Congress, 2nd Session, p. 136.

Chapter 3

1. This and the subsequent quotation are from Rhyne, Charles, *The Survey of the Law of Building Codes,* (American Institute of Architects, Washinton, D.C., pp. 7–8.

2. Williams, Young and Fischetti, *Survey of the Administration of Construction Codes in Selected Metropolitan Areas* (National Commission on Urban Problems Background Paper No. 29, 1968) p. 3. Ignored in large part is the home buyer, the consumer, who has little opportunity to influence the process of building regulation.

3. U.S. Department of Housing and Urban Development, *Guide Criteria for the Design and Evaluation of Operation Breakthrough Housing Systems*, Section A.4.1 (November 1, 1970).

4. Sanderson, Richard L. *Codes and Codes Administration* (Chicago: Building Officials Conference of America Inc., 1969) pp. 101–102.

5. 1970 Survey of Building Departments, conducted by Charles G. Field and Francis T. Ventre.

6. See Charles G. Field and Francis T. Ventre, "Local Regulation of Building Agencies, Codes and Politics," in *Municipal Year Book 1971* (Washington, D.C.: International City Management Association 1971), p. 142.

7. Manvel, Alan D. *Local Land and Building Regulations* Report No. 6 to the National Commission on Urban Problems (Washington, D.C.: U.S. Government Printing Office, 1968), p. 34.

Chapter 4

1. See Advisory Commission on Intergovernmental Relations, *Building Codes: A Program for Intergovernmental Reform*. (Washington, D.C.: Advisory Commission on Intergovernmental Relations, 1966.

2. Manvel, Alan D., *Local Land and Building Regulations* Report No. 6 for the National Commission on Urban Problems (Washington, D.C.: U.S. Government Printing Office, 1968).

3. U.S. Department of Housing and Urban Development research and technology demonstration—Operation Breakthrough—involved 22 different system builders operating in ten prototype sites (1969–73).

4. 1972 HUD Statistical Yearbook (U.S. Department of Housing and Urban Development) p. 338.

5. *Ibid.*, p. 357.

6. Sherman J. Maisel, *Housebuilding in Transition* (Berkeley: The University of California Press, 1953), p. 249.

7. Stockfrisch, J.A., *An Investigation of the Opportunities for Reducing the Cost of Federally Subsidized Housing for Lower Income Families* (Springfield, Virginia: Clearinghouse for Federal Scientific and Technical Information, September 1968)

8. Burns, Leland S. and Frank G. Mittelbach, "Efficiency in the Housing Industry" in *The Report of the President's Committee on Urban Housing: Technical Studies, Volume II* (Washington, D.C.: U.S. Government Printing Office, 1969).

9. Stockfrisch, *op. cit.,* p. 8.

10. Burns, *op, cit.*, p. 102.

11. The finding of the survey are reported in *Building the American City*, National Commission on Urban Problems (Washington, D.C.: U.S. Government Printing Office) p. 262.

12. *Ibid.*, pp. 271–272.

13. Copy of report submitted to the Home Manufacturer Association in response to 1967–68 study for the National Commission on Urban Problems. Information obtained from the files of the Home Building Corporation

14. National Association of Home Builders Research Foundation *Optimum Value Engineered Building System* (NAHB Research Foundation: Rockville, Maryland, 1972). Report done for the U.S. Department of Housing and Urban Development for Operation Breakthrough. NAHB Research Foundation built and tested this unit. Thus costs are specific to Montgomery County, Maryland, where the test took place.

15. U.S. Department of Housing and Urban Development *Statistical Yearbook 1972* (Washington, D.C.: U.S. Government Printing Office, 1974), p. 319, Table 343.

16. The history of the off-site preassembled combination electrical wiring harness is not provided because very few officials reported this code item as their most difficult item to adopt. That accounts for its number 10 ranking in Column C of Table 4–4.

17. Inadvertently, one of the 14 code items was deleted from the Home Manufacturer survey, that dealing with the spacing of 2″ by 3″ studs in non-load-bearing interior partitions.

18. In follow-up interviews, manufacturers indicated they understood the questions.

19. Source: 1970 Survey of Home Manufacturers. Eighty-two percent of

modular producers compared to 48 percent of panel producers reported
major or moderate problems in attaining local building code approval. $N =$
57 and 122 respectively.

20. See *The American Plumbing Engineer* (September 1970) p. 57.
21. *Ibid.*
22. Ibid., p. 58.

Chapter 5

1. *See* Appendix D, "State Building Regulatory Programs and Manufactured
   Buildings—A Summary" (Excerpts), NBS, 1974.
2. *E.g., North Carolina:* General Statutes of North Carolina, Secs. 143–136–
   143.2 (as amended 1971); *Virginia:* Code of Virginia, Secs. 36–70–85
   (as amended 1971); *Massachusetts:* General Laws Secs. 23B–16–22
   (adopted 1972); *Indiana:* Burns' Indiana Statutes Ann., Secs. 20–435–469
   (as amended 1971).
3. Code of Laws of South Carolina, Sec. 36–551 (Adopted 1970).
4. West Virginia Code, Sec. 8–24–50a (Adopted 1971).
5. Oklahoma Statutes Ann., Sec. 63–1084 (Adopted 1971).
6. *See, e.g., Slaughter House Cases* 83 U.S. (16 Wall) 36 (1873); Rhyne,
   supra note 24, at 7–9, 34–35.
7. *See, e.g., City of Little Rock* v *Raines*, 241 Ark. 1071, 411 S.W.2d (1967);
   Bennett v. *City of Hope*, 204 Ark. 147, 161 S.W.2d 186 (1942); *Kaveny* v.
   Board of Comm'rs, 71 N.J. Super. 244, 176 A.2d 802 (App. Div. 1962).
8. *See, e.g., People* v. *Sarnoff*, 302 Mich. 266, 4 N.W.2d 544 (1942).
9. *See, e.g., Loew* v. *Falsey*, 144 Conn. 67, 127 A.2d 67 (1956); State *ex rel.
   Gold* v. *Usher*, 138 Conn. 323, 84 A.2d 276 (1951).
10. *See, e.g., State* v. *Eckhardt*, 322 S.W.2d 903 (Mo. Sup. Ct. 1959); *Hays* v.
    Poplar Bluff, 263 Mo. 615, 173 S.W. 676 (1915); *State* v. *Kasten*, 382 S.W.
    2d 714 (Mo. Ct. App. 1964).
11. *See* Rhyne, *supra*, at 9–12.
12. *See, e.g., Camara* v. *Municipal Court* 387 U.S. 523 (1967).
13. Rivkin, Steven R. "Courting Change: Using Litigation to Reform Local
    Building Codes" *Rutgers Law Review* Vol. 26 (Summer 1973) pp. 774–802,
14. Although a review of reported cases reveals that the application of antitrust
    principles in this context would be novel, the operation of these principles
    to the building materials field is long established. *See, e.g., American
    Column & Lumber Co.* v. *United States,* 257 U.S. 377 (1921) (price fixing).
    Recently, the Department of Justice secured a consent order against the
    architectural profession for its "ethical" practices in discouraging competi-
    tive bidding. *United States* v. *American Inst. of Archts.*, 1972 *Trade Cas.*
    ¶73,981, *modified*, 1972 *Trade Cas.* ¶74,074 (D.D.C.)
15. *See, e.g., Northern Pac. R.R.* v. *United States,* 356 U.S. 1, 5 (1958).
16. A 1968 statistical sampling of building code provisions revealed that more
    than 20 percent of all governments with building codes, including model

codes, prohibit the following innovative and potentially cost-saving building methods and materials: plastic pipe in drainage system; 2″ by 4″ studs 24″ on center in non-load-bearing interior partitions; preassembled electrical wiring harness at electrical service entrance; preassembled combination drain, waste, and vent plumbing bathroom systems; 2″ by 3″ studs in non-load-bearing interior partitions; party walls without continuous air space; single top and bottom plates in non-load-bearing interior partitions; wood frame exterior for multifamily structures three stories or less; and ½″ sheathing in lieu of corner bracing in wood frame construction. Mannel, Local Land and Building Regulation 13–19 (1968) (Douglas Commission, Research Rep. No. 6). While these prohibitions may have eased in the ensuing years (more current figures have not been gathered) additional meritorious technology may also be assumed to have joined the prohibited list.

17. *Structural Laminates, Inc.* v. *Douglas Fir Plywood Association,* 261 F. Supp. 154 (D. Ore. 1966), *aff'd,* 399 F.2d 155 (9th Cir. 1968). The court also stated that a mistake made by the Association in formulating or maintaining standards would not be subject to antitrust violations. *Id.* at 159. *United States* v. *Johns-Manville Corp.,* 1967 *Trade Cas.* ¶72,184 (E.D. Pa., July 13, 1967).

18. *See, e.g.,* N.J. Const. art. I, Sec. 5.

19. *Boise Cascade Corp.* v. *Gwinnett County,* 272 F.Supp. 847 (N.D. Ga. 1967); *Kingsberry Homes Corp.* v. *Gwinett County,* 248 F.Supp. 765 (N.D. Ga. 1965).

20. 272 F.Supp. at 848.

21. *Ibid.* at 849.

22. *Ibid.* at 849–50.

23. *Ibid.* at 850 n.9.

24. *Ibid.*

25. By contrast, but still within the contours of a willingness to sift evidence to determine reasonableness, note that the Court of Appeals for the Fifth Circuit upheld the denial of an injunction in a rezoning case where the district court had found "there is no evidence here that will authorize a finding that the rezoning ordinance was arbitrary or unreasonable or that it had no substantial relation to the public welfare." *Mestre* v. *City of Atlanta.* 255 F.2d 401, 403 n. 1 (5th Cir. 1958).

26. U.S. Const. Art. I, §8.

27. 42 U.S.C. Sec. 1441 (1970).

28. Givens, *The Commerce Clause and the Interdependent Economy,* 53 A.B.A.J. 719, 720 (1967)

29. *E.g.,* 12 U.S.C. Secs. 1701z-1, 1701z-2 (1970), conferring sundry powers upon the Secretary of Housing and Urban Development to develop and promote new housing construction techniques, materials, and methods.

30. *E.g., Pike* v. *Bruce Church, Inc.,* 397 U.S. 137 (1970).

31. 340 U.S. 349, 354 (1951).

32. *Southern Pacific Co.* v. *Arizona,* 325 U.S. 761 (1945).

33. In the Fair Labor Standards Act of 1938, standards promulgated by the
     Administrator of the Wage and Hour Division of the Department of Labor
     are applicable to all employees "engaged in commerce or in the production
     of goods for commerce" (29 U.S.C. §206) with exemptions defined by
     statute with respect to the dollar volume of goods sold in intrastate com-
     merce and by regulation of the Administrator (29 U.S.C. §213). In the
     Meat Inspection Act, 21 U.S.C. §§601–695, all meat slaughtering establish-
     ments whose products "are to be used in commerce" are affected (21
     U.S.C. §603) but regulated products are flatly defined to be those "either
     in interstate or foreign commerce or substantially effect such commerce"
     (21 U.S.C. §602), e.g., by competing with those products that are in com-
     merce. Similarly, in the Metal and Nonmetallic Mine Safety Act, 30 U.S.C.
     §§721–740, "Each mine the products of which regularly enter commerce,
     or the operations of which affect commerce" are covered, although the
     Secretary of Agriculture may by published rules decline to exercise au-
     thority with respect to a class of mines where the effect "is not sufficiently
     substantial to warrant the exercise of jurisdiction . . . and the record of
     injuries and accidents . . . warrants such a declination of jurisdiction."
     30 U.S.C. §722 (a) and (b).
34. 42 U.S.C. Secs. 4901–4918, 49 U.S.C. Sec. 1431. (1972) See Section
     2 (b)
35. *Ibid,* Sec. 6(e).
36. For example, dating from the early years of the twentieth century, a key
     federal statute has rested on the device of a factually informed "statutory
     presumption" of evidence to equate mere possession of heroin to know-
     ledge of the substance's illegal importation (21 U.S.C. Sec. 174, *repealed*
     84 Stat. 1291 (1970)) as the essential basis for federal authority. See
     Turner v. *U.S.,* 396 U.S. 398 (1970).
37. 21 U.S.C. Sec. 844(a).
38. Nonetheless, limited mandates displacing local codes have long existed,
     typified by the provisions of the Lanham Public War Housing Act, 42
     U.S.C. Sec. 1521(b), which displaced state regulatory powers for certain
     federally-owned or leased lands used for defense housing.
39. For example, in *Wickard* v. *Filburn* (1942) (317 U.S. 111 (1942)) federal
     crop controls were upheld as they apply to produce grown and consumed
     entirely on the farm, inasmuch as they cast an appreciable shadow on
     product markets, and in *U.S.* v. *South-Eastern Underwriters Assn.* (1944)
     (322 U.S. 533 (1944)) the business of writing insurance on property—never
     considered previously to be "commerce" between the states—was brought
     under the standards of the Sherman Antitrust Act. And later cases, espe-
     cially those identified with the field of civil rights, go quite far to affirm
     federal powers every bit relevant to the field of building regulation. At this
     point, two broad principles underlying the sweep of federal power over
     conflicting state interests should be kept in mind. The first is the unambig-
     uous federal power under the Constitution through the "necessary and
     proper" clause (Art. 1, Sec. 8, cl. 18) and the interstate commerce clause to
     legislate over domestic economic activity, displacing state authority. As the

Supreme Court said in "The Shreveport case," *Houston & Texas Ry.* v. *U.S.*, 234 U.S. 342 (1913):

. . . It is unnecessary to repeat what has frequently been said by this court with respect to the complete and paramount character of the power confided to Congress to regulate commerce among the several States. It is of the essence of this power that, where it exists, it dominates. Interstate trade was not left to be destroyed or impeded by the rivalries of local governments. The purpose was to make impossible the recurrence of the evils which had overwhelmed the Confederation and to provide the necessary basis of national unity by insuring 'uniformity of regulation against conflicting and discriminating state legislation.' By virtue of the comprehensive terms of the grant, the authority of Congress is at all times adequate to meet the varying exigencies that arise and to protect the national interest by securing the freedom of interstate commercial intercourse from local control. At 350-1.

In addition, the Supremacy Clause of the Constitution (Article 6) imposes a reciprocal obligation on the states to yield to federal power, as follows:

This Constitution, and the laws of the United States which shall be made in Pursuance thereof; and all Treaties made, or which shall be made, under the Authority of the United States, shall be the supreme Law of the Land; and the Judges in every State shall be bound thereby, anything in the Constitution or Laws of any State to the Contrary notwithstanding.

40. 379 U.S. 241 (1964).
41. 379 U.S. 294 (1964).
42. 379 U.S. at 303-4.
43. The "rational basis" test was given a very wide reading by the Supreme Court in *Maryland* v. *Wirtz*, where a 1961 amendment to the Fair Labor Standards Act was upheld extending coverage under wage and hour standards from employees individually engaged in production for commerce to any "enterprise" engaged in commerce (regardless of the function of the particular employee). The extension of the original act from individual employees to *all* employees of a particular employer was fought as exceeding federal powers, but the court rejected that argument, finding a rational basis in two respects (lower wages in part of an enterprise and labor disruption through strikes both affect interstate competition). 392 U.S. 183 (1968).
44. The term "enterprise engaged in commerce or in the production of goods for commerce" was defined by 29 U.S.C. S203(s) to mean "an enterprise which has employees engaged in commerce or in the production of goods for commerce, including employees handling, selling, or otherwise working on goods that have been moved in or produced for commerce by any person, and which—[falls in any one of four listed categories]."

45. Even a country swimming-hole, six miles from the nearest state or inter-
    state road, where there was no special showing that any patrons had come
    interstate, was held within the Civil Rights Act of 1964, consistent with
    the interstate commerce clause, by the Supreme Court in *Daniel* v. *Paul,*
    (395 U.S. 298 (1969)) where the operators used 15 paddle boats leased
    from out-of-state. Again, the volume of commerce need not be great, once
    it is shown (or inferred) that the subject of regulation is within a consti-
    tutionally permitted class.

    In two criminal cases, *Perez* v. *United States* (402 U.S. 146 (1971))
    (loan-sharking) and *U.S.* v. *Dawson* 467 F.2d 668 (C.A. 8, 1972). (storage
    of explosive materials), federal courts have upheld federal criminal statutes
    involving the most localized subjects. Loan-sharking was revealed in Con-
    gressional hearings to be tied to the nationwide operations of the Mafia,
    and possession of explosives (without an explicit legislative finding to that
    effect) was seen by the Court as tied to political terrorism. Once again,
    these cases stand for judicial deference to the ability of Congress to relate
    local activities to national problems and legislate to control them.

46. 93 Sup. Ct. 1854 (1973).

Chapter 6

1. *New York Times* "Rights Unit Says U.S. Fails to Enforce Fair Housing"
   August 13, 1974, p. 1
2. "Housing and Community Development Act of 1974, House of Representatives, 93d Congress, 2d Session Report No. 93-1279. See Section
   401 (g), p. 62.

Bibliography

Public Documents

U.S. Congress, Joint Economic Committee, Subcommittee on Urban Affairs. *Hearings July 9, 23–24 on Industrialized Housing.* 91st Cong., 1st Sess., 1969.

U.S. Congress, Joint Committee on Housing. *High Cost of Housing.* 88th Cong., 1st. Sess., 1948.

U.S. Congress, Joint Economic Committee, Subcommittee on Economic Progress. *Public Facility Requirements Over the Next Decade: Hearings December 3 and 4, 1968.* 90th Cong., 2d Sess., 1968.

U.S. Congress, Joint Committee on Housing. *Study and Investigation of Housing.* 87th Cong., 2d Sess., 1947.

U.S. Congress, Joint Committee on Atomic Energy, *Understanding the National Energy Dilemma.* Washington D.C.: U.S. Government Printing Office, 1973.

U.S. Department of Housing and Urban Development, *Housing in the Seventies.* Washington D.C.: U.S. Department of Housing and Urban Development, 1973.

U.S. Senate, Committee on Banking and Currency. *Housing and Urban Development Legislation of 1969: Hearings before the Subcommittee on Housing and Urban Affairs.* 91st Cong., 1st Sess., 1969.

U.S. Senate, Select Committee on Reconstruction and Production. *Reconstruction and Production Senate Report No. 829.* 66th Cong., 3d Sess., March 2, 1921.

U.S. Senate, Committee on Banking and Currency. *Study of International Housing.* 88th Cong., 1st Sess., 1963.

Books

Adrian, Charles R. *Governing Urban America.* 2d ed. New York: McGraw–Hill Book Co., 1961.

Bain, Joe S. *Industrial Organization.* New York, New York: John Wiley & Sons, Inc., 1968.

Bauer, Raymond A., Pool, Ithiel de Sola, and Dexter, Lewis Anthony. *American Business and Public Policy The Politics of Foreign Trade.* New York: Atherton Press, 1963.

Baumol, William J. *Economic Theory and Operations Analysis.* 2d ed. Englewood Cliffs, New Jersey: Prentice–Hall, Inc., 1965.

203

Bemis, Albert Farwell. *The Evolving House: The Economics of Shelter*. Cambridge, Massachusetts: Technology Press, 1934.

Bemis, Albert Farwell. *The Evolving House: Rational Design*. Cambridge, Massachusetts: Technology Press, 1936.

Beyer, Glenn H. and Partner, James W. *Marketing Handbook for the Prefabricated Housing Industry*. Ithaca, New York: Cornell University, Housing Research Center, 1955.

—— and Yantes, Theodore R. *Practices and Precepts of Marketing Prefabricated Houses*. Washington, D.C.: U.S. Housing and Home Finance Agency, 1952.

Blalock, Hurbert M., Jr. *Causal Inferences in Nonexperimental Research*. Chapel Hill: University of North Carolina Press, 1964.

——. *Social Statistics*. New York: McGraw–Hill Book Co., 1960.

Bruce, Alfred and Sandbank, Harold. *A History of Prefabrication*. New York: John B. Pierce Foundation, 1943.

Carreiro, John. *The New Building Block*. Ithaca, New York: Cornell University Center for Housing and Environmental Studies, 1968.

Colean, Miles Lanier, *Your Building Code. What the Local Building Code Is, How it Works, and How it Can Be Made More Effective*. New York: National Committee on Housing, 1946.

Demarest, William. *Building Codes: Product Approvals*. New Haven, Connecticut: Ludlow and Bookman, 1964.

Drury, Margaret J. *Mobile Homes–The Unrecognized Revolution in American Housing*. Ithaca, New York: Cornell University, Department of Housing and Design, 1967.

Grebler, Leo. *The Production of New Housing*. New York: Social Science Research Council, 1950.

Henderson, James M. and Quandt, Richard E. *Microeconomic Theory*. New York: McGraw–Hill Book Co., 1958.

Herzog, John P. *The Dynamics of Large-Scale Housebuilding*. Berkeley: Real Estate Research Program, Institute of Business and Economic Research, University of California, Berkeley, 1963.

Kelly, Burnham. *The Prefabrication of Houses*. New York: Wiley, 1951.

——. *Design and the Production of Houses*. New York: McGraw–Hill Book Co., 1959.

Lochard, Duane. *The Politics of State and Local Government*. New York: The Macmillan Company, 1963.

Maisel, Sherman J. *Housebuilding in Transition*. Berkeley: The University of California Press, 1953.

Mansfield, Edwin. *The Economics of Technological Change*. New York: Norton & Company, Inc., 1968.

Merritt, F.S. (ed.). *Building Construction Handbook*. 2d ed. New York: McGraw–Hill Book Co., 1965.

Olson, Mancur, Jr. *The Logic of Collective Action*. Cambridge: Harvard University Press, 1965.

Owen, C.L. *Design and the Industrialized House*. Chicago: Institute of Design Press, 1965.

Rhyne, Charles S. *Survey of the Law of Building Codes*. Washington, D.C. American Institute of Architects and the National Association of Home Builders, 1960.

Robinson, E.A.G. *The Structure of Competitive Industry*. New York: Pitman, 1948.

Samuelson, Paul. *Economics: An Introductory Analysis*. New York: McGraw-Hill Book Co., 1951.

Sanderson, Richard L. *Codes and Code Administration*. Chicago: Building Officials Conference of America, Inc., 1969.

Schattschneider, E.E. *Politics, Pressures and the Tariff*. New York: Prentice-Hall, Inc., 1935.

Schon, Donald A. *Technology and Change*. New York: Delacorte, 1967.

Smith, Wallace F. *Housing The Social and Economic Elements*. Berkeley, California: University of California Press, 1970.

Sunichrast, Michael and Frankel, Sara A. *Profile of the Builder and His Industry*. Washington, D.C.: National Association of Home Builders, 1970.

U.S. Chamber of Commerce. *Building Codes and Construction Progress*. Washington, D.C.: Chamber of Commerce of the United States. 1951.

Wachsmann, Konrad. *The Turning Point of Building*. New York: Reinhold, 1961.

Williamson, Oliver E. *Innovation and Market Structure*. Santa Monica, California: Rand Corporation, 1964.

Articles and Periodicals

Allen, Frederick H. "New Way to Solve Industrial Housing Problem," *American City*, LXII, No. 12, (December 1947), p. 104.

Allen, H. William, III. "Restrictions of Building Permits as a Means for Controlling the Rate of Community Development," *Urban Law Annual*, II, (1969), pp. 184–189.

American City. "Building-Code Revision Urged," LIII, No. 4, (April 1938), pp. 78, 83.

———. "Cities Need Building-Code Revision for Low-Cost Housing," LV, No. 3, (March 1940), pp. 105, 107.

Architectural and Engineering News. "Building Codes," IX, No. 4, (April 1967), pp. 27–75.

———. "Housing As A Process," X, No. 8, (August 1968), pp. 18–33.

———. "Technology and the House, 1964," VI, No. 2, (February 1964), pp. 22–27.

Architectural Forum. "Prefabrication Gets Its Chance as FWA Allocates $153 Million for Demountable Houses, Offers to Buy Them F.O.B. for Assembly by Others," LXXVI, (February 1942), pp. 81–89.

———. "Prefabrication's Ups and Downs," LXXIV, No. 3, (March 1941), pp. 174–178.

Bosselman, Fred. "The Legal Framework of Building and Housing Ordinances," *The Building Official*, IV, No. 3, (March 1970), pp. 10–13.

"Building Codes, Housing Codes and the Conservation of Chicago's Housing Supply," *University of Chicago Law Review*, 31:180 (Autumn 1963).

Business Week. "Assembly Lines Bring Fresh Hopes for Housing," (October 26, 1968), pp. 82–86.

——. "Packaged Buildings Go Up Fast," (April 9, 1966), pp. 47–48.

——. "Prefab Housing Looks for a Home in U.S.," (March 1, 1969), pp. 44–46.

——. "Prefabs' Uphill Fight," (July 4, 1964), pp. 74–77.

Chase, Stuart. "Building Code Needed," *National Civic Review*, XLVII, No. 2, (February 1958), pp. 62–65.

Clayton, Kenneth. "The Nature of Industrialization," *Architect and Building News*, CCXXIX, No. 18, (May 4, 1960), pp. 789–792.

Davison, Robert L. "Technological Potentials in Home Construction," *Law and Contemporary Problems*, XII, No. 1, (Winter 1947), pp. 17–19.

Dietz, Albert G.H. "Current Patterns of Fabrication," in Kelly, Burnham *The Design and the Production of Houses*, New York: McGraw-Hill Book Co., 1959, pp. 137–187.

Divorkin, Philip. "Open System U.S.A.," *Architectural and Engineering News*, IX, No. 6, (June 1967), pp. 70–73.

Drewry, Austin. "Iinternal and External Problems of the Manufactured Home Industry," *Prefabricated Homes*, VIII, No. 4, (July-August, 1947), pp. 17, 25–28.

Engineering News Record. "Precast Slabs Keep Job Within a Budget," CLXXXIII, No. 17, (October 23, 1969), pp. 26–27.

——. "U.S. Looks to Europe in Systems Building Drive," (October 30, 1969), pp. 62–63.

——. "Union Backs Instant Housing," CLXXXII, No. 26, (June 26, 1969), pp. 21–23.

Field, Charles G. and Francis T. Ventre "Local Regulation of Building Agencies, Codes and Politics," in *Municipal Yearbook 1971*, Washington D.C.: International City Management Association.

Findlay, Alexander C. "Construction of Prefabricated and Conventional War Housing Projects," *Monthly Labor Review*, LXIII, No. 5, (November 1946), pp. 721–732.

Fortune. "F.O.B.: Fifty Houses a Day," XLI, No. 4, (April 1950), pp. 94–97, 177.

——. "That Lustron Affair: It's What Happens When Government Starts Handing Out "Risk" Capital," XL, No. 5, (November 1949), pp. 92–94.

——. "The Promise of the Shortage," XXXIII, No. 4, (April 1946), pp. 101–103, 126–131.

——. "The Strange Hold of the Building Trades on Construction," (December 1968).

Gilmore, C.P. "Money-Wasting Codes: One Model Set of Performance Standards Deemed Essential If Housing Needs of This Era Are to Be Met," *National Civic Review*, LVI, (November 1967), pp. 572–575.

Guy, Rolland B. "Industrialized Building," *Professional Builder*, (January 1968), pp. 44–47.

Harrell, Raymon H. "Mechanical Utility Cores," *Building Research*, I, No. 2, (March–April 1964), pp. 33–35.

Heineman, Hans. "The Mobilization of Housebuildings for Mass-production and Mass-sales," *Prefabricated Homes*, VI, No. 5, (April 1946), pp. 19–20, 31, 32.

Hooper, William. "Innovation in Housing: Pipe Dreams or Practical Reality?," *Technology Review*, LXX, No. 3, (January 1968), pp. 25–29.

House and Home. "Factory in the Field," XXI, No. 6, (June 1962), pp. 118–129.

——. "House and Home Round Table Ponders $1 Billion-a-year Cost of too Many Codes, Proposes a Simple 6-Point Program to Speed Reform," XIV, No. 1, (July 1958), pp. 112–119.

——. "Housing Technology: It's Time for a Realistic Appraisal," (December 1965), pp. 91–109.

——. [Issue on Prefabrication], X, No. 6, (December 1956).

——. "John Long's Researchers Are Spending $100,000 to Find New Ways to Build for Less," (March 1961), p. 131.

——. "Manufactured Houses," XXII, No. 5, (November 1962), pp. 96–115.

——. "Prefabber's New Stab at the Low-Income Market—Is This the Right House at the Wrong Time?," (April 1966), pp. 148–149.

——. "Shipping Costs Limit the Size of the Package, The Degree to Which It's Finished and The Distance It Can Go," (December 1966), p. 76.

——. "The Big Change in Today's Prefab Market," (December 1964), pp. 69–81.

——. "The Industrial Revolution on Housing is Inevitable in the 1960s; Standardization of Dimensions and Codes is the Next Essential Step," XVII, No. 1, (January 1960), p. 153.

——. "This $3,500 Investment Is Paying Back More Than $5,000," (April 1964), p. 140.

——. "What Does Prefabrication Mean to Everybody in the Building Industry?," VI, No. 6, (December 1954).

——. "What's Stopping Us From Building Low-Income Housing in Our Cities," (October 1967), p. 85.

——. "Who's to Blame for the Building Code Mess?," XXV, No. 4, (April 1964), pp. 146–150.

——. "6th Annual Report on Prefabrication," XIV, No. 6, (December 1958), pp. 86–111.

Johnson, R.J. "NAHM Research House and Code Problems," *Journal of Home-building*, XI, No. 6, (June 1957), p. 87.

Journal of Homebuilding. "Codes: Why a Building Code?," XII, No. 9, (September 1958), pp. 5–28.

——. "NAHB Research House Features New Products," XI, No. 4 (April 1957), pp. 133–137.

——. "Prefabrication," XX, No. 3, (March 1966), p. 58.

Journal of Housing. "Foreclosure of Lustron Ordered," VII, No. 3, (March 1950), p. 83.

——. "Is 'Mass Production' of Homes, or Home Parts, the Answer to High Building Costs?," XVIII, No. 1, (January 1961), pp. 24, 28–30, 43.

——. "Lustron's Tangled Affairs Stalled Awaiting Inquiry," VII, No. 7, (July 1950), p. 237.

——. "Lustron Under Study by RFC; Rumor Management Changes," VI, No. 11, (November 1949), p. 424.

——. "Pre-Fab: What's in it for U.S. Development Programs?," XXIII, No. 8, (August–September 1966), pp. 435–447.

——. "Some New Approaches to Industrialized Buildings," XXIV, (August 1967), pp. 431.

Kelly, Burnham, "The Future Builders," in Kelly, Burnham Design and the Production of Houses, New York: McGraw–Hill Book Co., 1959.

Klitzke, R.A. "Roman Building Ordinances Relating to Fire Prevention," American Journal of Legal History, III, (April 1959), p. 173.

Koch, Carl. "Component Design for the Urban Environment," Building Research, VI, No. 1, (January–March 1969), pp. 11–15.

Kuper, Irvin. "Getting Uniform Building Codes," National Real Estate and Building Journal, LVII, No. 11, (November 1956), pp. 46–48.

Loevinger, A. "Handicraft & Handcuffs: The Analomy of an Industry," Law and Contemporary Problems, XII, (1947), pp. 47–75.

MacGiehan Neal. "The Myth of the Low-Priced House," Prefabricated Homes, IV, No. 3, (January 1945), pp. 12–13, 17, 21.

McConnell, Campbell R. "Prefabricated Housing: Problems and Prospects," Current Economic Comment, XVIII, No. 2, (May 1956), pp. 23–41.

"Municipal Power to Regulate Building Construction and Land Use by Other State Agencies," Minnesota Law Review, XLIX, (December 1964), p. 284.

Myrdal, Gunnar. "Industrialized Housing: Have We overlooked True Value?," Journal of Housing, XXIV, No. 8, (September 1967), pp. 427–439.

National Real Estate and Building Journal. "Fifth Annual Special Report on Prefabrication," LXIII, No. 11, (November 1957).

——. "Fourth Annual Prefab Issue," LVII, No. 11, (November 1956).

——. "Going Up! Prefabs Break the Price Barrier," LVI, No. 10, (October 1955), pp. 40–43.

——. "Prefabbers Expect to Claim 10% of '56 Housing," LVII, No. 5, (May 1956), pp. 32–33, 37.

Pellish, David. "A New Approach to Codes," American Institute of Architecture Journal, (January 1969).

Practical Builder. "The Growing Battle with Codes and Building Officials," XXIII, No. 3, (March 1958), pp. 96–109.

Prefabricated Homes. "Inadequate Dealers' Mark Up Discourages Distribution Through Normal Channels," VI, No. 6, (May 1946), pp. 9, 16.

——. "Prefabricated Home Manufacturers Institute Organized," I, No. 6, (September 1943), p. 6.

——. "Prefabrication Defined," I, No. 5, (August 1943), pp. 6–7.

——. "The Prefabricated House—Its Legal Status and Financing Problem," II, No. 2, (December 1943), pp. 6–7, 22, 27.

——. "1946 and After—Prefabrication Looks Ahead," VI, No. 3, (January 1946), pp. 10–13.

——. "What Can be Done To Get Production Rolling?," VI, No. 5, (April 1946), pp. 14–15.

Progressive Architecture. "The Unchanging Building Industry," (August 1967), pp. 152–153.

Puglisi, Engo A. "Building Codes," *Construction Review*, XII, No. 9, (September 1966), pp. 4–7.

Richardson, Ambrose M. "Building Codes: Reducing Diversity and Facilitating the Amending Process," *Harvard Journal of Legislation*, V, (May 1968), pp. 587–611.

Rivkin, Steven "Courting Change: Using Litigation to Reform Local Building Codes" *Rutgers Law Review*, Vol. 26 (Summer 1973)

Robinson, Rita. "Prefabs: An Old Technique," *Architectural and Engineering News*, IX, No. 6, (June 1967), pp. 64–69.

Rothenstein, Guy G. "System Building in Europe," *Building Research*, IV, No. 5, (September–October 1967), pp. 29–31.

Royer, Richard. "The Case for Prefabs, " *National Real Estate and Building Journal*, LII, No. 8, (August 1951), pp. 22–24.

Safdie, Moshe. "A Case for City Living," *Habitat*, IV, No. 6, (November–December 1961), pp. 2–9.

Shire, A.C. "Why so Many Building Codes?," *American City*, LXIV, No. 11, (November 1949), pp. 101–102.

Stinchcombe, Arthur L. "Bureaucratic and Craft Administration of Production: A Comparative Study," *Administrative Science Quarterly*, (September 1959), pp. 168–187.

Stout, William B. "Your City's Building Code: Help or Hindrance to Post War Prosperity?," *American City*, LIX, No. 7, (July 1944), pp. 58–59.

Tabler, W.B. "Those Chaotic Building Codes," *Architectural Forum*, CIX, No. 1, (July 1958), p. 88.

Thompson, George N. "Revising the Local Building Code: To Prohibit Jerry-building While not Requiring Needlessly Expensive Construction," *American City*, LVII, No. 3, (March 1942), pp. 59–61.

Thompson, George N. "The Problem of Building Code Improvement," *Law and Contemporary Problems*, XII, (1947), pp. 95–110.

Wilson, James Q. "Innovation in Organizations: Notes Toward a Theory," In James D. Thompson, *Approaches to Organizational Design*, Pittsburgh, University of Pittsburgh Press, (1966), pp. 193–218.

Wilson, James Q. and Clark, Peter B. "Incentive Systems: A Theory of Organizations," *Administrative Science Quarterly*, VI, (September 1961), pp. 129–166.

Reports

Advisory Commission on Intergovernmental Relations. *Building Codes A Program for Intergovernmental Reform*. Washington, D.C.: Advisory Commission on Intergovernmental Relations, 1966.

——. *1970 Cumulative ACIR State Legislative Program*. Washington, D.C.: Advisory Commission on Intergovernmental Relations, 1969.

American Federation of Labor, Information and Publicity Service. *Report of the Housing Committee of the American Federation of Labor on the Fort Wayne Plan*, March 8, 1939.

Arthur D. Little, Inc. *Technology in Connecticut's Housing Delivery System*. A report to The Department of Community Affairs, July 1969.

Batelle Memorial Institute. *The State of the Act of Prefabrication in the Construction Industry*. Final report to the building and construction trades department AFL–CIO, September 29, 1967.

Bender, Richard. *Selected Technological Aspects of the American Building Industry*. A Report prepared for the National Commission on Urban Problems. Springfield, Virginia: Clearinghouse for Scientific and Technical Information, 1969.

Building Research Advisory Board, Special Advisory Committee on Industrialized Housing and Building Systems. "An Historical Evaluation of Industrialized Housing and Building Systems in the United States," in *The Report of the President's Committee on Urban Housing: Technical Studies. Volume II*. Washington, D.C.: U.S. Government Printing Office, 1968, pp. 172-190.

Burns, Leland S. and Mittelbach, Frank G. "Efficiency in the Housing Industry," *The Report of the President's Committee on Urban Housing Technical Studies, Volume II*. Washington, D.C.: U.S. Government Printing Office, 1969.

Chamber of Commerce of the United States. *Building Codes: An Essential Tool in Urban Development*, 1943.

——. Construction and Community Development Department. *Building Codes for Community Development and Construction Progress*, 1963.

Department of Commerce, Bureau of the Census. *Statistical Abstract of the United States 1961*. Washington, D.C.: Department of Commerce, 1961.

Department of Commerce, Bureau of Standards. *Status of Municipal Building Codes (May 19, 1933)*. Letter Circular LC–377. Washington, D.C.: Department of Commerce, 1933.

——. *Status of Municipal Building Codes (Revised to March 15, 1935)* Letter Circular LC–377. Washington, D.C.: Department of Commerce, 1935.

Department of Housing and Urban Development. *Housing and Urban Development Trends*, October 1970.

——. *1967 Statistical Yearbook*. Washington, D.C.: U.S. Government Printing Office, 1967.

Dietz, Albert G.H. *The Building Industry*. Report to the National Commission on Urban Problems, Springfield, Virginia: Clearinghouse for Federal Scientific and Technical Information, March 1968.

Dunlap, J.T. and Mills, D.Q. "Manpower in Construction: A Profile of the Industry and Projections to 1975." *The Report of the President's Committee on Urban Housing. Technical Studies Volume II*. Washington, D.C.: U.S. Government Printing Office, 1968.

F.W. Dodge Company, Marketing Research Department. "A Study of Compara-

tive Time and Cost for Building Five Selected Types of Low-Cost Housing,"
in *The Report of the President's Committee on Urban Housing, Technical
Studies Volume II*. Washington, D.C.: U.S. Government Printing Office,
1968.

Gaffney, Mason, *et. al*. Land As An Element of Housing Costs—*The Effects of
Public Policies and Practices. The Effects of Housing Demand*. Springfield,
Virginia: Clearinghouse for Scientific and Technical Information, October
1968.

Home Manufacturers Association. *H.M.A. Labor and Productivity Study*.
Washington, D.C.: Home Manufacturers Association, 1967.

————. *Wage and Labor Study*. Washington, D.C.: Home Manufacturers Association, 1967.

Kaiser Engineers. *In-Cities Experimental Housing Research and Development
Project, Phase I. Composite Report. Volume II. Constraints*. Springfield,
Virginia: Clearinghouse for Scientific and Technical Information, March
1969.

Klipple, G.C. *H.M.A. Income and Expense Study for Year 1968*. Washington,
D.C.: National Association of Building Manufacturers, 1969.

International City Managers' Association. *Municipal Building Inspection Practices*. Chicago: Management Information Report No. 241, February 1964.

Manvel, Alan D. *Local Land and Building Regulations*. Report No. 6 to the
National Commission on Urban Problems. Washington, D.C.: U.S. Government Printing Office, 1968.

Ministry of Works. *Methods of Building in the U.S.A*. The Report of a Mission
Appointed by the Minister of Works. London: His Majesty's Stationery
Office, 1944.

National Academy of Sciences. *Long Range Planning for Urban Research and
Development Technological Considerations*. Washington, D.C.: National
Academy of Science, 1969.

National Association of Home Builders Research Foundation. *Constraints to
Builders' Use of Cost Saving Innovations*. (Report done for the U.S. Department of Housing and Urban Development, Office of Research and Technology, 1971.)

National Commission on Mortgage Interest Rates. *Report of the Commission on
Mortgage Interest Rates for the President of the United States and to the
Congress*. Washington, D.C.: U.S. Government Printing Office, 1969.

National Commission on Technology, Automation, and Economic Progress.
Technology and the American Economy. Washington, D.C.: U.S. Government Printing Office, 1966.

National Commission on Technology, Automation, and Economic Progress.
Applying Technology to Unmet Needs. Washington, D.C.: U.S. Government
Printing Office, 1966.

National Commission on Urban Problems. *Building the American City*. Washington, D.C.: U.S. Government Printing Office, 1968.

————. *Hearings before the National Commission on Urban Problems* Vol. 1–5.
Washington, D.C.: U.S. Government Printing Office, 1968.

Parsons, Douglas E. "Building Codes and the Producers of Building Products."

Springfield, Va.: Clearinghouse for Federal Scientific and Technical Information, October 1966.

Platts, R.E. *Prefabrication in Canadian Housing.* Technical Paper No. 172 of the Division of Building Research. Ottawa, Canada: National Research Council of Canada, Division of Building Research, 1964.

Rowland, Norman. *Reston Low Income Housing Demonstration Program.* Springfield, Virginia: Clearinghouse for Scientific and Technical Information, April 1969.

Schlefer, Marion. *The Library of Congress Legislative Service, Industrialization of Housing: Today's Potential.* Washington, D.C.: Library of Congress, 1967.

Sims, Christopher A. "Efficiency in the Construction Industry," *The Report of the President's Committee on Urban Housing Technical Studies Volume II.* Washington, D.C.: U.S. Government Printing Office, 1968.

Stockfrisch, J.A. *An Investigation of the Opportunities for Reducing the Cost of Federally Subsidized Housing for Lower Income Families.* Springfield, Virginia: Clearinghouse for Federal Scientific and Technical Information, September 1968.

Stone, Peter A and Denton, R. Harold. *Toward More Housing.* A monograph for the Temporary National Economic Committee, U.S. Senate. Washington, D.C.: U.S. Government Printing Office, 1941.

U.S. President's Committee on Urban Housing. *A Decent Home.* Washington, D.C.: U.S. Government Printing Office, 1968.

Weiner, Neil S. *Supply Conditions for Low-Cost Housing Production.* Springfield, Virginia: Clearinghouse for Scientific and Technical Information, October 1968.

Williams, Lawrence A., Young, Eddie M. and Fischetti, Michael A. *Survey of the Administration of Construction Codes in Selected Metropolitan Areas.* A Report prepared for the National Commission on Urban Problems. Springfield, Virginia: Clearinghouse for Scientific and Technical Information, April 1968.

Williams, Young and Fischetti. *Survey of the Administration of Construction Codes in Selected Metropolitan Areas,* National Commission on Urban Problems Background Paper No. 29, 1968.

Index

213

About the Authors

Charles G. Field, a graduate of Cornell University, received the master's degree in urban planning from New York University and the Ph.D. from Harvard University. He has been involved both in building code reform and in social science research in the development of urban and housing policy. As a legislative aide, he assisted in the development of Massachusetts' statewide building code reform law. His writings concerning building codes have appeared in *Ripon Forum* and *The Municipal Yearbook: 1971* (International City Management Association, 1971). Since 1971 he has been affiliated with the Department of Housing and Urban Development, where he is working on the Experimental Housing Allowance Program, the nation's largest domestic social experiment.

Steven R. Rivkin, a practicing attorney in Washington, D.C., is a partner in the law firm Nicholson & Carter. He is a graduate of Harvard College and Harvard Law School. Since serving as Counsel to the White House Office of Science and Technology, his work has emphasized the interrelationship between technology, regulation and the antitrust laws. He is the author of two other books, *Technology Unbound: Transferring Scientific and Engineering Resources from Defense to Civilian Purposes* (1968) and *Cable Television: A Guide to Federal Regulations* (1973), and numerous articles in legal and general publications.

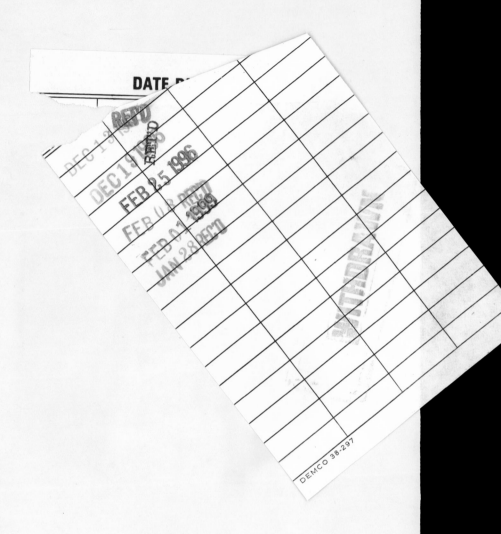